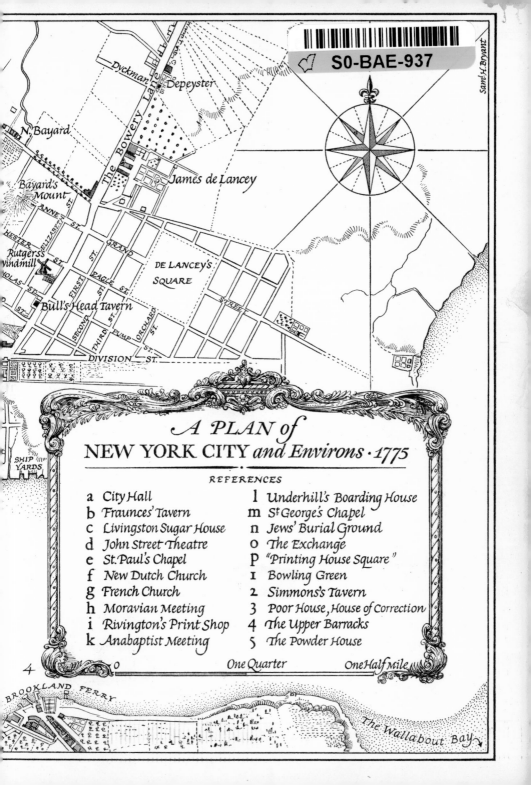

Sam'l. H. Bryant

Dyckman

Depeyster

N. Bayard

The Bowery Lane

James de Lancey

Bayard's Mount

ANNE ST.

ELIZABETH ST.

HESTER ST.

Rutgers's Windmill

NIOLAS ST.

GRAND ST.

FIRST ST.

EAGLE ST.

DE LANCEY'S SQUARE

Bull's Head Tavern

SECOND

THIRD ST.

PUMP ST.

ORCHARD ST.

STREET

DIVISION ST.

SHIP YARDS

A PLAN of
NEW YORK CITY and Environs · 1775

REFERENCES

a City Hall
b Fraunces' Tavern
c Livingston Sugar House
d John Street Theatre
e St. Paul's Chapel
f New Dutch Church
g French Church
h Moravian Meeting
i Rivington's Print Shop
k Anabaptist Meeting

l Underhill's Boarding House
m St George's Chapel
n Jews' Burial Ground
o The Exchange
p "Printing House Square"
1 Bowling Green
2 Simmons's Tavern
3 Poor House, House of Correction
4 The Upper Barracks
5 The Powder House

4   0   One Quarter   One Half Mile

BROOKLAND FERRY

The Wallabout Bay

A
Peculiar Service

A
Peculiar Service

✤✤✤✤✤✤✤✤✤✤✤✤✤✤✤

by COREY FORD

Little, Brown and Company • Boston • Toronto

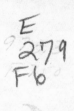

Published simultaneously in Canada
by Little, Brown & Company (Canada) Limited

PRINTED IN THE UNITED STATES OF AMERICA

For
A. Richard Barber

I am not influenced by the expectation of promotion or pecuniary reward; I wish to be useful, and every kind of service, necessary to the public good, becomes honorable by being necessary. If the exigencies of my country demand a peculiar service, its claims to perform that service are imperious.

— NATHAN HALE

A Personal Word

SOMEWHERE in the parched desert of Mongolia a paleontologist excavates the fossilized remains of a dinosaur. There are only scattered fragments: a femur, a section of backbone, part of the lower jaw, a few teeth. Near them he finds some giant footprints, left in the mud of an ancient lake bed back in Mesozoic times. The lengthy stride and narrow trackway tell him that the creature was long-legged and walked upright. The bones and vertebrae, fitted together, reveal its shape and structure. A comparison with living members of the same species suggests its probable coloration. Combining his scientific knowledge with his imagination, the paleontologist fills in the missing parts of the skeleton with plaster of Paris, covers the frame with a skin of painted fabric, and restores the dinosaur as it was a couple of hundred million years ago.

It is a long way from Mongolia to New York, a long way from the Mesozoic age to the American Revolution; but my point is that the process of restoration is the same with a writer of history. There are only a few scattered facts: some names and dates, a faded newspaper clipping, an entry buried in an old journal. The historian must excavate them from the parched pages, fit the parts together to reveal the shape and structure of the period, consult his own living experience to suggest its color, combine knowledge with imagination to recreate the past as it was a couple of hundred years ago.

So it has been with this book. Every word is true, as true as I could make it. The names and characters are real, the events are documented, even the smallest details of foliage and flowers are the result of long and conscientious research. (Gilliflower and corn flag for stock and iris; lime tree for basswood.) Here is New York as it was in 1775, the way it looked, the way it smelled. The crooked cobbled streets, so uneven that Dr. Benjamin Franklin of Philadelphia observed: "You can always tell a New Yorker by his gait, like a parrot on a mahogany table." The spicy aroma of the waterfront, the fly-blown sewage in the gutters, the pervading odor of cedar smoke that could be detected fifty miles at sea and would guide the mariner into port as surely as a compass. The boisterous taverns, the rumble of water carts and shouts of hawkers, the grunt of wild pigs that roamed the city, the tinkle of a spinnet behind drawn shutters, the strident chirp of tree toads in the elms along the Broad Way.

History is narrative, by the old Greek definition, and this is told as a story. Here and there, to give reality, I have used the device of conversation, as the paleontologist uses plaster and fabric and paint. Some purists may object that this is an unwarranted liberty by an amateur, that the professional historian quotes only those speeches recorded in a memoir; but the speeches he quotes were themselves written long after the event, often second or third hand. (Hale's last statement was repeated by Montresor to Hull, who set it down from memory half a century later.) At least, I have been honest; my dialogue is based on known facts, and there is no invention save the words themselves.

Similarly the motivations I have ascribed to the characters are indicated by their own letters, or by descriptions in contemporary diaries and journals. George Washington's secret correspondents were a strange lot, no two alike; but they were living people, and I have tried to bring them back to life. Nathan Hale the zealot, glazed of eye, welcoming martyrdom as the fitting climax to a dedicated career; in another age he might have been a Savonarola or a John Brown. Abraham Woodhull the shy neurotic, living in constant dread of discovery but carrying out his duties in spite of that dread. Caleb Brewster the heavy-fisted extrovert, boasting of his whaleboat exploits to anyone who would listen. Robert Townsend, lonely and introspective, the troubled victim of a Quaker conscience, so ashamed of his spy role that he never acknowledged it in his lifetime and carried the secret to his grave.

A final word. Any history of espionage is bound to contain some blank pages, where the writer can find no documentation or record to guide him. The Manhattan agents destroyed every letter they received from Washington, for fear it might be found by the enemy; but Washington saved all their letters to him, and painstakingly made copies of his own correspondence, and these are preserved in the Library of Congress. Still there are several sections of the story which have been the subject of endless argument among historians, or have been lost alto-gether: the movements of Hale during the last seven days of his mission; the part played in the secret service by the enigmatic James Rivington; the identity of the lady known only as 355. In each of these three cases I have considered all the evidence, weighed the conflicting statements one against another, and — again the use of plaster, the combination of knowledge with imagination — filled in the missing part with what seemed to me the most logical solution to the mystery.

The idea of this book has been in my mind for twenty years. During World War II, I was a colonel in the Air Force, as-signed to temporary duty on the staff of the late Major Gen-eral William J. Donovan, the fabulous "Wild Bill" who held the Congressional Medal of Honor and was selected by Presi-dent Roosevelt to organize the Office of Strategic Services, forerunner of today's Central Intelligence Agency. General

Donovan was an avid collector of books on espionage — his magnificent library belongs to Columbia University now — and one night at his apartment he took down from his crowded shelves a copy of *George Washington's Spies* by Morton Pennypacker and asked me: "Why don't you write a book about the beginnings of American intelligence in the Revolution?" (This is an example of the dialogue I mentioned above; I have invented the words, but it is based on a known fact.)

I had always been fascinated by this period in New York's history. I was born in New York, and my earliest memory — so vague that it is like remembering a dream — is of a Revolutionary sword and epaulets which hung on my bedroom wall. I have no idea whose they were, or whatever became of them; they are gone now. I do not even know the location of the house where I was born. Somewhere in upper Manhattan, I think. Probably it is gone, too. Nothing in New York lasts very long.

But there was a deeper compulsion that moved me, a haunting sense of personal identity with the long past. Perhaps it was the early memory of the sword. It came over me strongly when I visited the Setauket area of Long Island, in the course of my research, and set foot on the sandspit that is still called Old Man's Point, and felt the sudden emanations of yesterday. I was halfway through my manuscript last winter when I happened to discover, in an old steamer trunk in the attic, a package of letters wrapped in brown paper and tied with string, labeled in my father's handwriting: "Family Records." The package had evidently followed me all my life, but I had never noticed it before. Since I knew nothing of my background on my father's side, I carried it downstairs out of curiosity and cut the string. The letters went back to the Revolution; and I learned for the first time that my great-great-grandfather served as a sergeant in Colonel Samuel Webb's raid on Setauket in 1777. They crossed the Sound in the *Schuyler*, the same vessel that had carried

Nathan Hale on his mission the previous year. A British frigate-of-war drove their sloop onto the sandspit of Old Man's Point, and the entire personnel was captured or slain. Then I knew why I had wanted to write this book.

COREY FORD

Introduction

ESPIONAGE is one of those ancient professions that has from its very nature always been conducted in such anonymity and with such fragmentary documentation that no one could be so bold as to claim to write its definitive story, certainly not for the Revolutionary War. Bits and pieces have come to light from time to time. Thanks to revelations in the English archives we now know that Dr. Edward Bancroft, a confidant of Benjamin Franklin, was a British counterintelligence agent, transmitting data from the American mission at Passy to his employers across the Channel. Thanks, too, to the splendid collection of General Sir Henry Clinton's Headquarters Papers, we now have in rich detail the facts of Benedict Arnold's apostasy.

Because the American Revolution was a bitter civil war, as well as a war for liberation of a colonial people, spies chose to conceal their espionage roles even long after that war was over and the bitterness had subsided. In *The Spy* James Fenimore Cooper recorded the remarkable tale of one such secret agent which he heard from the lips of John Jay, only revealed to him years after the war and when that revered patriot had been long in retirement.

In *A Peculiar Service* Corey Ford has given us the fullest and

xvi   INTRODUCTION

most convincing account of the extraordinary operations of
Washington's Manhattan agency, known as the Culper Ring.
He traces the undercover operations not only out of Manhattan,
solidly held redcoat territory, but on the Neutral Ground, the
section of Westchester County which lay between the two opposing lines.

A Peculiar Service reads like exciting fiction, but it is a
scrupulously documented and thoroughly researched book. Mr.
Ford has shown remarkable ingenuity as a spy-hunter and has
put together a jigsaw puzzle based on fragments of letters, allu-
sions in papers, and other fugitive data relating to persons, often
posing as Loyalists, who engaged in undercover activity for
General Washington. He has exploited fresh discoveries, including the rich vein of data contained in the William J. Donovan Papers at Columbia University's Special Collections, and
other recent revelations, notably the discovery by Mrs. Catharine
Crary that the opportunistic James Rivington, the notorious
Tory newspaper printer, was in fact a secret agent of Washington during the closing days of the Revolution, evidence which
confirms old legends repeatedly discredited by historians.

Corey Ford brings us face-to-face with bribery and subversion.
We catch the taint of treachery and corruption, the sense of peril
and the atmosphere of fear which overhung these espionage
operations. We can almost handle the phials of invisible ink,
and itch to get hold of the cryptic ciphers and the code names
used in messages smuggled out of Manhattan between the
bound covers of a book or in the sole of a boot. But this is more
than a cloak-and-dagger story. Corey Ford captures New York,
before and after the Great Fire, its crooked streets, its waterfront aroma, its boisterous taverns, and its divided loyalties.
Above all, and with that expert literary craftsmanship we have
come to expect of him, the author has penned memorable por-
traits of spies famous and others until now relatively unsung.

Heroic Nathan Hale stands out unforgettable, and so do Benjamin Tallmadge, Abraham Woodhull, Robert Townsend, and, perhaps most of all, No. 355, whose identification is one of the central problems of a fascinating book.

RICHARD B. MORRIS

Department of History
Columbia University
New York City

Contents

Contents

A
Peculiar Service

The Shape of Yesterday

WHETHER through expediency or indifference or an urbane distaste for sentimental display, New York has done away with almost every vestige of its past. Other great world metropolises not only venerate their monuments of antiquity, they do a sizable business showing them off to tourists; but New York has neither time nor space for ruins. The city is in a perpetual flurry of moving day, and anything which is not needed is set out on the curb to be hauled away. Instead of an historic shrine, with roped-off rooms and visiting hours, there is an efficient bronze plaque on the side of a modern skyscraper which occupies the site. Generally it is illegible, and sometimes inaccurate — the plaque on the Yale Club marking the location of Nathan Hale's execution is off by twenty blocks — and it is seldom seen by the hurrying pedestrian with his eyes on the sidewalk. New Yorkers never look up, or look back.

Of the city which existed at the time of the American Revolution, only three buildings have survived. St. Paul's Chapel on Broadway at Fulton Street was saved during the fire of 1776 because the flatness of its roof enabled parishioners to stand aloft with leather buckets and douse the flying embers. Fraunces' Tavern at Broad and Pearl, where Washington bade farewell to his officers, became successively a warehouse and German tenement and beer parlor, until it was salvaged by the Sons of the Revolution; the interior is largely a restoration. At 160th Street and Edgecomb Avenue is the Roger Morris mansion, which Washington occupied briefly after the Battle of Manhattan; but it is better known by the name of a later and more permanent resident, Madame Jumel, whose French Empire furnishings and flowered brocade gowns in the upstairs bedrooms give a misleading impression of life at Continental command headquarters.

There is little else. A stone hut in Dyckman Park of uncertain history; an exposed ledge in a children's playground, daubed with kindergarten chalk, that was the site of Fort Washington; some hollowed-out logs from the city's first aqueduct system. Bulldozers in lower Manhattan, digging a cellar hole on the former grounds of King's College at Barclay Street, discovered two pieces of cannon, believed to have been hauled from the Battery and secreted on the campus by an undergraduate named Alexander Hamilton. In 1871 a remote farmyard yielded the leaden tail of a horse, hidden there a century before by Loyalist sympathizers; it is a section of the gilded equestrian statue of King George III which was pulled down by the mob in Bowling Green on the night the Declaration of Independence was read. A few other artifacts have been unearthed in the middens of Manhattan: charred Holland bricks, cannonballs, Hessian bayonet blades, broken camp utensils, pewter buttons. All told they fill only a corner of a room at the Museum of the City of New York, part of one hall at the New-York Historical Society.

The very size and shape of the island has altered almost beyond recognition. Its original shoreline has been straightened and extended, the backwaters and bights filled in until in places the city is more than half a mile wider. Ninth Avenue was the Hudson shore in 1775. The East River, once so broad that it was called New York Sound, is little more than a ship's channel now. Turtle Bay, at the foot of 46th Street, was a deep sheltered cove; on a rocky island at its mouth stood the Royal arsenal which a group of Liberty Boys raided shortly after the news of Lexington. The cove is gone and the island rests beneath the United Nations Building, a concrete and glass headstone. A little downriver was a larger indentation called Kip's Bay, extending from 38th to 32nd Street and cutting inland to Second Avenue. Here the British troops made their landing on Manhattan in September of 1776, under a covering cannonade from the frigates lying offshore. The Franklin D. Roosevelt Drive runs almost exactly along the line where the enemy ships rode at anchor. Most of the Lower East Side below 14th Street was a broad salt flat which flooded at high tide; waterfowl fed in the reeds, and muskrats scampered along the banks of the muddy sloughs. In the center of this marsh, near what is now Tompkins Square, rose a dry mound covered with native oaks. There was a popular rumor that Captain Kidd, a onetime resident of New York, had cached his pirate gold on this knoll, and it was pock-marked with holes dug by eighteenth century treasure-seekers. Perhaps a fortune in Spanish doubloons still lies a few feet beneath some East Side tenement subcellar.

Walk the streets of New York late at night, when the flow of traffic has ceased, and you are aware of ghostly climbs and steep descents, the skeletal structure of Manhattan. Once it was a rugged terrain, some of it all but impassable, with sheer cliffs and ravines and bare limestone outcroppings — the rough northern section of Central Park is typical of the whole island — and several rather imposing elevations. Commanding lower Manhattan was Bayard's Mount, a sugarloaf hill which reared a hundred feet above the present intersection of Mott and Pell Streets, in the heart of Chinatown. Its cedar-crested summit looked west across the Hudson to the Newark Mountains, east to the fertile green plains of Long Island, south to the gabled roofs and spires of the little city a mile away. At its base, about Foley Square, was New York's main source of fresh water, a natural lake called Collect Pond (after the Dutch word *kolk*, meaning rippling water) which was supposed to be bottomless and to hold a sea monster. Bayard's Mount has been leveled to fill the bottomless lake; the sea monster is locked forever beneath New York's Municipal Court.

Sometimes a steam shovel, grubbing at the bottom of a deep excavation, encounters an underground seepage, and work halts until the flow can be pumped away. The bedrock of the island was honeycombed with these freshwater springs, which bubbled to the surface to form countless small ponds and streams. In winter it was possible to cross Manhattan on the ice. Parties of skaters would start from the East River where the abutments of Brooklyn Bridge stand today, skim across Collect Pond and the flooded Lispenard Meadows, now Broadway and Canal Street, and zigzag down a small outlet creek to the present entrance of the Holland Tunnel. Small wonder the first settlers, remembering the canals and interlocking waterways of their native Holland, named it Nieuw Amsterdam.

Many of New York's winding streets trace the course of forgotten brooks. Maiden Lane was a footpath along a crystal stream which tumbled over flat stones in cascades and rills, forming occasional pools where Dutch *vrouws* and their dimpled daughters came to do their washing. Minetta Street marks a willow-lined meadow rill which started in a swamp at Fifth Avenue and 21st Street and meandered west through Greenwich Village to the Hudson. Crommessie Brook, later called Gramercy, originated in the same swamp, but perversely flowed southeast to empty into the East River at First Avenue and 18th Street. The pronounced dip in Park Avenue at 31st Street, where the underpass emerges, is the ancient bed of Sunfish Pond, the loveliest fishing lake on the island. Its grassy banks were shaded by hickories and oaks, and boys with willow poles angled in its spring-fed water for sunnies and sticklebacks and yellow-bellied cobblers, the sweetest perch of all. The only sound was the creak of a well sweep at Robert Murray's estate on Inclenburg Mount, now called Murray Hill, the thumping of a butter churn in Jacobus Kip's stone farmhouse over by the East River, the rumble of a stagecoach along the Post Road which skirted its eastern shore.

Even as late as 1775, Manhattan was pretty much as the Dutch had found it. Porpoises and sharks and an occasional whale cruised off the black rocks of the Battery, and sturgeon plunged and rolled up the Hudson as far as the Highlands. Lobsters were plentiful in the unpolluted water of the East River, planted there accidentally late in the seventeenth century when a ship from Massachusetts Bay foundered on the reefs of Hell Gate and several barrels of live shellfish broke open. The muddy banks abounded in oysters and clams, the latter prized not only for their meat but also their shells. Each purple shell was carefully sorted out, to be sold as wampum to the Indians north of Albany. The rest were gathered up by farmers and scattered for fertilizer, whitening their plowed fields like an April blizzard.

It was a beautiful and bountiful island, still largely uninhabited, profligate with native cherries and plums and mulberries. Wild strawberries grew in such profusion that "people lay down in the fields and gorged themselves." In the fall and spring, the migrating geese traced their cobwebby skeins across the sky, to settle and feed in the barren Harlem Flats. Flights of passenger pigeons descended on the island in such numbers that they were netted and sold in the markets six for a penny. Heath hen and quail raised their broods in the low gravelly hills that ran west of Broadway from Canal to 42nd Street, wild turkeys roosted in the groves of tall chestnuts north of Times Square, and the drumming of cock grouse could be heard in Bayard's Woods, now the heart of the Bowery. After several hunting accidents, an act was passed by the Assembly in 1765 imposing a fine of twenty shillings on anyone who "fires a gun in an orchard, garden or cornfield" within the city limits. Local sportsmen, outraged by this restriction, insisted that "the citizens should have some place for that manly diversion, otherwise they will be in danger of forgetting to use their firearms with dexterity, however necessary they may be for their own defense, and of sinking into effeminacy and meanness." Ten years later their long-barreled flintlocks and fowling pieces were virtually the only weapons for the defense of New York.

The sole land access to Manhattan was the King's Bridge over the Harlem River near Spuyten Duyvil. A stagecoach from Boston would rumble over the oak planking of the bridge and follow the Post Road south, hugging the precipitous bluffs of Harlem Heights for several miles and gradually descending to cross the Harlem Flats, the lowest point on the island. What is 125th Street today was a boggy bottomland, where ducks and teal nested in the rye grass and lanky herons, startled into flight by the approaching stage, loped with downswept wings toward the Hollow Way and the Hudson. On the other side of the Flats, the horses would labor up a long rock-strewn grade to McGown's Pass, a narrow defile between the crags which is still visible in Central Park at 106th Street, just west of Fifth Avenue. Looking back and to the east, the traveler could see the sleepy Dutch village of Haarlem, huddled on the shore of the river near Montresor's Island, now Randall's Island.

The highway zigzagged downhill in a series of switchbacks, through stands of cedar and giant oak, and bore southeast across the present Madison and Park Avenues to Third. On the corner of 66th Street stood the Dove Tavern, a modest wayside inn with a swinging sign depicting a Colonial gentleman smoking a clay pipe. Behind the tavern was the apple orchard where Nathan Hale was hanged. Here the land fell away sharply, and the road cut across Third and Second Avenues toward the river, past the elegant James Beekman mansion with its formal gardens and glass-enclosed greenhouse in which Hale spent the last night of his life. P.S. 135, an antiquated and condemned school building at the northwest corner of First Avenue and 51st Street, marks its approximate site. Skirting Turtle Bay, the highway swung west again to Lexington Avenue, climbed Inclenburg Mount to the entranceway of the Murray estate, about Park Avenue and 36th Street, and dropped down the far side to a wooden bridge over the outlet of Sunfish Pond. A Franklin-stone beside the bridge read *NY 2½ M,* and the Boston stage-driver usually halted here to water his horses for the final run to the city. The 71st Regiment Armory squats stolidly on the spot today.

From Sunfish Pond the Post Road angled inland to avoid James Duane's country seat, Gramercy Rest, and at Madison Avenue it joined the Bloomingdale Road. This second main highway to New York ran down the west side of the island from the Hoaglandt farm, at Riverside Drive and 115th Street, along the present-day course of Broadway to 25th Street. Here both roads terminated, and below the fork the main thorough-fare south was the Bowery Lane.

Drab shops and saloons and flophouses line it now, pushcarts with vegetables or cotton print dresses clutter the sidewalk, drunks sprawl in doorways to sleep off last night's escape from reality; but then it was a dusty country lane, bordered with elms and poplars, winding through a fertile farmland dotted with the neat Dutch *bouwerijs* from which its name derived. On the left, from Union Square to Cooper Square, were the vast baronial holdings of the Stuyvesant family, their well-tended orchards extending all the way east to the river. On the right at Grand Street, instead of the Bowery Savings Bank, was a small snuff mill, and beyond it the canvas sails of Rutgers's wind-mill turned lazily against the sky. A high brick wall ran from Grand to Rivington Street, hiding the James de Lancey estate, but through an arc-shaped recess and wrought-iron gate the traveler could catch a glimpse of the handsome three-story mansion and stables and private paddock for his blooded race-horses. At Hester Street the stage-driver might haul on his reins while a drover herded his pigs or steers into the corral beside the Bull's Head Tavern, largest hostel in Bowery Village. The stage swung west at the Plough and Harrow Inn, and crossed Chatham Square, and the soft thud of hooves on packed dirt changed suddenly to the ring of steel against the stone paving of Chatham Street, now Park Row, the outskirts of the city. Peddlers filling their water carts at the Tea Water Pump turned to stare, and the passengers held scented handkerchiefs to their noses to smother the stench of the unsightly tanyards and limekilns on the south shore of Collect Pond. The horses trotted faster, past Catiemut Hill, and the alley that led to the Jews' Burying Ground, and the Brick Presbyterian Church at Beekman Street, facing the Commons. Past the broad stubble-covered field, three times the size of the present City Hall Park, framed on the north by the grim facade of the Debtors' Gaol and the new Bridewell Prison, still unfinished in 1775. Around the corner and down the Broad Way, past the timeless gray columns of St. Paul's Chapel, lurching and jolting over the uneven cobblestones toward the busy brawling waterfront town that was New York two centuries ago.

*   *   *

It was a small town, wedged between two rivers at the island's southernmost tip, only a dozen blocks long and five blocks wide. Its population was about twenty-five thousand, less than that of Boston or Philadelphia. The eastern boundary was Queen Street, now called Pearl Street; Water Street beyond it was actually a series of wharves and docks and quays built out into the East River and connected by wooden bridges. The western limit was Broadway, lined with fashionable residences whose terraced gardens descended to the Hudson, separated by stone walls resting on the rocky beach. To the north the city ended at the Commons, though a few small settlements had sprung up in the Out Ward along the Bowery Lane, and on the upper Hudson shore at Chelsea and Greenwich.

It had been a walled city until the beginning of the eighteenth century. All the early dwellings were inside a log barricade, erected by the Dutch for protection against marauding Indians, which was the origin of Wall Street. The Fields, as the Commons was then called, was a sort of community pasture; a town herdsman would gather up the cattle in the evening, drive them down Broadway and through the gates of the stockade, and deliver each animal to its owner with a toot on his trumpet. Near the site of the present Stock Exchange, a farmer named John Robinson killed a black bear in his peach orchard by knocking it on the snout with a club. Bulls and bears in Wall Street even then.

Slowly but surely, in the decade before the Revolution, New York had changed from a Dutch village to a provincial English town. Fat Holland *vrouws* still smoked clay pipes and kept warming pans under their skirts in the winter; but it was no longer necessary to understand the Dutch language in order to shop at the Fly Market or Old Slip. The Flemish-style houses, with their glazed tiles and gabled ends fronting on the street, were being supplanted by new residences whose gambreled roofs and classical doorways were "after the London taste." The open-air slave market at the foot of Wall Street had been removed; and the adjoining Merchants' Coffee House, once a hangout for privateersmen and freebooters with convenient rear doors through which they could escape to their boats in an emergency, had turned into a dignified meeting place for the leading tradesmen and importers. Here in 1774 young John Jay drew up the first proposal for a Continental Congress, the genesis of the republic.

Then as now it was a commercial city, ideally situated at the mouth of the Hudson, with a generous harbor which seldom froze over and was protected by islands from the open Atlantic. It faced on the East River — the Hudson shore was too rocky for vessels to dock — and cartage to any retail shop was nowhere more than a quarter mile. At noon the Coffee House Bridge, a raised wooden platform in the center of lower Wall Street, echoed with the voices of traders haggling before the Merchants' Exchange, the strident bellow of auctioneers, the singsong of longshoremen at a ropewalk beside the river. Shipping from the seven seas tied up at its crowded wharves, and the waterfront was aromatic with spices and coffee and rum from the Sugar Islands, mules and Madeira from the Spanish Main, logwood from Honduras, dry goods from England, cotton from St. Thomas, lime juice and mahogany from Nicaragua, oxnabrigs and tea from Hamburg and Holland. Nor was all of it imported in accordance with British trade regulations; many of New York's first families acquired their fortunes by discreet smuggling.

Dominating the town, ecclesiastically and socially, was Trinity Church, the Anglican house of worship, on Broadway at Wall Street. It had been erected in 1696, on a tract of land conveyed outright to the vestry by Her Majesty Queen Anne through her cousin, Viscount Cornbury, then the Royal governor of the colony. Lord Cornbury was a man of numerous eccentricities, including an obsession that he bore a striking facial resemblance to the Queen. He appeared so frequently in feminine attire that his Council made a formal complaint to the British Colonial Secretary about the Governor's habit of "dressing publickly in woman's cloathes." Shortly thereafter Governor Cornbury was recalled to England, where he became the Earl of Clarendon and had his portrait painted in a low-cut evening gown which had belonged to Her Majesty.

The structure was Gothic in design, square and squat, with an ostentatiously tall steeple, the highest in New York, and a rounded apse which protruded at the rear like a bustle. Its peaked roof was cedar-shingled, but the walls were of solid limestone blocks, quarried on upper Manhattan Island and lifted into place with the help of Captain Kidd, who according to vestry records "lent a Runner & Tackle for the hoisting of stones." It stood in an elm-shaded park, enclosed by a white picket fence which ran along Broadway. The entrance faced west, looking down a sloping meadow to the Hudson, but piously averting its eyes from the grove of locusts on the river-bank which had become a trysting place for local lovers. With serene Episcopalian detachment, its back was to the city.

Adjoining it along the west side of Broadway — the fashionable side of the street — were the stately mansions of the rich. This lower section of New York's main avenue was sometimes called the Mall; it was bordered with lime trees and water beeches, and its brick sidewalk, carefully laid in herringbone design, was the favorite promenade of bewigged gentlemen in flowered taffeta and ladies in pastel silk and satin, the ostrich plumes in their bonnets bobbing and their three-inch-high heels clicking along the pavement. On warm evenings the residents sat on their balustraded rooftops, kissed by the salt spray of the harbor, raising their voices to be heard above the incessant shrill of tree toads which drowned even the clatter of hooves and crack of bullwhips in the street below.

The Mall began at the Bowling Green, an elliptical park surrounded by an iron railing and ornamented by a leaden statue of His Majesty George III in flowing Roman toga. Number One Broadway, near the glacis of Fort George, was the home of former Captain Archibald Kennedy of the Royal navy, wealthy heir to the Earldom of Casillis, who had been cashiered from the service for cowardice during the Stamp Act riots. It was constructed in the approved English fashion, with ornate cornices and Palladian windows and carved front doorway. From the paneled entrance hall, a grand staircase with mahogany hand-rails led to the spacious upstairs parlor, fifty feet in length, whose graceful bow opened onto a porch large enough for a cotillion party. Next door, at Number Three, was the equally palatial town house of his father-in-law John Watts, connected to the Kennedy mansion by a second-story bridge. Beyond it were the Van Cortlandt and Robert R. Livingston residences, imposing brick edifices with brownstone water tables and lintels and jambs.

Social life in New York was as gay as London or Paris, if you happened to be one of the gentry, of course. "Balls, concerts, dancing, all of us mad in the pursuit of pleasure," enthused young Gouverneur Morris, just graduated from King's College, "grim phizzes are grinned out of countenance." Business hours were from ten to two, affording ample time for leisure, and the town offered a wide diversity of entertainment. Dilettantes could visit the crude red-painted theater in John Street for a performance of Farquhar's licentious new comedy *The Beaux' Stratagem*, or while away an evening at the gaming tables. Puppet shows and waxworks exhibits vied in popularity with such mechanical novelties as an "unparalleled Musical Clock which played upon the organ, French horn pieces, German and common flute, flageolet, etc." or a Solar Microscope whose magnifying power was guaranteed to reveal "the circulation in the Blood of a Frog's foot, a Flea, a Fish's Tail, and many small Insects with their young in them." At the Sign of the Dolphin, a Mr. Dugee advertised that his wife, known as The Female Samson, would "lie with her body extended between two chairs, bearing an anvil of 300 lbs. on her breast, and suffer two men to strike it with sledge hammers." Not to be outdone, a rival showman near Whitehall Slip displayed "a creature called a Japanese of about 2 Feet high, his Body resembling a Human Body in all parts except the feet and tail" who would perform "Various Actions to Admiration such as walking upon a Line, exercising the Firelock, dancing to any Tune, and Sundry other Things too tedious to mention."

For the sporting bloods, there was tennis at the Sign of the

Hurlers, horse-racing on the New Market Course at Hempstead Plains, or bullbaiting in a pit near Chatham Square. Cockfighting was much patronized by the elite, and good gamecocks could be obtained at the Dog's Head in the Porridge Pot or at the print shop of James Rivington, publisher of the *New York Gazetteer*, who further augmented his income by selling imported battledores and shuttlecocks, cricket balls, racquets for fives, and backgammon tables, boxes, and dice. Sleighing and ice-skating on Collect Pond north of the Commons helped pass the winter months, and on summer weekends the younger set would climb into Italian chaises and travel up the East River for a turtle feast, or mingle with the commoners at a fireworks display in Ranelagh Gardens on upper Broadway.

Women's styles followed the European mode, though sometimes they lagged a season or so behind. The broad-brimmed straw peasant hat, introduced in France the year before by the new queen Marie Antoinette, was just coming into vogue in New York in 1775. The wide pannier or farthingale at the hips had yielded to a bustle in back, and the current trend was toward a higher waistline, Empire bust, and form-fitting gown designed to reveal the female form. In order to achieve the desired slim figure, stay-makers turned out elaborate corsets of whalebone or buckram to make "crooked women appear strate," and young girls wore steel collars with long needles stuck upright in front to keep their heads erect. Fashionable ladies affected ivory-handled umbrellas, feather muffs with ermine tippets, fancy stomachers, and bosom bottles, small water-filled phials worn at the breast to hold fresh flowers. Every coquette knew the language of the fan, twisting it timorously, or sweeping it in an angry flutter, or opening it with a snap and smiling seductively over its silken spread.

A Colonial belle spent so much time on her make-up that "it took a whole morning to put on what it took a whole evening to take off." No boudoir table was complete without an assortment of paste pots, scent bottles, bags of perfume, boxes of rouge, beauty patches, breath-sweeteners, and bowls for mixing compounds to improve the skin, eyebrows, lips, hands, and hair. A favorite bloom was called Bavarian Red Liquor, which was also "taken internally." Members of the English clergy, who viewed these feminine enticements with alarm, proposed an Act of Parliament to prohibit every "woman, wife, maid or widow from entrapping any of His Majesty's subjects by the aid of perfume, false bosoms, or rouge."

Milady's headdress was her crowning triumph. The natural hair was built up with pads and cushions and puffs until it was "of twice natural size, frizzled to imitate the shock head of a Negro," and ornamented with lappets, gauze, lace, poufs, feathers, ropes of pearls, sequins of gilded fish scales, and artificial flowers or vegetables. The sardonic Hannah More described eleven females of her acquaintance who "had among them on their heads an acre and a half of shrubbery, besides grass plots, tulip beds, peonies and kitchen gardens." After the hair was arranged and powdered, it was left intact for months at a time, and the wearer dared not disturb it with comb or brush. Since the powder was common white flour, a headdress had a tendency to attract unwelcome visitors. Ivory wig-scratchers were in great demand, and one enterprising manufacturer offered a cage made of thin wire mesh, which could be placed over a lady's head while she slept to protect her from hungry mice which might creep across her pillow.

The New York gentleman of fashion was equally sensitive to changing Paris styles. The shorter coat was just coming into vogue, cut away and worn unbuttoned, with white ruffles at the cuffs to show that its owner did not soil his hands by manual labor. The latest breeches no longer fastened in front but had a wide fall, like a sailor's pants, which extended to either hip. To give his legs a more shapely appearance, he sometimes wore false calves under his white stockings. His shoes were low and square-cut, made to fit either foot, and ornamented with silver or jeweled buckles. He shaved daily, of course; a moustache or beard was considered a sign of uncleanliness. Before setting out for an evening, the fastidious man-about-town would sprinkle his peruke with heavily perfumed blue powder, don his Barcelona muslin cravat, adjust his stock and buckle, tie a solitaire ribbon to his bagwig and drape it over a shoulder, scent his snuff handkerchief, fasten his sword to his side, and clasp his beaver under an arm, ready at last to saunter down the Mall. He carried his snuffbox and coins in an embroidered silk pocketbook, and in chilly weather his unsoiled hands were protected by a fur muff.

He devoted as much care to his headdress as the fair sex. His choice of smart tonsorial arrangements included the pigeon's wing, the comet, the cauliflower, the royal bird, the staircase, the temple, the rhinoceros, the corded wolf's paw, the she-dragon, the negligent, the snail-back, the spinach seed, and the artichoke. For the exquisite, there was the new Macaroni toupee, which was brushed erect a foot above the forehead and sported large curls over each ear. This latest London craze originated with a group of effete young Oxonians who had toured the Continent and formed a club named after Italy's famous dish. A Macaroni was defined by the *Oxford Magazine* as "a kind of animal, neither male nor female, which talks without meaning, smiles without pleasantry, eats without appetite, and rides without exercise." He wore gold-spangled frogs on his coat, tight knee-breeches of striped or polka-dot silk, and a knot of fresh flowers on his breast. His walking stick, festooned with tassels, was used to lift off the tiny tricorn hat perched on top of his towering hair-do. Efforts of Colonial dudes to imitate their foppish British cousins were ridiculed in a popular song, just published in England, about a "Yankee Doodle Dandy" who stuck a feather in his hat and called himself a Macaroni.

During the hot months, when the city grew sultry and the

odor of the tanyards offended their nostrils, the plutocrats moved out of town to their country seats along the Hudson or East River, surrounded with rolling green lawns and fish ponds and private deer parks. Their banquet tables were laden with fresh-killed pheasant and quail raised on their game preserves, muskmelons and English strawberries and Battersea asparagus grown in their greenhouses, apricots and quinces and nectarines from their exotic orchards. In the fall they reopened their town houses for another social season of cotillions and routs, pirouetting past the lighted windows of their mansions on the Mall, indifferent to the hostile eyes that watched them from the other side of the street.

East of Broadway, in narrow lanes and tortuous alleys, were the homes of the poor. They lived in log huts floored with dirt, or in rickety frame tenements with three or four families crowded into as many rooms. In winter the bitter wind from the bay rattled the loose planking and snow sifted through the eaves; but fuel was dear, and save at mealtime the single hearth was unlighted. The back streets were unpaved and the gutter ran down the center, forming an open sewer. Slops and human filth were tossed out the windows, and droves of wild hogs wallowed in the muck and fed on garbage left to rot in the passageways between the houses.

The only source of pure drinking water was the Tea Water Pump by Collect Pond, and peddlers hauled the limited supply in carts and hawked it from door to door. Since the poor could not afford such luxury, they used the public wells, filled with contaminated surface seepage, or dipped their leather buckets in the brackish coves of the East River. Recurrent epidemics of dysentery swept the city. There were no doctors, at least in the poor section, and apothecaries compounded their own remedies of herbs and simples: the powdered bark of white oak to cure the flux, a jelly of boiled linden roots for the ague, sage leaves mixed with lemon juice for the prevalent malarial fever which was popularly supposed to be "caused by vapours" from the stagnant swamps of lower Manhattan. Smallpox inoculations were given by scratching the arm with a dirty fingernail, and were more apt to spread than curb the disease. Scores died of the plague every year, and were laid in unmarked trenches in the public Potter's Field beside the Bloomingdale Road.

As the patriot embargo on British goods began to take effect, trade fell off and unemployment mounted; and the sheriff made frequent visits to the slum areas to carry off debtors to the jail on the Commons. Many of the destitute turned to crime or commercialized vice to keep from starving. Pickpockets plied their trade in the marketplaces, and armed highwaymen held up stagecoaches on the Bowery Lane. Prostitution did a flourishing business, encouraged by the gentry. So many ladies of pleasure "kept lodgings contiguous within the consecrated liberties of St. Paul's" that the district was known as the Holy Ground. Several fancy houses were located in the shadow of City Hall, and the street leading to King's College was the resort of such notorious Manhattan bawds as Katie Crow, "Quaker Fan" Bambridge, and Hannah Bradshaw, whose popularity with British sailors earned her the alias of "Man-of-War Nance."

Punishments ranged from the ducking stool and pillory to branding or mutilation or hanging. John Morris, found guilty of sheep-stealing, was "burnt in the hand," and Daniel Martin received "fifteen lashes for the theft of fiddlestrings." For defrauding and cheating, Richard Ely was "exalted upon a wooden horse on a triumphal cart with labels on his breast" and conducted to the public whipping post. Offending slaves were paraded up and down Wall Street, receiving a fixed number of lashes at each intersection. The city lived in mortal fear of an uprising by its large colored population. During the so-called "Negro Plot" — New York's own version of the Salem witch-hunts — fourteen suspected slaves were burned at the stake on Catiemut Hill.

Hangings were held on the Commons, and were sometimes private affairs. A bill from John Aynscough to James Mills, debtor, listed: "To cash paid for the execution of a negro man, £5.8.0. To the horse and cart, 0.12.0. To a cord, 0.5.0. For burial of body, 0.6.0. To liquor for the hangman, 0.2.9." Even the hangman, one Van Johnson, was convicted of robbery and ordered to be executed on the gallows, a sentence which could not be enforced because he stubbornly refused to hang himself and no one else was willing to do it. The problem was solved by lightening his sentence to thirty-nine lashes, the severing of an ear, and banishment to Staten Island.

The bulk of the population — the leather-aprons, mechanics, dockworkers, seamen, carters, apprentices, day laborers, servants, slaves — were denied the suffrage. Ridden by poverty and disease, unable to voice their protests, they were easy prey for local prophets of discontent who saw, in the mounting resentment toward England's oppressive measures, an opportunity to topple the existing Tory oligarchy and substitute their own radical leadership. Some of the gentry saw it also. Gouverneur Morris, looking down at their sullen faces from a balcony of the Merchants' Coffee House, uttered a prophetic warning: "The mob began to think and to reason. Poor reptiles! it is with them a vernal morning; they are struggling to cast off their winter's slough, they bask in the sunshine, and ere noon they will bite, depend on it. I see, and see with fear and trembling, that if the disputes with Great Britain continue, we shall be under the worst of all possible dominions; we shall be under the domination of a riotous mob."

The quarrel between the Colonies and the mother country had been a long time in the making, first breaking out in mob violence ten years ago during the controversy over the Stamp Act. The British Ministry had argued, with some justice, that the King's subjects, who enjoyed the benefits of Royal protection, should bear their share of the cost; but the proposal to tax them without their consent was loudly denounced by the demagogues of rebellion. A secret organization calling itself the Sons of Liberty, masterminded by an impoverished and palsied Boston politician named Samuel Adams, spread rapidly through New England and down to New York, inciting the unenfranchised workers with inflammatory slogans: *Taxation without Representation! Rights of Man! Slavery! Tyranny! Enemies of Liberty, Beware!* The masses echoed the phrases without understanding their meaning. They made no distinction between Ministerial oppression and that of New York's upper classes. Tyranny was tyranny, whether abroad or at home. Their long winter's slough was ending, and they stirred in the sunny promise of better living conditions and equal voting rights. Though they had no property to tax, they banged their tankards in protest against the Stamp Act and rallied to the heady cry of *Liberty*.

On a black November night in 1765, a motley crowd two thousand strong had paraded down Broadway to Fort George, demanding that the acting governor, aging Cadwallader Colden, surrender ten bundles of the hated stamps which had just arrived from England. Their flaring torches revealed a giant Negro balancing a chair on his head, with a paper effigy of the Governor holding a sheet of stamps and a second effigy of the Devil peering over his shoulder and urging him to "persevere in the cause of slavery." Ignoring the armed guards on the parapets, they tacked a proclamation to the gate of the Fort defying Colden to fire on them "lest he die a matir to [his] own villainy." When he refused to turn over the stamps, the rioters broke into his coach house beside the gate, hauled his carriage across the street to the Bowling Green, placed his effigy on top and fired it with their torches.

Committees of Correspondence spread the alarm through

New England, and blustering old Colonel Israel Putnam of Pomfret, leader of the Sons of Liberty in Connecticut, offered to send ten thousand men to New York to aid in the struggle. General civil war was averted when a fast packet from London brought word that the Stamp Act had been revoked, and newspapers hailed the "Glorious news for America and no more Shim Shams." Churchbells rang all night, an ox was roasted whole on the Commons, and Captain John Montresor, a British engineering officer stationed in New York, noted whimsically in his diary: "Grand illumination throughout the city, throwing of Squibbs, Crackers, firing of muskets and pistols, breaking some windows and forcing Knockers off the doors. A large mob of the Sons of Liberty went to the Fort to congratulate the Governor, three of which, drunk as they were, had admittance." The grateful Assembly voted funds to erect a statue of King George III in Bowling Green, and broadsides were posted in all the coffeehouses: "Peace proclaimed."

It was an uneasy peace, marred by occasional clashes between the Sons of Liberty and the Royal garrison quartered in the city. The tension exploded, late in 1769, when the British soldiers, weary of epithets and brickbats, revenged themselves on their persecutors by chopping down the "pine post where they daily exercised, called by them the Tree of Liberty." After four successive Liberty Poles had been destroyed, the Sons secured a tall ship's mast, bound it with iron bands, and set it in a deep hole on the Commons. Some members of the Sixteenth Regiment, during the dead hours of night, blew it up with gunpowder and insolently deposited the fragments on the doorstep of the Widow de la Montagne's Tavern on Broadway, the rebel rendezvous. In retaliation the mob collared three lobsterbacks next morning and marched them toward the mayor's office. A group of comrades in arms came to their rescue, wielding musket butts and bayonets, but the civilians defended themselves so vigorously with canes and cart stakes that the soldiers retreated

Nathan Hale on his mission the previous year. A British frigate-of-war drove their sloop onto the sandspit of Old Man's Point, and the entire personnel was captured or slain. Then I knew why I had wanted to write this book.

COREY FORD

Introduction

ESPIONAGE is one of those ancient professions that has from its very nature always been conducted in such anonymity and with such fragmentary documentation that no one could be so bold as to claim to write its definitive story, certainly not for the Revolutionary War. Bits and pieces have come to light from time to time. Thanks to revelations in the English archives we now know that Dr. Edward Bancroft, a confidant of Benjamin Franklin, was a British counterintelligence agent, transmitting data from the American mission at Passy to his employers across the Channel. Thanks, too, to the splendid collection of General Sir Henry Clinton's Headquarters Papers, we now have in rich detail the facts of Benedict Arnold's apostasy.

Because the American Revolution was a bitter civil war, as well as a war for liberation of a colonial people, spies chose to conceal their espionage roles even long after that war was over and the bitterness had subsided. In *The Spy* James Fenimore Cooper recorded the remarkable tale of one such secret agent which he heard from the lips of John Jay, only revealed to him years after the war and when that revered patriot had been long in retirement.

In *A Peculiar Service* Corey Ford has given us the fullest and

most convincing account of the extraordinary operations of
Washington's Manhattan agency, known as the Culper Ring.
He traces the undercover operations not only out of Manhattan,
solidly held redcoat territory, but on the Neutral Ground, the
section of Westchester County which lay between the two opposing lines.

A Peculiar Service reads like exciting fiction, but it is a
scrupulously documented and thoroughly researched book. Mr.
Ford has shown remarkable ingenuity as a spy-hunter and has
put together a jigsaw puzzle based on fragments of letters, allu-
sions in papers, and other fugitive data relating to persons, often
posing as Loyalists, who engaged in undercover activity for
General Washington. He has exploited fresh discoveries, including the rich vein of data contained in the William J. Donovan Papers at Columbia University's Special Collections, and
other recent revelations, notably the discovery by Mrs. Catharine
Crary that the opportunistic James Rivington, the notorious
Tory newspaper printer, was in fact a secret agent of Washington during the closing days of the Revolution, evidence which
confirms old legends repeatedly discredited by historians.

Corey Ford brings us face-to-face with bribery and subversion.
We catch the taint of treachery and corruption, the sense of peril
and the atmosphere of fear which overhung these espionage
operations. We can almost handle the phials of invisible ink,
and itch to get hold of the cryptic ciphers and the code names
used in messages smuggled out of Manhattan between the
bound covers of a book or in the sole of a boot. But this is more
than a cloak-and-dagger story. Corey Ford captures New York,
before and after the Great Fire, its crooked streets, its waterfront aroma, its boisterous taverns, and its divided loyalties.
Above all, and with that expert literary craftsmanship we have
come to expect of him, the author has penned memorable por-
traits of spies famous and others until now relatively unsung.

toward Golden Hill, a waterfront section near Burling Slip. Here a lively street fight ensued, one citizen was slain and several wounded, and the mob leader, a burly waterfront boss named Isaac Sears, received a bayonet scratch on his arm. The Battle of Golden Hill marked the first bloodshed of the Revolution, two months before the Boston Massacre.

Now Sears was a popular martyr, and the Sons of Liberty, more or less inactive in politics since the Stamp Act repeal, renewed their agitation. They were aided by a serious rift in the coalition of conservative Tories and moderate Whigs who had thus far held the radical faction of the city in check. The conservatives urged conciliation with the Royal government, hoping to influence Parliament by persuasion but balking at any overt measures which might jeopardize the privileges they enjoyed under the Crown. The moderates, though equally concerned with protecting their private interests, insisted on some more vigorous assertion of Colonial rights. Their schism tipped the political balance in favor of the self-styled patriot party. All the rebels needed was a cause; and in 1773 the bumbling British Ministry obligingly supplied one. Lord North's government, which maintained a token tax on tea, granted the East India Company a monopoly on the tea trade with America.

This was the issue on which the Sons of Liberty seized, joining forces with such active New England smugglers as John Hancock of Boston and Benedict Arnold of New Haven. In mob demonstrations reminiscent of the Stamp Act riots, they paraded with torches and banners, they published broadsides denying the right of Parliament to tax the Colonies, they pledged themselves to "regard as enemies all those who took part in the tea business." In December, a courier of the Boston Committee of Correspondence, Paul Revere, galloped to New York in the record-breaking time of four days with news of the Tea Party in Boston Harbor. The local Liberty Boys prepared Mohawk disguises of fringed buckskin, sharpened their hatchets, and waited grimly for the first tea ship to arrive at New York.

On April 22nd the merchant ship *London* slipped through the Narrows and tied up at Murray's Wharf, with eighteen chests of tea in its hold. While the city leaders met at the Merchants' Coffee House and drew up a formal resolution declaring that the tea should be returned to England, the mob took matters in their own hands. Scorning Indian disguises, they boarded the *London,* broke into the hold, and tossed its cargo into the East River. As the smell of water-soaked tea wafted from the harbor the following morning, cannon boomed at the Battery, the patriots' flag, a Union Jack cantoned on a red field, was raised on the Liberty Pole, and a parade led by Isaac Sears escorted the *London*'s captain back to his ship to the ironic strains of "God Save the King."

Day by day the mob grew more defiant of law and order. Tenants rioted, debtors broke jail, the eighty-seven-year-old Cadwallader Colden fled for his life to his country retreat in Flushing, Long Island. When the British government closed the port of Boston, hoping to starve its inhabitants into submission, thousands of sympathizers surged through the New York streets, carrying effigies of the King's Ministers and one of Satan bearing a placard: "Devil do thy office! With tartarean sulphur destroy these pests of mankind." The Sons of Liberty declared an embargo on shipments of supplies to the British troops blockading Boston Harbor, and offered violence to any merchant who dared to disobey. Isaac Sears — who preferred the nickname "King" Sears — was arrested for disturbing the peace, and his followers freed him at the jail door and carried him off triumphantly on their shoulders. Homes of Loyalists were daubed with tar and their windows shattered by stones, Royal arsenals were plundered, the Crown's authority flouted.

Now there was little doubt in anyone's mind that an open break with Great Britain was inevitable. Warlike rumblings in the city were growing louder. Patriots cleaned and oiled their long-barreled fowling pieces, and sent to Holland and even England for supplies of gunpowder. Their wives held pewter parties to collect lead plates and window weights and door knockers which could be melted down for bullets. A shocked visitor from London in early 1775 saw "nothing but rubbing up of arms, enlisting, exercising and other preparations denoting a vigorous resolution in the people to defend themselves against all aggressors to the very last." King George III declared the New England Colonies in a state of rebellion. "Blows must decide," he told Lord North, "whether they are to be subject to this country or independent." A Virginia tobacco-planter, Colonel George Washington, wrote that "the crisis is arrived when we must assert our rights." And in March the red-headed rabble-rouser Patrick Henry made an impassioned speech to the Virginia Convention in Richmond: "Gentlemen may cry Peace! Peace! — but there is no peace. The war is actually begun. The next gale that sweeps from the north will bring to our ears the clash of resounding arms . . ."

Shortly before noon on the 23rd of April — a year to the day after the New York Tea Party — the doors of Trinity Church swung open at the end of Sunday service, and the fashionable congregation emerged blinking into the bright sunshine. It was a vernal morning, soft and breathlessly calm. No trace of a breeze stirred the lacy branches of the elms, their leaf buds already unfolding in the early spring. The least sound carried a long way in the noonday stillness; quail were calling in the green meadows sloping to the Hudson, and curlews whistled along the rocky shore, bright with shadbush in bloom. The humid air bore the heavy scent of narcissus and hyacinths, imported from Holland and arranged in neat borders along the brick walk that led to the rear of the church and the Broadway gate. Even the city was hushed, and the voices of the parishioners were unnaturally loud as they strolled toward the deserted avenue.

There was another sound in the distance, a gale of wind sweeping out of the north. It seemed to swell in volume, building to hurricane force, punctuated by the far-off crackle of muskets and guttural cheers. The bell of the Brick Presbyterian Church near the Commons began clanging erratically, like a harbor buoy tossed in a storm, and above the tumult the listeners made out the clatter of hooves coming down Broadway.

The express courier was riding full gallop. He stood in the stirrups and his arm rose and fell regularly, flogging his horse on. He had been a long time in the saddle; mud caked his boots and spattered his blue homespun breeches, and their inseams were stained with lather from his horse. He reined to a halt before the church, and took a dispatch from his leather pouch and read it in a hoarse voice. The message was dated four days ago:

Watertown, Massachusetts,
April 19, 1775,
Wednesday morning near 11 of the clock.

To all friends of American liberty, be it known that this morning before break of day, a brigade, consisting of about 1000 or 1200 men, landed at Phipp's farm at Cambridge and marched to Lexington, where they found a company of our militia in arms, upon whom they fired without any provocation and killed 6 men and wounded 4 others . . . The bearer Israel Bissel is charged to alarm the country quite to Connecticut, and all persons are desired to furnish him with fresh horses as they may be needed. I have spoken with several who have seen the dead and wounded.

J PALMER,
One of the Committee of Safety.

Israel Bissel wheeled his mount and lashed it with the reins, rounded the corner into Wall Street, and galloped toward the Committee of Correspondence chambers in the Merchants'

Coffee House. The roar of the mob was growing louder, starting down Broadway, and the aristocrats climbed hastily into their gilt and crimson chariots. The clash of arms, resounding from Lexington, had ended a genteel and decadent way of life forever.

*   *   *

New York fell to the British almost without a struggle. The fleeing patriot army lost only fifty-odd killed or wounded and two hundred taken prisoner; the enemy casualties were a mere handful. Within a couple of hours after General Howe's assault forces landed on September 15th, 1776, the whole island south of Harlem was secured. When Fort Washington surrendered, two months later, the last gun was fired in Manhattan during the war.

But another war was waged in the captive city, a silent war which never ceased during the seven long years of British occupation. It was fought in the coffeehouses and taverns where Royal officers talked indiscreetly in their cups, in the intimacy of perfumed boudoirs, behind the closed doors of Royal command headquarters. Its strategy was bribery and subversion and treachery. Its weapons were phials of invisible ink, cryptic ciphers and code names, messages smuggled out of town between the bound covers of a book or in the sole of a boot.

As neutral Geneva was the focus of international espionage in World War II, so New York was the spy center of the Revolution. The very character of the city lent itself to intrigue. Its crowded streets afforded good cover, and furtive agents could slip in and out on market boats, or cross on the ferry between Manhattan and Brooklyn, on the pretext of trading with Long Island. The divided loyalties of its inhabitants — some of them Whigs who had concealed their devotion to the patriot cause, others impoverished Tories who would sell their information for a price — enabled Washington's confidential correspondents in New York to supply him with a steady flow of military intelligence throughout the war.

They worked anonymously, either through caution or a sense of shame at their deceitful occupation. Save for Nathan Hale, their names are little known today, and there are some whose identities were so carefully guarded that they are lost to history. Their duty was as hazardous as that of any soldier, but they wore no uniform and received no medals or public acclaim. Instead they bore the stigma of desertion, despised by family and neighbors who believed they had gone over to the enemy. They lived in constant fear, for they were well aware that detection meant death upon the gallows, the customary penalty inflicted on spies. Their only reward was the inner knowledge that they had served their country.

The members of the Culper Ring — code name for Washington's Manhattan agency — were amateurs, untrained in the business of spying: a schoolteacher, a Setauket farmer, an ex-whaler, a tavern keeper, a Quaker merchant; but through ingenuity or divine Providence or both they managed to outwit the British to the end of the Revolution. Hale's capture and death had pointed the need for a more efficient undercover operation; their unit was the result of his sacrifice. Naive and temperamental and absurd in terms of today's techniques, still it was America's first organized espionage service, the beginning of our modern intelligence.

BOOK ONE

❀❀

The Inglorious Tree

He died upon the "inglorious tree," not the death of the
soldier, but for his country's sake.

— SERGEANT STEPHEN HEMPSTEAD

I

A Spy from the Enemy

Head Q^{rs} New york Island Sep^r: 22^d: 1776
A spy f^m the Enemy (by his own full Confession) Ap-
prehended Last night, was this day Executed at
11 oClock in front of the Artilery Park
—BRITISH HEADQUARTERS ORDER

SUNDAY morning was bright and hot, unseasonably hot
for late September. Today would be another scorcher, Captain John Montresor reflected. It was not yet ten o'clock, but
thermal waves danced on the sailcloth shelters slung between the
apple trees, and the sun-baked grass crunched underfoot as
sentries paced the perimeter of the Artillery Park. The canvas
sides of his marquee had been lifted to encourage any passing
breeze, and he had discarded his scarlet coat, heavy with epaulets and gilt braid, and unbuttoned his buff-colored waistcoat,
and was working in shirtsleeves at his drafting table.

The tent stood a little apart from the others, with its back
turned to the camp to afford him greater privacy. Captain Montresor preferred to be alone. He was Chief Engineer of His
Majesty's forces in North America, aide-de-camp to General Sir
William Howe, but he had few close friends; something in his
mocking manner discouraged any intimacy. His lean face ta-
pered to a sharp chin, elevated in a perpetual attitude of amused
disbelief, and his mouth was pursed in a small skeptical smile.

His hair, already gray at forty, was lightly powdered and tied back in a neat club. He was an old campaigner, urbane and cynical and hardened to war.

His brush moved with practiced strokes, shading a relief map of Manhattan Island. He worked from memory; he knew every elevation and valley in the wild uneven terrain. Most of his military life had been spent on this side of the water. He had come to America as a young engineer in 1754, had served under Braddock during the French and Indian War, and had plotted the overland route from Maine to Quebec for General Amherst. After the war he had been stationed in New York, surveying the uncharted coastline of Manhattan and drafting the first authentic maps of the little city at its lower tip. Montresor's Island in the East River was named for him. It was on his maps that General Howe had relied when he landed his invasion troops at Kip's Bay last Sunday, just a week ago.

The British forces were currently deployed on Manhattan in two main positions, facing the rebel army dug in on Harlem Heights. At the northern front — Captain Montresor drew a series of boxes across the top of his map from Hell Gate to the Hudson — was the First Division, commanded by Sir Henry Clinton. The Second Division under General Lord Percy, ten regiments of artillery, was encamped about midway down the island, in a line west of the Post Road; the Brigade of Guards was a little below them; and here in the Artillery Park, a cultivated orchard adjoining the Dove Tavern, were the reserve artillery and the Provost Marshal's headquarters and Montresor's own Engineer Corps. From the Dove Tavern, the Post Road dipped southeast a mile to the Beekman Mansion, a handsome white-pillared residence situated on a bluff overlooking Turtle Bay. He marked the site with another box and lettered it: *Gen. Howe's Hq.*

His palm left a damp print on the map, and he took a scented handkerchief from his sleeve and dried his hands delicately and dabbed his beaded face. The air was sultry, and tainted with the sickly sweet smell of charred timbers and smoldering cellar holes. A pall of smoke still darkened the sky to the south over the gutted city. The fire had started Friday midnight and had not been brought under control until yesterday afternoon; nearly a third of New York lay in ashes. Rebel incendiaries, no doubt. Several had been caught red-handed, so the rumor went, and bayoneted or tossed alive into the flames, and other suspects were being rounded up hourly by the patrols. Now the British would have to scratch for winter quarters.

It did not seem like Sunday without the tolling of churchbells in the city. The rebels had carried them off when they fled, to be melted down for bullets, and the morning was breathlessly still. Soldiers lounged in front of their canvas lean-tos, weary after a night and day of firefighting, and puttered at off-duty chores: cleaning and oiling their muskets, polishing their boots, whitening their leather belts and cross-straps with pipe-clay paste. Here and there an iron cauldron of water was heating over a bed of coals, salmon-pink in the blazing sunlight, and men were doing their laundry or standing knee-deep in the tubs, soaping their naked flanks. The only sounds were the muted drone of conversation in the tents, a snatch of ribald song from the Dove Tavern, the dull insistent beat of a single drum somewhere in the distance.

The drumbeat was growing louder, and he saw the bulky figure of William Cunningham, the Provost Marshal, emerge from a rear door of the tavern. Captain Montresor's thin aristocratic nose wrinkled in distaste. He had no liking for this slovenly Irishman, his black broadcloth coat always wrinkled and stained, his stockings sagging, his face as red as his unkempt hair. His cheeks were disfigured by several taut scars, patches of glazed skin which turned livid white when he was angry. Souvenirs of his encounter with the Sons of Liberty, Montresor understood. Cunningham had come to New York in 1774 with a shipload of indentured servants whom he had kidnaped in Ireland; some had died of mistreatment on the voyage, and the Liberty Boys had freed the rest. When Cunningham protested, the mob had seized him on the Commons, torn the clothes from his back, and dragged him face down across the cobblestones to the base of the Liberty Pole. His features skinned and bleeding, he had escaped to the British man-of-war *Asia* and joined the Royal forces in Boston, where he had volunteered his services, as he phrased it, "in order to wreak vengeance on the Americans." He was a petty tyrant, profane and habitually drunk and despised throughout the army; but since he was a civilian, employed directly by the Ministry, he was independent of the authority even of General Howe.

He made his way across the orchard past Montresor's tent, swaying a little as he walked. It was apparent that he had put his time to good use at the tavern. Behind him trotted the half-wit boy Richmond, a giant young mulatto, his upper body bare save for a hand-me-down waistcoat of flowered brocade. He was only thirteen, but his developed chest muscles and solid arms were those of a grown man. A coil of rope was looped around his neck; he was the hired hangman. Cunningham stumbled to the front of the Park and steadied himself against an apple tree, and peered down the Post Road in the direction of the approaching drum.

Over its slow measured beat came the sudden shrill of a fife, and Captain Montresor recognized the derisive strains of "The Rogue's March." He turned his head in curiosity, and watched a small procession coming up the long grade in a swirl of choking dust. The drummer and fifer were in the lead, followed by a hollow square of guardsmen in blue coats faced with red, carrying primed muskets with bayonets fixed. The prisoner, his hands bound behind him, marched in step in the center of the square; even at a distance, Montresor was aware of his erect carriage, the broad shoulders straining against the unnatural pull of his pinioned arms. At the rear of the procession were two more guardsmen, hauling a cart which held an oblong box of rough pine boards.

They swung off the Post Road and halted before the Provost Marshal, and he took a step toward the prisoner and began cursing him in a low ugly voice, his mouth turned down at the corners. The young mulatto, aping him, glowered and jabbered unintelligibly. Cunningham turned away with a final oath, and gave an order, and a detail of soldiers with shovels set to work digging a hole beside the tree. The two rear guardsmen, their duty ended, lowered the shafts of the cart and started back toward the Post Road. Captain Montresor hailed them as they passed his tent, and acknowledged their salute with a perfunctory flip of his hand. "Who is our guest?"

"Rebel spy, sir. Picked up last night as he tried to go through the lines. The General ordered him hanged this morning."

"Without a trial?"

"No need, sir. They found the evidence in his stocking. Papers and maps of our positions."

Montresor cocked a quizzical eyebrow. "A fellow draftsman," he murmured. "Perhaps his maps are more accurate than mine."

He rose and buttoned his waistcoat, shouldered into his red uniform coat, and buckled a sword at his belt. A hand resting negligently on the hilt, he strolled toward the group under the apple tree. The prisoner stood in the broiling sun, watching the diggers; he was half a head taller than the guards around him, and Montresor studied him as he would survey a new terrain, objectively and without emotion. Broad-brimmed round hat, plain suit of brown homespun, low square-toed shoes without buckles. Young, no more than twenty-one, he guessed, and strikingly handsome: the skin was fair, the short-cut hair flaxen and the brows a shade darker, giving his blue eyes a deep shadowed look. He blinked them repeatedly as the salt perspiration trickled down his forehead, and now and then he ducked his face into the hollow of his shoulder to wipe it dry. He seemed composed and unafraid, and there was a shining quality in his face that baffled Montresor. On an impulse, he turned to Cunningham. "Marshal, would it be permissible for the prisoner to wait in the shade of my marquee until the preparations are completed?"

Cunningham assumed an important frown. He was not prone to grant favors, but Montresor was the General's aide, and he might want a favor in return someday. Moreover, his throat was well-nigh parched in this infernal heat; he could do with another flagon of rumbo. He said curtly: "Mind he's kept under guard," and set off toward the Dove Tavern with the mulatto at his heels, a dark shadow.

Montresor led the way to his marquee, and the cordon of guardsmen stationed themselves around the tent at a proper distance. He gestured courteously toward a chair. His young guest hesitated, indicating his bound hands, and Montresor apologized and untied them. The prisoner flexed his cramped arms in relief and rubbed his wrists; there were raw rope burns under the fine gold hair. Montresor sat down opposite him. "Your name, sir?"

"Hale. Nathan Hale. Captain in the Continental Army."

The eyebrow cocked again. "A fellow captain, too? We have much in common. I understand you are also a map-maker." He indicated the chart on the table with a small smile. "Would you have any suggestions?"

Hale bent over the map for a moment. "Haven't you overlooked Leslie's light infantry and the Forty-second Regiment of Highlanders under General Cornwallis, sir? When I saw them, they were encamped just east of the Bloomingdale Road."

"Hmm?" The smile faded. "Yes, of course. Quite right. Thank you." He added several boxes to the upper left-hand corner of his map, and regarded the prisoner with new interest. "You're very observant. Though I suppose you have to learn that in your trade."

"This isn't my trade," Hale corrected him. "I'm a school-teacher." He saw the skeptical lift of Montresor's chin, and took a folded parchment from his pocket. "Here's proof of my calling."

It was a Yale diploma, signed by President Naphtali Daggett, dated September 1773. Hale's own name was inscribed on the document; it did not appear to be a forgery. Montresor picked up a long-stemmed clay pipe and methodically tamped tobacco into the bowl, turning over a thought in his mind. "Pity you're not working for our side, you know." His voice was casual, but the eyes were shrewd. "We could offer you more than the rebels."

"I take that as a compliment, sir, but I'm not seeking any reward."

"A promotion, then? Perhaps a title?" Hale's indifference was beginning to irritate him. "You could save your neck if you came over to us."

"There are things I value more," Hale said quietly.

Captain Montresor held a candle to the bowl of his pipe, bending the flame with short sucking drags. He had never entertained any illusions about patriotism and duty and sacrifice. War was a business, and you worked for pay, and did no more than you were told. There were no heroes. He leaned back in his chair, and peered at the prisoner through a veil of curling blue smoke. His carefully nurtured cynicism was being challenged by something he did not understand, something in this stranger's face that set him beyond fear.

Hale broke the little silence. "If it is not imposing on your hospitality, Captain, I should like to write a couple of farewell letters."

Montresor indicated paper and quill with a nod of his head,

and Hale dipped a sharpened point in the inkpot and began the first letter. It was a formal report to his commanding officer, Lieutenant Colonel Knowlton of Knowlton's Rangers, stating the circumstances of his capture. He finished it quickly, and addressed a second letter to his brother Enoch Hale. Enoch was a year older, and closest to him in the family of twelve children; he would know how to break the news to their father. He wrote *Coventry, Connecticut,* and his pen slowed as past memories crowded out the present, and he could see the white frame farmhouse, and the stone walls he had helped to build, and the apple trees behind the house; they were more real than these trees around him now. There would be a stir of autumn in the tawny sunshine, and the first stabs of color would be showing in the rolling hills where he had hunted grouse as a boy. He wondered if his flintlock still rested on pegs above the kitchen hearth. It was fall pickling time, and the kitchen would smell of spice and boiling vinegar and cucumber relish. He shut his eyes to see it all better. The bell in the Congregational meeting-house would be chiming its final call at this moment, and Deacon Hale, in a black satin coat with white lace ruffles at the sleeves, would be leading the rest of the family into the house of worship, and they would kneel in the ancestral pew, and he would be there in their prayers.

He looked up at the heavy clump of boots. Cunningham was standing in front of the marquee, his face flushed with rum. The scars on his cheeks were like streaks of white war paint. "Who untied the prisoner?" he demanded.

"I did, Marshal." Montresor could not conceal the dislike in his voice. "He wished to write some letters."

Cunningham lurched toward the table, and swept up the letters and college diploma. "I'll take care of these," he said, crumpling them in his fist and ramming the wad into his pocket. He lowered at Hale. "On your feet, rebel."

Hale rose with dignity. "I request the services of a clergy-man, sir."

"Ask the Devil for absolution." Cunningham beckoned to Richmond, and the mulatto's vacant face split in an eager grin. "Make the prisoner ready."

It was done quickly. They stripped him to his body linen, and dressed him in a coarse white shroud edged with black, and placed a white hat with black trim on his head. His hands were bound again, and he was led to the front of the Artillery Park, escorted by armed guards. The shallow hole under the apple tree had been finished, and the pine coffin unloaded from the cart and set by the grave. A rope was tied to a high branch of the tree, the dangling end looped in a noose, and the empty cart stood directly beneath it.

Richmond leapt onto the cart with a catlike spring, and tested the rope with his weight, the biceps knotting in his thick brown arms. He nodded, and the guardsmen picked up Hale like a sack of grain and tossed him face forward onto the flooring. He strug-gled for a moment, his arms tied behind him, and reared to a squatting position, and the thrust of his powerful thighs lifted him to his feet. He steadied himself and looked down on the im-personal faces.

There were not many spectators; it was too hot to stand around in the sun for another routine hanging. A few artillery-men had strolled over from their tents in mild curiosity, and several camp-followers from the Holy Ground, their cheeks bright with rouge, giggled and whispered. Captain Montresor hovered at the rear of the crowd, impelled to watch against his will. His head was tilted back, the chin elevated in cynical amusement, but his gray eyes were unsmiling. They were fixed on the lone figure on the cart.

Cunningham raised his voice above the murmur of the spec-tators. "Does the prisoner have any last statement?"

Hale's lips moved silently, shaping the words he would say. His expression was exalted, as though his whole life were dedicated to this supreme moment. That was the quality in his face which had eluded Montresor, he realized: a kind of dedication, a fanatic devotion to an ideal that was more important than life itself. He spoke slowly, and Montresor had the fleeting impression that he was quoting something long remembered:

> ". . . What pity it is
> That we can die but once to serve our country."

Cunningham's impatient shout came over the final words. "String the rebel up!" The grinning mulatto adjusted the noose around Hale's neck and drew it tight, and tied a handkerchief over his eyes. He leapt lightly to the ground, and two guardsmen seized the shafts of the cart, bracing themselves to pull. The low steady roll of the drum could not quite drown the creak of cartwheels turning. Montresor lowered his head, and a shadow swung across the patch of sunlight before him.

He turned away from the crowd to hide the sudden moisture in his eyes. He did not know why he was moved, and it angered him. War was a business, and you lived or else you died, and that was all. There were no heroes.

⚜⚜

II

"Boston Is a Yankey Town"

NATHAN HALE was nineteen when the war began, an instructor in classical languages at Union Grammar School in New London. He had accepted the position after graduation from Yale, and it was greatly to his liking. "I have a school of 32 boys, about half Latin, the rest English," he wrote his friend and classmate Benjamin Tallmadge, who was teaching at Wethersfield Academy. "In addition to this I have kept a morning school, between the hours of five and seven, of about 20 young ladies." Tallmadge may have wondered wryly whether the young ladies arose at this unlikely hour because of their interest in Latin declension, or in their handsome young schoolmaster with his quick blush and shy unsure smile.

His love for the classics dated back to early boyhood in Coventry. He had been prepared for college by the local Congregational minister, the Reverend Dr. Joseph Huntington, a devout scholar of Latin and Greek; and in the little parsonage on Coventry Hill he had listened spellbound to the soaring cadences of Vergil and Cicero and Homer. He would recite whole passages from memory as he went about his farm chores in the evening, posturing and declaiming to the indifferent cattle in their stalls. The influence went deeper; in his impressionable and deadly serious young mind, he identified himself with the heroes of antiquity — Cyrus the Great, and Philip of Macedon, and Marcus, son of Cato, who "resign'd his life a sacrifice to his country's liberty" — and adopted their code of honor and martyrdom as his own. Even as a boy his appearance resembled a Roman statue, reminding one observer of Michelangelo's David: the round symmetrical limbs, the well-set head and chiseled features. Their perfection was marred by a powder burn on his forehead, the result of a hunting accident, and a brown birthmark at the nape of his neck where the hair was knotted in a club. His youthful companions used to twit him about it; they said it was a sign that he would be hanged.

When he entered Yale, at the age of fourteen, he had already made up his mind to be a Latin teacher. He was an average student, but excelled at athletic sports. His body, hardened by Spartan training, possessed a remarkable agility; he could put his hand on a fence as high as his head and clear it at a bound, or jump in and out of three hogsheads in a row. He held the college wrestling championship, Graeco-Roman style, and friends recalled that he "could kick a football higher than the elms" on the New Haven green. He was president of the debating society, and at Commencement Day exercises he and Benjamin Tallmadge were selected to argue the question: "Whether the Education of Daughters be not, without any Just Reason, more Neglected than that of Sons." To the delight of the daughters in the audience, Hale took the affirmative.

They had formed a deep bond of friendship, signing their letters "Damon" and "Pythias"; though in fact the two were opposites in many ways. Tallmadge was half a year older, the son of a Presbyterian minister in Setauket, Long Island, small-spoken and a trifle austere, with a sly caustic wit. Hale was outgoing and amiable, but his too ready laugh betrayed an insecure sense of humor. He was fond of feminine company and a favorite with the ladies, and rumors of his romances would reach his friends from time to time. "I should be very glad to have some news from you, I assure you," Tallmadge wrote him in New

London, "for by the latest accounts, you was all over (head and heels) in love . . ." His affairs were never serious; he was too engrossed in his career to consider matrimony at the moment, and lately there had been disturbing talk of war.

The storm clouds were gathering ominously, that spring of 1775. Wherever he went, visiting in the parlors of the town gentry or strolling along the busy New London waterfront, the conversation would turn to the recent melancholy events in Massachusetts Bay. The British Ministry had closed the port of Boston, in retaliation for the Tea Party riots last year, and New Londoners made no secret of their sympathy for the neighboring colony. They considered themselves loyal subjects of the Crown, but like all Americans they resented England's determination to tax them without their consent. A husky young dockworker named Stephen Hempstead expressed the general feeling. "We always governed ourselves," he told Hale. "We always mean to. They don't mean we should." There was bound to be bloodshed before the issue was settled, Hale was convinced. Captain Coit's volunteer company of militia mustered daily on the New London green, and the local Committee of Correspondence, keeping in close touch with its affiliated Committees in Massachusetts, warned that a clash was imminent.

The storm broke on the evening of April 20th, when Israel Bissel galloped down from Boston with the Lexington alarm. An emergency meeting was called in the Long Room of Miner's Tavern that same night, while Bissel was catching a few hours' sleep in an upstairs bedroom before setting out again at dawn for New Haven and New York. The argument was heated; some called for drastic action, others urged a more temperate course in hope of achieving an accommodation with Great Britain. The Honorable Richard Law, district judge of Connecticut, was in the chair, and he recognized the young Latin teacher. Hale's high musical voice, trained in college debating, grew eloquent as he addressed the meeting. "Let us march at once,"

he concluded, "and never lay down our arms until independence
is won." Several townsfolk gasped at such seditious talk; the
word "independence" was seldom uttered aloud.

Captain Coit's company started for Boston the following
morning, joining the rivulets of volunteers from other New
England villages and crossroad hamlets who were trickling
north to swell the spring flood. Hale stood with the older men
and women and children, watching them parade across the
green with haversacks loaded and flintlock fowling pieces shouldered. Some were in homespun smocks and manure-caked farm
boots; others wore fringed hunting shirts and doeskin breeches
and hatchets at their belts; a few were dressed in faded red
uniform coats and tricorns trimmed with tarnished lace, brought
down hastily from attic trunks where they had been stored since
the French and Indian War. The drums beat a quick flam, and
the fifes squealed "The White Cockade," the same tune the
minutemen had played as they marched to meet the British at
Concord, and the motley company swung smartly up the Post
Road and were swallowed in the dust.

The town seemed strangely deserted after they had gone, and
Hale settled back to teaching with an uneasy conscience. His
bold words at Miner's Tavern came back to taunt him; he had
urged his fellow townsmen to march, and he had stayed behind.
Three of his brothers had joined up after the news of Lexington; every post brought word of friends and classmates who
were enlisting; but he had pledged himself to remain at Union
Grammar School until his year's engagement ended in July,
and his rigid sense of obligation would not let him go back on
his word. He lectured his classes dutifully in Latin grammar,
but over his words, like an insistent drum, echoed the stirring
news in June of Bunker Hill, and the raw untrained volunteers
who had manned the shallow breastworks on Charlestown
Heights and the stone walls leading down to the Mystic, and
sent the British regulars tumbling back on their heels in wave

after wave until their powder gave out. Colonel Washington of Virginia had just been appointed commander-in-chief of the Continental Army, the *New London Gazette* reported, and was on his way to Cambridge to direct the siege of Boston. Early in July the Connecticut Assembly approved a new state regiment, designated the Seventh, under Colonel Charles Webb of Stamford. Recruits were being drawn from all the towns along the Sound, and Hale was offered a commission as first lieutenant.

It was a troubled letter from Benjamin Tallmadge that resolved him. Tallmadge was likewise torn between his desire to serve and his duty to teach; and his note was full of self-analysis. He had learned of Hale's proposed commission, he wrote, and was not certain of the proper advice to offer. "Liberty is closely connected with learning . . . When I consider you as a Brother Pedagogue, engaged in a calling, useful, honourable, & doubtless to you very entertaining, it seems difficult to advise you to relinquish your business . . . On the other hand, when I consider our Country, a Land flowing as it were with milk & honey, holding open her arms, & demanding Assistance from all who can assist her in her sore distress, Methinks a Christian's counsel must favor the latter . . . Was I in your condition, notwithstanding the many, I had almost said insuperable, objections against such a resolution, I think the more extensive Service would be my choice."

Hale wrote to the proprietors of Union Grammar School the next day, asking to be excused from the last few weeks of the term. Unconsciously he used Tallmadge's phrase in his own letter. "Schoolkeeping is a business of which I was always fond; and since my residence in this Town, every thing has conspired to render it more aggreeabble. I have thought much of never quitting it but with life; but at present there seems an opportunity for more extensive public service."

When he marched to Cambridge under the blue banner of Webb's Seventh Connecticut, his ozier camp basket was heavy with classical books to be reread during the campaign: Pope's *Iliad*, the *Aeneid*, the *Odes* of Horace, and Joseph Addison's *Cato*, a drama in verse which had been one of his favorites at college. Characteristically, his farewell remark as he departed was a quotation from Horace: *Dulce et decorum est pro patria mori.*

*   *   *

On its arrival at command headquarters in Cambridge, the Seventh was assigned to General John Sullivan's brigade at Winter Hill, near Medford, two miles by direct road from the British entrenchments on Charlestown Heights. Winter Hill marked the extreme northern end of the American line of investment; other Connecticut regiments were south of Cambridge at Roxbury, guarding the main approach to Boston; and the rest of the Colonial forces were deployed at strategic points in a semicircle around the besieged city. At some places the opposing armies faced each other across a narrow tidal marsh, so close that either side could see what the other was doing. Advance picket guards on Ploughed Hill could hear the redcoats digging entrenchments all night, and make out clearly the voices of sentries giving the countersign.

The Seventh encampment was a hodgepodge of makeshift shelters, no two alike, facing haphazardly in all directions like an Indian village. A few officers had regular tents, but most of the men were housed in crude huts topped with sailcloth. Their walls were constructed of piled stones and lumps of turf, or birch and other small brush bound together with willow branches, or halves of hogsheads set one atop another and smelling sourly of molasses or rum. Some were dank hovels without ventilation; others had doors and windows cunningly wrought with wreaths and withes in the manner of a woven basket. Since planks for flooring were scarce, the men slept on straw spread on the packed dirt, and cooked over open bonfires.

There was no proper sanitation, the camp smelled of decaying refuse, and was loud with the buzz of flies and hollow honk of scavenging ravens and the quarrelsome voices of soldiers who had imbibed too much Medford rum at Brown's Tavern.

Hale saw it all with starry eyes. The mud, the stench, the drinking and brawling were all part of the great adventure, and even the daily drills held an exciting promise of action to come, of a chance to serve with valor on some classic battlefield. In his first enthusiasm he sought to describe the scene in verse, though he admitted to Tallmadge that rhyme and meter were not his forte:

> *The hills with tents their Whiteness show*
> *Resembling much Mid winter's snow.*
> *(For some such cause perhaps the same,*
> *Our hill is known by winter's name.)*
> *When coming here from Watertown,*
> *Soon after ent'ring Cambridge ground,*
> *You spy the grand & pleasant seat*
> *Possess'd by Washin[g]ton the great . . .*

Soldiering was a far cry from schoolkeeping, but he trained himself diligently in his military duties. "Studied the method of forming a regiment for a review, of arraying the companies, also of marching around the reviewing officer," he wrote in his camp diary. "A man ought never to lose a moment's time. If he put off a thing from one minute to the next, his reluctance is but increased." He was popular with the men and joined in their sports, playing football and organizing wrestling matches between his company and the troops on adjoining Prospect Hill. "Evening prayers omitted for wrestling," a diary entry noted. "This hill stumped by Prospect," and, two days later, "Grand wrestle on Prospect Hill no wagers laid." Stephen Hempstead, the big dockworker from New London, was a member of his company; and after the meet, urged by the men, Hale stepped into the ring with him and flipped him expertly over a shoulder and pinned him to the turf. From that moment on, Hempstead attached himself to Hale with the mute idolatry of a stray pup who has found a master, following devotedly at his heels until they parted at Huntington Bay and Hale set out alone on his fateful mission.

There was ample leisure time that fall, as the siege of Boston dragged on. His off hours were spent at "Jabber & Chequers," or reading the Latin books he had brought, or riding into town with a college classmate, William Hull of Derby, aide to Colonel Webb. Hull made much of his acquaintance with his superior officers, and one night in November he brought Hale with him to the Cambridge quarters of General Israel Putnam. "W^t to Cm^{ge} with Capt. Hull, dined at Genl Putnams," he recorded in his diary. The legendary "Old Put" of the French and Indian campaign was in his late fifties, paunchy and boisterous and given to telling and retelling tall tales of his shipwreck off the coast of Cuba or his escape from being burned at the stake. He was a genial host, proud of his ability to stow a flagon of Madeira under his sword belt and lead the tableful in the Maggie Lauder song. A bold military leader, Hale judged, though he displayed little interest in such matters as logistics and strategy.

Opposite him at the General's table was a heavyset colonel, Benedict Arnold, whom Hale remembered from college days as an apothecary in New Haven, generally disliked by the students. Arnold was about to lead an overland expedition against Quebec, and he described his plans to Putnam with vehement confidence, his black eyes snapping as though he expected to be contradicted. He semed to be nursing a cancerous grudge toward society; his conversation was filled with curses against the political generals, as he called them, who were persecuting him and seeking to wreck his career. Hale was more impressed by the tall and modest major seated beside him, a thirty-six-year-old farmer from Ashford, Connecticut, named Thomas Knowlton. He had been a ranger under Putnam in the French wars, taken part in the capture of Ticonderoga, fought in Cuba against Spain, and served with valor at Bunker Hill. Hale listened in silent envy as Knowlton told how he had been sent with his Ashford troops to hold the right flank, a low stone wall surmounted by the remains of a rail fence. He had filled the gaps in the fence with straw, and his heroic stand had enabled the American defenders, their powder exhausted, to retreat in safety. Hale wondered when he might have a like chance to lead his men in battle.

For all the agreeable camp life, he was beginning to chafe for action. The military situation had developed into a stalemate. The Americans maintained their blockade of the lone road leading into Boston, but they lacked the weapons for an attack; there were never more than ten rounds of powder per man, and over two thousand soldiers were still without muskets. For their own part, the British did not feel their forces were sufficient to break the siege, and General Sir William Howe, who had succeeded General Gage in command, had no stomach for any more stone-wall fighting such as the regulars had faced in their costly assault on Charlestown Heights. As winter approached, both armies held to their established lines, and contented themselves with sporadic cannonading. The troops grew so inured to this daily bombardment that they made a game of it, holding an open knapsack and trying to catch a cannonball lobbed by the British, or scooping it up like a football before it stopped rolling, and putting it in one of their own cannon to fire back at the enemy.

Now the ground was furry with frost each morning, and the receding tide left a thin sheet of ice draped over the marsh grass, and the citizen army began to think of home. There were cattle to be rounded up before the snows came, and cornstalks to be gathered for fodder, and cider to be pressed, and soft beds waiting and wives to warm them. They could not see what good they were doing here. Rallying to the Lexington alarm was one thing; sitting idle month after month with scant rations and no pay was another. Men began to drift away in increasing numbers. Deserters were forced to straddle a sharp board with weights tied to their feet, or given thirty-seven lashes across the bare back, but the purple welts only made them more determined to quit. One whole Connecticut regiment marched home in a body. The rest counted the days until their short-term enlistments would be up in December, and they would be mustered out.

Washington appealed to Congress to raise money and recruit new levies to meet the emergency. At the Commander-in-Chief's personal request, Colonel Webb and all his officers re-enlisted when their terms ran out, and on New Year's Day Hale was promoted to the rank of captain. He pleaded earnestly with the men of his company to follow his example and volunteer for a few weeks more, and even offered his own salary as an inducement. "Promised the men if they would tarry another month, they should have my wages for that time." The entries in his army account book listed payments to four soldiers "in consequence of enlisting in the Continental service for another year," and one of them, his drummer, received "1 pr. Deerskin breeches and 32 shillings."

Thousands declined to sign again, despite the efforts of their officers, and those who stayed on were sullen and defiant to the point of mutiny. They refused to parade, they entertained prostitutes in their tents, they were fiercely resentful of the disciplinary measures ordered by George the First, as they nicknamed Washington. The General's long-suppressed temper boiled over at his army's "dearth of public spirit, want of virtue, stock-jobbing, and fertility in all the low arts to obtain advantage . . . an exceedingly dirty and nasty people. Could I have foreseen what I have to experience, no consideration upon earth should have induced me to accept this command."

The British in Boston were no better off. They were feeling the pinch of the long blockade, but General Howe was loath to swallow his pride and admit defeat. Scurvy and smallpox raged in the streets of the beleaguered city. All food except fish had to be brought in from England or Canada or the West Indies, and many vessels were lost in the Atlantic storms. Fuel was so scarce that soldiers tore down the remaining houses in burned-out Charlestown, ripped paneling and balustrades from the Whig mansions in Boston, destroyed barns and fences and shade trees, including the Liberty Elm where the patriots used to gather, and even removed the steeple of the Old North Church to burn for winter heat. Unaware of the American army's critical shortage of muskets and powder, the British were in a "tremble lest the Provincials should force their way into the town, and put us all to the sword for our cruelty at Lexington, and for setting fire to the ancient and flourishing town of Charlestown."

News of Arnold's failure at Quebec plunged the American camp into deeper gloom, and Washington realized that some offensive action was necessary to bolster the morale of his troops. Late in January he had two providential strokes of fortune. The British supply ship *Nancy* was captured by a rebel privateer, and the American arsenal was augmented by 2000 muskets, 30,000 round shot, and 100,000 flints. A week later Colonel Henry Knox, a chubby young Boston bookseller, arrived from Ticonderoga with 43 cannon and 14 mortars, which had been hauled on sledges from Lake Champlain, through the snowbound passes of the White Mountains, and down to Cambridge.

At last Washington was able to seize the initiative, and the British presented him with a golden opportunity. Through an incredible oversight, they had neglected to fortify Dorchester Heights, to the south of Boston. The American cannon in Roxbury started a diversionary bombardment of Boston Neck; and under cover of this feint, shortly after dark on March 4th, General John Thomas and two thousand men crept onto the strategic heights. Since trenches could not be dug in the frozen ground, Washington had cunningly arranged to send several hundred oxcarts carrying timber frames stuffed with hay, and hogsheads full of scrap iron and stones. All that night the men worked to set up their prefabricated barricades, chopped down fruit trees to form an abatis of sharpened timbers, and placed the loaded barrels on the edge of the cliff to be hurled down in an avalanche if the enemy attempted to scale its sheer sides. In the morning the British awakened to stare at an apparently impregnable series of breastworks dominating the city.

General Howe had had enough. He made hasty preparations for the evacuation of Boston, and arranged, through Loyalist intermediaries, that if the Americans would hold their fire while his troops were boarding their ships, the British would not put the city to the torch. On St. Patrick's Day the Royal forces marched to the waterfront, taking the precaution to strew the streets with sharp-pointed chevaux-de-frise lest the Americans should pursue them. Soldiers and over a thousand Tory refugees crowded onto men-of-war and transports, and the fleet stood out to sea, and Howe headed north to Halifax to mount his next attack.

Washington had little doubt where that blow would fall. New York's strategic location, midway between New England and the southern colonies, offered the British a central base of operations from which to strike in either direction at will. Its harbor was sufficient to shelter the entire Royal fleet, and the city would provide comfortable winter quarters. More important, New York was the gateway to the Hudson, and the Hudson was the gateway to Canada. The chain of connecting waters from the Hudson to Lake George to Lake Champlain to the Richelieu River to the St. Lawrence, if seized and made secure, would isolate New England and cut the American Colonies in twain.

As early as January General Charles Lee, next in command

to Washington, had proceeded to Manhattan to prepare its defenses; and with the release of Boston General William Heath
was ordered to organize a special command and start for New
York at once to meet the expected enemy invasion. Webb's
regiment, redesignated the Nineteenth Foot, was assigned to his
brigade. Hale packed his ozier basket with undisguised eagerness.
He had been too late for the battle of Bunker Hill; he had
seen no action during the long siege; perhaps in New York he
would have his chance to serve.

The Nineteenth marched south by easy stages, leaving Cambridge on March 18th, with cooked rations for five days, and
supplementing their food supply by overnight stops at Green's
and Burnham's and other inns along the way from Providence
to Connecticut. On the 26th they arrived in New London, and
the following day, the *Gazette* reported, Heath's brigade "embarked in high spirits on board 15 transports and sailed for
New York."

The weather was prosperous for the first two days of their
voyage; but on Friday evening a driving nor'easter lashed the
Sound to whitecaps, the gray sky met the water, and the transports were forced to weigh sail off Flushing and lay to until
morning, in order to navigate the treacherous shoals of Hell
Gate by daylight. All night long they wallowed in the heavy
rollers, seasick and miserable, and their high spirits faded fast.
It was still pouring on Saturday morning, and the sloops felt
their way cautiously past Montresor's Island and through the
rock-strewn channel into the East River. A choppy sea was running, and they were glad to pull into Turtle Bay and drop
anchor in the sheltered waters of the cove, pebbled with rain.

Hale stood on the forward deck, impatient for his first sight
of New York. The shoreline was barren and unpromising, lined
with salt grass and reeds; but, as he watched, the curtains of rain
parted for a moment, and he made out a high bluff to the north.

On its crest he saw a handsome white-pillared mansion and beside it a greenhouse whose glass panes reflected the unreal
pewter light.

The eddying curtains drew together again, and he stepped
over the side and descended a rope ladder to one of the small
boats, waiting to ferry the troops ashore.

*   *   *

They were coming and still coming, slogging down from
Turtle Bay in a long ragged line. The morning cloudburst had
turned the Post Road into a quagmire. Mud rose above the tops
of their half-boots and canvas spatterdashes, and their dragging
feet could not keep in step. Sunfish Brook was a swollen torrent,
curling over its low plank bridge, and they broke ranks to walk
the rails single file, balancing themselves with their muskets.
Sometimes a man would halt to take a slab of pressed tobacco
from his knapsack, bite off a chunk, and plod on again, his
jaws moving rhythmically to the muffled cadence of the drums.

The transports had dropped downriver to the city wharves to
unload the heavy baggage, but each man carried his personal
equipment. A sodden blanket roll high on his back; haversack
and woven camp basket and wooden canteen slung from white
straps crossed on his chest; a sheathed bayonet on his waist belt,
a cartridge box at his right hip. A few had rifles, but most of
them shouldered smoothbore Brown Besses. They leaned forward with the weight of their packs, and water funneled from
the upturned brims of their tricorns and spilled down their lean
Yankee faces.

Each company of Webb's Nineteenth had its distinctive uniform: Captain Bostwick's company in light gray surtouts and
buckskin breeches; Captain Perritt's company in green short-
coats with brass buttons and black velvet jackets; Captain Tuttle's company in blue coats and small castor hats with black
bands and silver buckles; Captain Hale's company in butternut-

colored coats with green lining. Hale marched at the head of his men, a sword at his belt and the yellow cockade of a captain on his hat. He was taller than the two lieutenants who flanked him on either side, and longer of stride; they had to jog a few steps now and then to keep abreast of him. The uniform coat was tight across his broad shoulders, and his thighs strained against the snug-fitting buckskin breeches as he pulled his boots from the clinging mud and planted them again in time with the drumbeat. He faced ahead with soldierly discipline, but his eyes stole right and left to observe the strange Manhattan countryside.

The downpour had settled into a cold March drizzle, dripping from the branches of the overhanging elms and poplars as they swung into the Bowery Lane. Everything had an oddly foreign look. Instead of the familiar stone walls of New England, the fields were enclosed by fences of split rails set in forks and held by withes, and white oyster shells were scattered over the freshly turned earth. The narrow hip-roofed farmhouses and barns were built of brick, their gabled ends decorated with exotic painted tiles, and clumps of Holland tulips were in early bloom beside their doorsteps. The Connecticut troops frowned in disapproval; no frugal Yankee would waste time prettifying his buildings like that.

The farms appeared deserted, though smoke curled from the chimney pots and cattle huddled in morose groups in the flooded barnyards, their heads lowered in submission to the rain. There were no cheers to greet the marchers, no handkerchiefs waved in welcome. Now and then a furtive face appeared in a dormer window, watching them with frightened eyes. A dog bristled and started toward them, its lips curled back in a snarl which changed to a yelp as a thrown stick caught it in the ribs. Once a barn door slammed and a plump Dutch *juffrouw* scampered terror-stricken through the mud toward the house, her skirts held high. A soldier called after her in a high Yankee twang: "H'ist 'em higher,

missie," and his comrades took up the remark and passed it glee-
fully down the line in a receding echo: "H'ist 'em higher,
missie." "Higher, missie."

They could see increasing signs of defense as they approached
the city. A group of riflemen were bivouacked in the Stuyvesant
orchard, huddled around a bonfire made from one of Mynheer
Stuyvesant's choice pear trees. The De Lancey mansion on
Lower Bowery Lane had been commandeered from its Tory
owner for a hospital; the iron gates of the estate stood open,
and carts of medical supplies rumbled up the beech-bordered
driveway. Side streets in the Out Ward were barricaded with
felled trees and wooden boxes of dirt, and on top of Bayard's
Mount the cedars had been leveled and the half-finished sides
of an earthen redoubt stood against the leaden sky. The sails of
Rutgers's windmill were motionless; the mill was being used for
billets. A block below it, the Bull's Head Tavern had been
taken over for officers' quarters, and tents for the enlisted men
were pitched behind the white palings of the stock corral. One
of the marchers recognized the gray surtout and striped waistcoat of a Massachusetts militiaman, and shouted to him: "I see
they got ye sleeping with the cows."

"You're lucky if you sleep anywheres in this town," the militiaman retorted. "Them New York bug-tits grabbed all the
barracks."

They turned right at the Plough and Harrow Inn and crossed
Chatham Square, wading knee-deep in mire churned by the
troops preceding them, and on the far side their weighted boots
struck the cobblestones of Chatham Street. A group of towns-
people loitered in front of the Tea Water Pump, and the New
Englanders gazed at them sullenly. They had no love for these
New Yorkers with their Macaroni wigs and tasseled walking
sticks and foppish London airs. New York had not come to the
aid of Boston; why should they come here to defend New

York? Lay the city in ashes so the British couldn't have it. Half the people were Loyalists anyway, they had heard, ready to take up arms against their own countrymen. They spat contemptuously in the mud.

The New Yorkers returned their gaze with hostile eyes. Food was scarce enough in the city without having to share it with these thieving New Englanders, who peddled wooden nutmegs and sold clay pellets for coffee beans. Their shops would be looted, their women molested, their taverns filled at night with illiterate farmhands and drovers and lobstermen. One of the group muttered in derision: "Yankees . . . "

Yankees! Their heads snapped back, their knobby jaws set. Yankees, eh? They trimmed ranks and marched in step with the drums. At the head of the line, the fifes started playing "The Lexington March," the parody ballade which had been written to mock the New Englanders and which they had adopted and christened "Yankee Doodle." Bostwick's company began to sing the words, and Perritt's company took them up, and Tuttle's joined in, and Hale's company swelled the chorus:

> *Sheep's Head and Vinegar,*
> *Butter Milk and Tansy.*
> *Boston is a Yankey town,*
> *Sing Hey Doodle Dandy . . .*

They were stepping proudly now, muskets shouldered in an even row, nasal voices raised in defiance:

> *First we'll take a Pinch of Snuff*
> *And then a drink of Water,*
> *And then we'll say How do you do*
> *And that's a Yankey's supper . . .*

West on Chatham Street, past the smoking tanyards on the shore of Collect Pond and Martling's Tavern and the Brick

Presbyterian Church, chanting in unison as Hale led his company onto the rain-soaked Commons:

> *Two and two may go to Bed,*
> *Two and two together,*
> *And if there is not room enough,*
> *Lie one a top o' t'other.*

The Tory Nest

GENERAL CHARLES LEE — no relation to the distingished Lee family of Virginia — was a disgruntled former officer in the British army, spindle-legged and plain to the point of ugliness and so racked with gout that he had to be borne on a litter. By nature a misanthrope, he preferred the company of his twelve pet poodles at the dinner table. "When I can be convinced that men are as worthy as dogs," he explained, "I shall transfer my benevolence." He was a consummate egoist, eaten out by jealousy of his Commander-in-Chief, whom he described to Horatio Gates as "that dark designing sordid ambitious vain proud arrogant and vindictive knave." His neurotic hatred of Washington would lead him eventually to betray his country as basely as the archtraitor Arnold.

Congress had been so impressed by Lee's own stories of his military successes in Europe that they had made him second-ranking general in the Continental Army; and in January of 1776, at his request, he was given the Manhattan defense command. The idea had been in his mind since last November when Isaac Sears, exiled from New York, had made his way north to Lee's quarters in Cambridge. After several months of despotic mob rule, "King" Sears had been deposed by the moderate faction under John Jay and Livingston, and in his bitter resentment he claimed that New York was a "Tory nest" and the majority of its citizens favored the British cause. Lee's twisted face lighted; he would punish the Loyalist city, and at the same time enhance his own chances of succeeding Washington as supreme commander.

News that General Lee was bringing fifteen hundred troops from Boston, with the vengeful Sears as his Adjutant General, threw the populace into a panic. Two British men-of-war, the *Phoenix* and the *Asia,* were anchored in the East River with their guns trained on the New York waterfront, and an open clash with Lee's approaching forces seemed inevitable. The frightened citizens pictured their streets raked with grapeshot, their homes shelled, their city leveled. As Lee was carried down the Post Road, his gouty leg propped on pillows, he met a steady stream of refugees passing him on their way north, women and children and household goods piled into carts. Every vehicle and horse in town was pressed into service in the mass stampede, but many of the poor had to leave their belongings behind. Some fled into Westchester, others rowed in small boats across the ice-choked Hudson to seek safety in New Jersey. He entered an almost deserted city, its total population less than five thousand.

Lee did nothing to alleviate the fears of those who remained. He saw himself more as an avenger than the city's defender. Sears and his bully boys roamed the streets with tar buckets and feathers, in search of lurking Loyalists, while Lee, defying the British guns, set his men to work chopping down shade trees, digging trenches, throwing up barricades across Broad and Wall Streets, erecting batteries at Fort George and on the Whitehall docks, and building redoubts on Bayard's Mount and other eminences. Troops broke open and quartered themselves in any residences they found vacant, and the stately mansions on lower Broadway swarmed with rough soldiers who tore down the mahogany balustrades for firewood and despoiled the teakwood floors with their filth. "Oh, the houses of New York, if you could but see the insides of them, occupied by the dirtiest people on the continent," a resident mourned. "If the owners ever get possession again, I am sure they must be years in cleaning them."

Early in March, Lee was transferred to Virginia to head the new Department of the South, and Isaac Sears retired to private life in New Haven, where he amassed a fortune during the war as a privateer. Temporary command was given to William Alexander, a hard-drinking and hard-fighting patriot who claimed a lapsed Scottish earldom and preferred to be called by his assumed title of Lord Stirling. Advised by Washington that the British were about to abandon Boston, General Stirling called for reinforcements, and regiments were sent from the adjoining colonies, taking over such billets as the local militia had not appropriated for themselves. Over five thousand troops were already in New York on March 30th when Webb's Nineteenth Foot marched down from Turtle Bay.

Captain Hale's company was stationed on the west side of the Bowery Lane at Grand Street, guarding the redoubt on Bayard's Mount. They were lucky enough to find quarters in an old snuff mill, long in disuse; the roof kept out the rain, but snuff had permeated the walls and sifted into the cracks between the floor boards, and every footfall raised a fine powdery cloud that set them to coughing and sneezing. There were no furnishings, and they spread their blankets side by side on the hard floor. Hale shared a room with Sergeant Hempstead, who curled at the door like a huge watchdog protecting its master.

More and more troops poured down from Boston as the siege ended. By early April there were fourteen thousand soldiers in the city. General Israel Putnam took over the New York command from Lord Stirling, and moved into the elegant Kennedy mansion at Number One Broadway. The adjoining residence of John Watts was assigned to Putnam's staff, including his young aide Major Aaron Burr. On April 10th, twenty-three transports sailed through Hell Gate with General John Sullivan's brigade of six regiments; a couple of days later General Nathanael Greene disembarked his brigade at Cruger's Wharf; and on April 13th the Commander-in-Chief and his entourage trotted down the Post Road into town. Citizens lined the highway, curious for their first glimpse of the great General who had routed the enemy from Massachusetts Bay; and the ten-year-old William Dunlap, later the author of the first history of the American theater, stood wide-eyed as the party of military horsemen drew nearer, dressed in blue and buff coats and red waistcoats and buckskin breeches. "They were gallantly equipped and mounted," he recalled, "with glittering gold epaulets on either shoulder. But the center figure was the tallest of the group, and I knew that I saw in him the man on whom every thought centered. The salutation of taking off my cocked hat was performed with the feeling which probably my face expressed. Instantly the salute was returned in the same manner by the chief, and each hat in the company was lowered with its waving plume to me. They passed and I gazed after them. I had seen Washington."

Now the deserted city was coming back to life as the military capital of America. Its waterfront, long idle, teemed with sloops unloading supplies and ammunition, and the streets echoed to the rattle of munition carts, the beat of drums, the barked commands of officers, the endless shuffle of marching men. Their uniforms were as varied as their regimental colors. Marylanders in green shirts and leggins to match. Some New Jersey riflemen in short red coats and striped trousers, others in blue coats and leather breeches and wool hats bound with yellow. Pennsylvanians in all the hues of the rainbow, brown and buff, or blue and red, or brown and white with pewter buttons. Virginians in white smock frocks furbelowed with ruffles at the neck and elbows and wrists, black stocks, and their hair in queues. New Hampshiremen in homespun tow frocks, frontiersmen from the Vermont Grants in fringed hunting shirts with powder horns

slung from their shoulders and tomahawks at their belts, seamen from Rhode Island with knitted stocking caps pulled down
over their ears.

New York had turned into a garrison town, with all the pag-
eantry and all the vices. Shopkeepers took down their shutters,
hung out their silhouetted metal signs, and trebled their prices
to take advantage of the booming military business. Taverns
mushroomed overnight; a survey showed 267 in New York by
May. Cockfights were held daily in the alleys, gambling houses
invited the visitors to risk their wages at a game of Pharaoh, and
ladies of easy virtue beckoned seductively from darkened doorways. "The inhabitants of the Holy Ground have brought some
of the officers and a number of the soldiers into difficulty,"
Colonel Baldwin wrote his wife in Woburn, Massachusetts.
"These bitchfoxly jades, jills, haggs, strums, prostitutes and
whores (by information) continue their imploy which is become very lucrative." He hastened to assure her that "I was
never within the doors nor changed a word with any of them except in the execution of my duty as officer of the day in going
the grand round with my guard of escort, have broke up the
knots of men and women fighting, pulling caps, swearing, crying
'Murder' etc — hurried them off to the Provost dungeon by
half dozens, there let them lay mixed till next day . . . Hell's
work."

Inevitably the animosity between the Yankees and the residents of Manhattan erupted into violent quarrels. The New
Englanders claimed that local merchants were overcharging
them; the New Yorkers retorted that the troops from the north
received higher wages and therefore could afford to pay more.
Charges of "Tory turncoat" and "Loyalist pimp" resulted in
so many bloodied noses and broken skulls that Washington
issued a headquarters order: "The General most earnestly en-
treats the officers, and soldiers, to consider the consequences;
That they can no way assist our cruel enemies more effectually,

than making divisions among ourselves; That the Provinces are all United to oppose the common enemy, and all distinctions sunk in the name of an American."

The accusations of the New Englanders were not without foundation. It was common knowledge that the enemy was receiving accurate reports on the American strength and positions, which could only be sent by informers in the city. As early as April, the British War Office was in possession of a complete description of the "State of the Fortifications in New York," with an itemized account of every battery, location of guns, and number of troops. Infuriated by the evidence of Loyalist espionage, the Sons of Liberty took it on themselves to clean out the Tory Nest. Suspected citizens were routed from their beds, stripped and coated with boiling tar and sprinkled with feathers, and then turned loose by the mob to run in blind circles like decapitated white hens, crazed with pain. Others were pelted with stones, or paraded with lighted candles in their hands which they were ordered to hold aloft on pain of having them pushed in their faces, or carried naked through town astride a rail, jouncing up and down on the sharp edge until they were maimed for life. A letter from a New York patriot reported enthusiastically: "We had some grand Tory rides in this city this week; several of them handled very roughly, their clothes torn from their backs and their bodies pretty well mingled with dust . . . There is hardly a Tory face to be seen this morning."

To avoid mob violence, the ministers of the Anglican churches removed the Royal coat of arms from the walls behind their pulpits, and most of them prudently omitted the usual prayers for King George and his family. The Reverend Charles Inglis, rector of Trinity, was threatened with lynching if he persisted in using the regular liturgy; he replied that to abstain from the mention of England's monarch would be to violate his oath. On Sunday morning, as he was holding services, a company of one hundred soldiers marched into the church with drums beating and fifes playing, bayonets glinting at the ends of their loaded muskets. The congregation expected that Mr. Inglis would be slain at the sacred desk if he read the collect for the King, but he ignored the troops in the aisle and continued the service to the end. It was the last service held in old Trinity; the vestry elected to close its doors for the emergency, and they never reopened.

Loyalist sentiment was equally strong on Long Island, and observers reported that sloops filled with provisions and fresh water were slipping out of creeks and coves under cover of darkness to supply the British warships. In May Washington sent an expedition to round up the ringleaders; and Hale was assigned to the regiment on temporary duty. They crossed on the ferry to Brooklyn, a peaceful village of neat Dutch homes clustered around an octagonal white church, and marched east through the rolling countryside. Quail were calling in the fields of wild asparagus, and heath hens hurried their new spring broods across the Jamaica Road. Benjamin Tallmadge had boasted to him of the fine hunting on Long Island, Hale remembered. It reminded him that several months had passed since he had heard from Tallmadge last. He wondered if he was still teaching in Wethersfield.

The regiment spent three weeks on the island, working their way as far east as Oyster Bay and Huntington. They were aided by patriot residents who confided the names of Tory neighbors known to be supplying the enemy. The quarry proved elusive; as the searching party approached, they took to the swamps or concealed themselves in caves and hollow trees. John Harris Cruger, son of former New York Mayor John Cruger and one of Governor Tryon's counselors, was discovered hidden beneath a farmer's haymow. The aristocratic Augustus Van Cortlandt was shielded for ten days in the cowshed of a friendly Quaker, his conscientious host taking pains to walk backwards when he brought the fugitive his meals in order to be able to swear he had not seen him. "It would grieve every good man to consider what unnatural monsters we have as it were in our bowels," Hale wrote to his brother Enoch. "Numbers in this Colony, and likewise in the western part of Connecticut, would be glad to imbrue their hands in their Country's blood."

He returned to find the city buzzing with excitement. A monstrous Loyalist plot had just been revealed. Washington had declined a dish of peas, so the camp gossip ran, and his housekeeper had scattered them to the chickens, and all had died. One report claimed that the conspirators had planned to poison both Washington and Putnam and stab them while drugged; another said they hoped to take them alive and deliver them to London for punishment. Day after day the rumors grew wilder. The Tories were secretly plotting a mass uprising when the British arrived. They would blow up the powder magazine, spike the cannon, loot the arsenal, and attack the Continental Army from the rear with its own guns. The whole affair had been concocted by Governor Tryon, who was keeping in daily contact with Loyalist spies from his safe haven aboard the *Duchess of Gordon*.

William Hull, as Colonel Webb's aide, was in a position to give Hale more official information. David Matthews, Mayor of New York, had been taken into custody, Hull said, along with a gunsmith named Forbes, a drummer, a fifer, and a member of Washington's own bodyguard, Sergeant Thomas Hickey. Mayor Matthews was deported to jail in Litchfield; Forbes and the others saved their necks by telling all they knew; but Sergeant Hickey, who refused to talk, was tried by a court-martial and sentenced to be hanged by the neck until dead.

He had other news for Hale. A letter from a friend in New Haven mentioned that Benjamin Tallmadge had just accepted a commission in Colonel Chester's Connecticut regiment, and was on his way to New York.

*　　　*　　　*

It had not been an easy decision for Benjamin Tallmadge. His oldest brother William had served as a sergeant during the Boston siege, and two of his younger brothers were now privates in Captain Daniel Roe's Setauket unit of the Suffolk Guard, his father had written. Benjamin was his namesake and favorite son, and the Reverend Tallmadge, failing in health, had begged him to remain at his schoolteacher's desk in Wethersfield. But in June, when the academic term ended, he was offered a commission as lieutenant by Colonel John Chester. It was a particular honor; Chester's Wethersfield minutemen were famed as the only company in uniform at Bunker Hill, though the men had pulled hunting shirts over their blue coats so they would not present too tempting a target to the enemy. He found himself confronted with the same problem which Hale had faced a year ago; and, like Hale, he chose the more extensive service. His only request was that he be allowed to break the news personally to his father in Setauket before reporting for duty in New York . . .

The Reverend Benjamin Tallmadge was pastor of the Setauket Presbyterian Church, a gray shingled structure located on one side of a small triangular park, facing the white-steepled Caroline Episcopal Church across the green. The parsonage was a short distance from the church, on the side of a gently sloping hill. As Benjamin started down the familiar path, his two youngest brothers, barely in their teens, raced to meet him. They halted abruptly, awed into silence by his blue uniform coat faced with red, his shining officer's boots, the sword at his side. He put his hands on their shoulders, and they walked together toward the parsonage, and the Reverend Tallmadge was waiting in the open doorway.

Benjamin and his father were alike in appearance: tall, well proportioned, with angular features and outthrust jaw. Both were taciturn and reserved, but they had always been unusually communicative in a deep unspoken way. It was an understanding that did not require words. The Reverend Tallmadge's expression betrayed no emotion at the sight of his son's uniform. He took his hand in a long hard clasp. "Well, Benjamin," he said after a moment, and led him into the parsonage.

That afternoon, after midday dinner, Tallmadge strolled down the Old Town Road to the village. A drum was thudding, and some sixty members of the Setauket Guard were holding their daily muster in the field opposite Austin Roe's Tavern. He paused in the shade of an oak beside the tavern, and watched them parade in and out of step, Captain Daniel Roe bawling orders at the head of the awkward unit. Some were in hunting shirts, others in faded homespuns; only a few had muskets. His younger brothers John and Samuel, twenty-one and twenty, marched with earnest faces, carrying broomsticks on their shoulders. He picked out other faces in the ranks. Austin Roe, the tavern keeper, lanky and laconic. Abraham Woodhull, whose farm was on the neck of the peninsula fronting on Conscience Bay, pale and hollow-chested and looking older than his twenty-six years.

Austin Roe spotted him first, halted in the line of march to shade his eyes incredulously, and then yelled: "Ben, you old hellion!" The others turned, and broke ranks and ran across the road to greet him. Captain Daniel called a tardy "Company dismissed" and hurried to join the group which had gathered around Tallmadge, grinning and gaping at his uniform and making a mock show of saluting. Austin linked an arm in his, and they all crowded into the little taproom of the tavern, and seated themselves around the trestle table. Austin's young wife Catherine set foaming tankards before them, and Tallmadge leaned back in a barrel-chair and sipped his small beer. The floor had been freshly sanded, and the dark oak-beamed room had a comfortable smell of tobacco smoke and whale-oil lanterns and spilled ale. It was good to be home.

They plied him with town gossip, all talking at once. Did he know that Judge Selah Strong and Nathaniel Woodhull, Abraham's uncle, were the Suffolk delegates to the New York Provincial Congress now meeting in White Plains? Was he aware that Woodhull had been elected its president? Well, then, had he heard that Woodhull had just resigned his office, to take an appointment as Brigadier General in command of the Long Island militia? Austin Roe winked at Abraham Woodhull across the table. "You picked the right tit, Abe. You'll be a colonel pretty soon, sure'n God made little green apples."

Abraham gave him a wispy smile, and retreated behind his tankard. He was diffident in a crowd, and his low shaky voice could not make itself heard.

One friend that Tallmadge missed was Caleb Brewster. Caleb was the local blacksmith, a jovial young giant, great-grandson of the first minister of Setauket; he had shipped before the mast as a boy, and had returned with salty language and a notable proficiency with his fists. Why wasn't he drilling with the rest, Tallmadge wondered. "Cale?" Austin Roe grinned. "Hell, he's been a regular since last April, him and Josh Davis. You know how Cale's always spoiling for a fight. He's a second lieutenant now with Colonel Smith's county regiment."

Tallmadge set down his empty tankard. "There's a lot of others I didn't see today."

"Well, some of them was sick," Austin said, "or they had their farms to tend, or else there was other reasons." He paused until Catherine had served a second round, and leaned forward and lowered his voice. "A lot of 'em are King's men in this town. Half Setauket is Tory, I'd reckon. Folks like Dr. Muirson, and the Reverend Lyon of Caroline Church, and of course Richard and Benjamin Floyd. Funny thing how families like the Floyds is split up. Here's their own sister married to General Woodhull, and their brother William a member of the Continental Congress down to Philadelphia. Took his wife and little girl with him. Remember Mary Floyd?" he asked Tallmadge. "She's twelve now, and pretty, s'I, you'd never know her."

Abraham Woodhull licked his colorless lips, and his voice was so faint that the others bent their heads to hear him. "There's going to be trouble in this town if the British come, all these Tories."

"Now, Abe," Austin drawled, "no sense gettin' all haired out about it. They won't come here." He appealed to Tallmadge. "Will they, Ben?"

Tallmadge hesitated a moment. "Howe's fleet is supposed to be on its way down from Halifax. They might land on Long Island in order to attack New York. Maybe they won't get this far out."

"Well, if they come, I'll aim right at 'em." Austin Roe gestured to his wife for more beers. "Best we get rid of this barrel before the redcoats grab it."

*   *   *

The execution of Sergeant Hickey was scheduled for eleven in the morning of Friday, June 28th. A gallows had been erected in a field near the Bowery Lane, between Colonel Huntington's and Colonel McDougall's camps; and all the brigades in New York were ordered to assemble at ten o'clock, and march to the site of the hanging. Washington was determined to drive home the moral lesson to his troops. "The unhappy fate of Thomas Hickey, executed this day for mutiny, sedition, and treachery," his headquarters order read, "the General hopes will be a warning to every soldier in the Army."

Tallmadge had arrived in the city the previous night, and reported to his assigned regiment, encamped by the Merchants' Coffee House at the foot of Wall Street. On Friday morning he took his place in the ranks for the first time, and they paraded up Queen Street and east to the Bowery Lane and joined the throng of over twenty thousand spectators, soldiers and civilians, gathered to witness the military drama.

Promptly at eleven they heard the funereal beat of drums, accompanied by a constant roll on the snares, and the fifes struck up "Poor Old Tory." The procession came down Chatham Street and crossed the square to the field, eighty soldiers with loaded muskets guarding the sullen Hickey. All the buttons had been slashed from his uniform coat, and the red cloth epaulette of a sergeant ripped from his right shoulder. The prisoner broke down only once, at the foot of the gallows, when the chaplain shook his hand in farewell. He recovered his composure quickly, wiped the tears from his face, and assumed a scornful smile as he mounted the steps of the movable platform. The noose was placed around his neck, the blindfold adjusted, the platform yanked away. His body swung outward, writhed for a moment, and then hung limp.

The brigades were dismissed, and the troops shoved and milled across the field, like an impatient audience when the drama is over. Tallmadge made his way slowly through the crowd. Near the gallows he saw an officer standing alone, gazing at the dangling form above him. There was no mistaking the erect carriage, the well-set head. Tallmadge shouted "Nathan!" and they embraced, and walked together toward the Bowery Lane. Hale turned his head for a last thoughtful look at the gibbet as they left the field.

At nine the following morning, June 28th, lookouts with spyglasses detected a thin column of smoke rising on Staten Island, the prearranged signal that the British fleet from Halifax had been sighted. Shortly after noon an express arrived from the island to report that forty-five square-rigged vessels were anchored off Sandy Hook. More ships and transports kept coming in all day "like a swarm of locusts escaped from the bottomless pit," their deck rails lined with redcoats. By nightfall 113 enemy masts rocked in the shadow of the Atlantic Highlands, with six thousand veterans of the Boston siege, other seasoned troops from Royal garrisons in the West Indies and Gibraltar and the British Isles, and several thousand German mercenaries from Hanau and Hesse: the most formidable armada ever employed by a European power outside the Continent.

Hale's company assembled that night to hear him read aloud General Washington's proclamation to the army: "The time is near at hand which must probably determine whether Americans are to be slaves or freemen. The fate of unborn millions will now depend (under God) on the courage and conduct of this Army . . . We have therefore resolved to conquer or die."

*   *   *

General Israel Putnam had embarked on a desperate plain to seal off the Hudson. Fort Washington was nearing completion on the northernmost heights of Manhattan Island; almost opposite it was Fort Lee on the Jersey Palisades. On a line across the river between the two forts, a number of weighted hulls had been scuttled to block the main channel and divert enemy shipping within range of the shore batteries. Atop these sunken obstacles were mounted chevaux-de-frise, long sharpened timbers framed together and submerged just below the surface, so that their elevated points would rake the bottom of any vessel passing over them. One secret passageway was left open in the barrier to allow American ships to pass through unharmed.

Loyalist spies had watched, listened, made notes. A little north of the city at Bloomingdale was the Apthorpe country seat, an austere stone mansion overlooking the river. Charles Ward Apthorpe, a scholarly gentleman in his late fifties, and his neighbor Oliver de Lancey, scion of one of New York's leading families, were both members of Governor Tryon's council and ardent Tories; they were suspected of bribing men to enlist in the King's service, and the Committee of Safety had summoned them to appear for trial. On a dark midnight Apthorpe and De Lancey climbed into a small canoe, paddled down the Hudson unchallenged, and crossed the heavy swells of the harbor to take refuge aboard the *Duchess of Gordon*, lying just below the Narrows. There they gave Governor Tryon a detailed description of the barrier across the river, and charted the exact location of the safe passage.

They arrived just as the British fleet at Sandy Hook hoisted sail and stood for the Narrows. Soldiers working on the barricades of New York gathered on the sea wall, and gazed in dismay at the forest of masts that filled the Lower Bay. The fleet came to anchor about two miles off Gravesend; and the following day, July 2nd, General Sir William Howe disembarked his 10,000 troops on Staten Island without opposition. His brother, Admiral Lord Richard Howe, followed shortly with some 150 transports from England; Generals Henry Clinton and Lord Cornwallis brought their forces back north after their defeat at Charleston; further reinforcements of several crack Highland regiments swelled the invading army to a total of 32,000 trained combatants, including 7800 German professionals hired by King George at the bargain rate of $34.50 per man killed, three wounded counting as one dead.

Staten Island proved to be a delightful encampment for the British soldiers and sailors. "The fair nymphs of this isle are in wonderful tribulation, as the fresh meat our men have got here has made them as riotous as satyrs," young Lord Rawdon wrote gaily to the Earl of Huntington in London. "A girl cannot step into the bushes to pluck a rose without running the most imminent risk of being ravished, and they are so little accustomed to these vigorous methods that they don't bear them with the proper resignation, and of consequence we have the most entertaining courts-martial every day . . . A woman who had been forced by seven of our men came to make a complaint to me 'not of their usage,' she said, but of their having taken an old prayer book for which she had a particular affection."

The landing of British troops under their very noses threw the New York defenders into a frenzy of activity. Officers and soldiers sweated side by side in the early summer heat, digging trenches and felling trees and dragging cannon to hastily constructed redoubts. All civilians were ordered by the Committee to work on the fortifications, the Negroes every day and the whites every other day. From morning to night the city echoed to the thud of pickaxes and scrape of spades. Mahogany logs were taken from West Indian cargoes and piled in barricades across every street leading to the river. The Commons was almost entirely enclosed; Broadway was obstructed in front of St. Paul's Chapel; a bulwark was thrown up behind Trinity Church, another in Chatham Square, another at the Jews' Burying Ground on Catiemut Hill. Batteries were located at Horn's Hook on the upper East River, to cover the Hell Gate channel, and at Paulus Hook in Jersey, fronting the bay. A citadel and outworks were erected on Governor's Island, the strongest position around Manhattan. A fort with seven guns rose on Brooklyn Heights, which commanded lower New York and its harbor much as Dorchester Heights had dominated Boston. Washington realized that an island surrounded by navigable waters would be hard to hold against a British naval attack, particularly since an American navy did not exist; but he was determined to make New York an advantageous field of battle and contest every inch of ground if the enemy gained a foothold.

While the onetime peaceful city was changing into a bristling fortress, a more profound change was taking place in the minds of the people. Even as late as the end of 1775, the thought of independence was voiced only by a few hotheads and extremists. The Colonies had taken up arms to defend their rights as Englishmen, not to severe their allegiance with the mother country. Both Washington and Jefferson were opposed to independence;

John Adams said he wanted only "a restoration to the state of things before the contest began"; Benjamin Franklin assured Lord Chatham that he "had never heard from any person drunk or sober the least expression of a wish for separation."

But by the spring of 1776 public sentiment had begun to change. The British had shown no intention of yielding to Colonial demands, they were employing foreign troops to slaughter their own countrymen, they had incited Indian raids on isolated settlements; and there was a growing desire to end all ties with England. The feeling was galvanized by the publication in January of an inflammatory pamphlet, written by an obscure British expatriate, entitled *Common Sense*. "Everything that is right or natural pleads for separation," Thomas Paine declared in purple prose. "The blood of the slain, the weeping voice of nature cries 'Tis time to part." Within three months the tract had sold a hundred thousand copies, and suddenly the word "independence" was on every tongue. Strangers halted in the street to debate the burning issue, soldiers argued it over their campfires, and the coffeehouses of the city echoed to the new slogan: *'Tis time to part.*

Hale discussed it heatedly with Tallmadge as they strolled down Queen Street toward Fraunces' Tavern on a Sunday evening in early July. It was the first time they had met since the Hickey execution, and there was stirring news from Philadelphia. Richard Lee of Virginia had proposed a resolution calling for a confederation of American states, and a dissolving of all allegiance to Britain. The Congress was debating it at this moment.

Tallmadge was more reserved. "It would mean a long and bloody war."

"But aren't we at war now?" Hale pushed open the tavern door. "Even the King has said so. Independence is already a fact, save that we haven't yet declared it."

The taproom was crowded, but there were two vacant chairs at a corner table, and they joined an officer and a middle-aged civilian. Hale recognized the young man in uniform; he was Captain Alexander Hamilton, whose local company of artillery had been cited as the best-disciplined in the city. Although his men respected him, they resented his arrogant manner, and there was some ugly whisper about him that Hale could not recall at the moment. The civilian was a genial chubby-faced Irishman who introduced himself as Hercules Mulligan, proprietor of a New York tailor shop. Hamilton broke through the pleasantries impatiently, and resumed his conversation with Mulligan which their arrival had interrupted. "Look at it from an economic standpoint. Business stagnating, importation all but ceased, communication between the colonies hampered or halted altogether. The city's actually suffering for lack of food. It's impossible to trade with Britain, and impossible to open our ports to ships of other nations. Well, then, there are only two alternatives: submission, which would re-establish trade with the Old Country, or independence, which would provide trade with the rest of the world."

Hale studied Hamilton with interest as he talked. He was just nineteen, small-boned and slight of frame, with delicate features and a feminine softness to his fair complexion. His reddish-brown hair was brushed back from his forehead and tied in a neat powdered club, his uniform was studiously correct, his boyish smile charming. The charm seemed to Hale contrived; the gray eyes were cold and calculating. Something in his manner was defensive, and now he remembered what they called Hamilton behind his back: "That bastard brat of a Scotch peddler."

He had been born in the British West Indies, the natural son of Rachel Faucette Levine, a French Huguenot married to an elderly Jewish planter, and a shiftless Scottish adventurer named James Hamilton; and the stigma of illegitimacy was to shadow him all his life. The aggressiveness, the overriding ambition, the hunger for wealth and position that would ultimately wreck his career, derived in no small measure from a basic insecurity, a need to compensate for his lack of a respectable family background. James Hamilton had abandoned his common-law wife, and Rachel died penniless when Alexander was twelve years old. His only legacy was his father's Scotch hardheadedness and practicality, a strain of French romanticism inherited from his mother, and a brilliant and restless mind of of his own.

In St. Croix he had found employment as an apprentice clerk in the trading house of Nicholas Cruger, nephew of the former New York Mayor. He displayed such a natural aptitude for finance and administration that at fifteen he was able to board a packet and sail for America, with enough funds in his pocket to pay for a college education. He carried a letter of introduction from Nicholas Cruger to Hugh Mulligan, and Hugh's younger brother Hercules took the cocky youngster under his wing. Hamilton had boarded with the Mulligan family while he was an undergraduate at King's College, and under the influence of Hercules, a secret member of the Sons of Liberty and an ardent patriot, he had espoused the rebel cause with fervor, and founded his own military corps at King's College, the basis of the artillery company he now commanded.

Mulligan waited till his young protégé had finished, and his plump cheeks dimpled in a bland smile. "There's a more important reason for declaring independence, Sandy." His voice had a soft Irish brogue. "We need the help of France to drive the British fleet from our waters, and King Louis isn't interested in championing the rights of the people, not him surely. No, it's only if America breaks away from the Empire that France will ever be aiding us."

Tallmadge remarked courteously: "You seem well informed, sir."

"I keep me ears open." Mulligan gave him an owlish wink. "Generals have a way of talking sometimes when they're being fitted for a new embroidered waistcoat. Sure I hear the French Foreign Minister himself said that if we want their loan, we'll have to declare ourselves. 'We might join you if you're fighting for independence,' said he, 'but we'll not be after sacrificing one French soldier to uphold the liberties of Englishmen — ' "

There was a stir outside, a rising murmur of excited voices. All around the room, officers were pushing back their chairs and hastening to the street, and Hale and Tallmadge joined the crowd in front of a hastily printed broadside posted on the tavern door. By the flickering light of a whale-oil lantern they read: "New York, Sunday, July 7, 1776. THIS INSTANT arrived here an Express from Philadelphia, with Important News, as follows: On July 2nd a majority of nine States approved the resolution . . .."

Early Tuesday morning an order was issued to every encampment:

Headquarters, New York.
July 9, 1776

The Honorable Continental Congress, impelled by the dictates of duty, policy, and necessity, have been pleased to dissolve a connexion which subsisted between this Country and Great Britain, and to declare the United Colonies of North America free and independent states. The several brigades are to be drawn up this evening on their respective parades at six o'clock, when the Declaration of Congress, shewing the grounds and reasons of this measure, is to be read with an audible voice. The general hopes this important point will serve as a fresh incentive to every officer and soldier to act with fidelity and courage, as knowing that now the peace and safety of this country depend (under God) solely on the success of our arms. By order of his Excellency, General George Washington, Commander in Chief of the Continental Army.

* * *

All day long the glass had been dropping. The city sweltered under a blanket of steam, and sweat blackened the shirts of the fatigue parties digging entrenchments. Not a breath of air stirred the leaves of the elms around the Commons, and even the tree toads had ceased their incessant chirping.

Across the flat shimmering expanse of the Hudson, a bank of black thunderheads was piling up over the Newark Mountains, lit by occasional flashes of lavender. The distant rumbling grew louder, and the troops cast uneasy glances overhead as they hurried back to quarters to prepare for six o'clock assembly. The clouds in the west had taken on an ominous brown color, and heavier growls of thunder mingled with the rolling flam of the drums.

Hale's company took its place in formation at the south of the Commons, on one side of a hollow square. Sergeant Hempstead gave a sharp command, the men stiffened at attention, and a group of horsemen clattered down Broadway and crossed the Commons to the center of the square. An aide dismounted and stepped forward, unrolled a sheet of paper, and strained his eyes to read it in the fast-settling darkness.

"In Congress, July 4, 1776. The unanimous declaration of the thirteen states of America. When in the course of human events . . ."

Hale was looking steadily at the tall cloaked figure in the middle of the group. A violent flash of lightning illuminated for a moment the purple sash across his chest, the long plumes in his black tricorn. The ensuing crackle and clap of thunder made his horse shy and jerk its head sharply, but the rider

remained immobile. A sudden wind, rushing ahead of the
storm, whipped the top branches of the trees, and the aide raised
his voice to be heard above the roar.

"We hold these truths to be self-evident . . ." The wind
died as abruptly as it had come, and the first fat drops of rain
pelted the men in rigid formation. ". . . let Facts be submitted
to a candid world . . ." The rolls of thunder were growing less
frequent, moving eastward toward Long Island, and the downpour increased. "We, therefore, the Representatives of the
united States of America . . ." The steady drum of rain all
but drowned the final words. ". . . mutually pledge to each
other our Lives, our Fortunes and our sacred Honor."

The aide stepped back, rolling up the spattered paper, and
the troops bowed their heads as the Reverend Mr. Leonard
recited the Eightieth Psalm: "Restore us, O Lord God of Hosts!
Let thy face shine, that we may be saved." The group of horsemen wheeled and cantered back across the Commons toward
Broadway, and the soldiers gave three hearty huzzahs. Hale
watched until the central figure was lost in the sheets of driving
rain.

The storm was over by dark, but the riotous celebration in the
city continued through the evening. Soldiers and patriot civilians
crowded the taverns, clinking tankards and shouting toasts to
the new republic. As the night wore on, a huge throng gathered
in the Commons, the light from their torches glistening on the
wet cobblestones, and started down Broadway with drums and
fifes playing.

Hercules Mulligan, at the head of the procession, led them
to the Bowling Green at the foot of Broadway. In the center of
the oval park stood the massive lead statue of King George III,
covered with gold leaf. Mulligan smashed the locked gate of the
iron fence around the park, and the cheering mob surged after
him across the green. He climbed onto the marble pedestal,
fastened a rope around the statue, and a dozen men grabbed

the other end and toppled it with a mighty heave. As horse and rider crashed to the ground, they fell on it with knives and hatchets, chopped off the King's head, and hacked the gilded laurel wreath from his brow. The dismembered body was carried triumphantly through the main streets of the city, and later the fragments were sent to Connecticut and cast into precisely 42,088 lead bullets "to assimilate with the brains of our infatuated adversaries," the *Pennsylvania Journal* reported, "who, to gain a peppercorn, have lost an empire."

The celebrants had barely recovered from their hangovers on Wednesday morning when a courier arrived from Westchester with news that sent them into further ecstasy. The Provincial Congress, meeting in the White Plains courthouse at the same moment that the troops were assembling in the Commons, had approved the Declaration by the Continental Congress, authorized the New York delegates in Philadelphia to sign their names to the document, and declared that New York had begun to exist as a State on April 20, 1775. The Tory province had placed itself definitely in the patriot ranks, and challenged the enemy to battle.

The enemy was not long in meeting the challenge. At three o'clock on Friday afternoon, the booming of six cannon sounded a warning to the city. As the drums beat "To arms" and officers and soldiers raced to their alarm posts, the 44-gun frigate *Phoenix* and the 28-gun *Rose*, with a schooner and two tenders, appeared in the harbor and headed toward the mouth of the Hudson. American batteries on Paulus Hook and Governor's Island and lower Manhattan opened up with all their guns. The smoke of the engagement covered the city with a gray cloud, the air was acrid with powder, and women with children in their arms fled sobbing from the districts near the waterfront and sought refuge along the Bowery Lane. Solid shot screamed across the river; but the *Phoenix* and *Rose*, their decks protected by sandbags, sailed through the bombardment unscathed, replying with a few random volleys which crashed through deserted houses without doing injury. Virtually the only casualties were two members of Captain Alexander Hamilton's artillery company, who were killed when their cannon burst the first time it was fired.

Aided by a favorable southerly wind and the incoming tide, the men-of-war moved past the last shore batteries, and approached the sunken barrier in the river. To General Putnam's chagrin, they threaded their way through the secret passage as accurately as though they had a chart, and proceeded up the Hudson thirty miles to the Tappan Zee. One British sailor, to show his contempt for the American defenses, perched nonchalantly on the topgallant yard of the *Phoenix* as it ran the entire gauntlet.

The British had effectively demonstrated that they could encircle New York at will. The Hudson was their river.

IV

Death and Jack Boots

J ULY melted into August, and the city was like an oven.
Sailcloth lean-tos and unventilated board shacks became unbearable, and men crawled out at night to sleep naked in the
open, and malaria broke out in the camps. Improper sanitation
and polluted drinking water bred typhus, known as camp
fever, and dysentery, called the flux. Typhoid made its dread
appearance, and smallpox raged unchecked until Dr. Malachi
Treat, Washington's Surgeon General, moved all those stricken
with the plague to the isolation of Montresor's Island. Many
soldiers attempted crude self-vaccinations, which only spread the
epidemic, and an order was issued that any man who tried to
inoculate himself would be cashiered as an enemy to his country. Hospitals were filled to overflowing; King's College was
taken over to care for the sick, as well as the Tory estates along
East and Hudson Rivers; but trained physicians were scarce,
knowledge of the diseases even scarcer, and medical equipment
all but nonexistent. During the defense of New York, illness
cost the Continental Army more men than British bullets.

As the heat grew more oppressive, and weeks passed without
any movement by the enemy, tempers began to fray. Most of
the troops were convinced that New York was indefensible, and
that the attempt to hold it was inviting disaster. The *Phoenix*
and the *Rose* had proven that the British could strike wherever

they pleased. Suppose they moved an assault force up the Hudson or East River and landed north of Kingsbridge. The entire American army would be trapped on the island and starved into surrender. Why not evacuate the city, the New Englanders argued, burn it to the ground, and retire to a more maneuverable position on the mainland? New Yorkers resented the suggestion and the old quarrel flared anew, fights broke out among the troops, and three men were killed in a riot on the Bowery Lane.

No one saw the danger more clearly than Washington. His forces, decimated by illness and desertions, numbered less than seventeen thousand men fit for duty, of whom only six thousand had seen actual service. To split this weakened army in half, in order to defend Long Island and Manhattan at the same time, was little less than suicidal. He submitted to Congress the suggestion that it might be prudent to abandon New York; but the political strategists, safe in Philadelphia, replied loftily that the effect of such a retreat would be too demoralizing. New York must be defended at all costs, as well as the heights of Brooklyn, Governor's Island, and Paulus Hook in Jersey — points separated by water and some as much as fifteen miles apart. Washington believed that the military should be subservient to civil authority; and, against the counsel of his staff and his own better judgment, he broke a cardinal rule of warfare by dividing his forces on either side of a mile-wide river, and waited for Howe's next move.

General Howe was in no hurry about moving. Both he and his brother, Admiral Lord Howe, were members of the Whig party in England and had sympathized strongly with the Colonies in their appeals to the Ministry. Howe had reluctantly accepted his appointment as commander of the British forces in America, on the understanding that his mission was to be that of peacemaker, and that he would make every endeavor to bring about a reconciliation. Though he regretted that the

Colonies had been so rash as to declare their independence, he still hoped for some happy solution, and even made overtures to Washington, under a flag of truce, indicating his desire to heal all difficulties and grant full pardons. Washington replied, with stiff Virginia courtesy, that since the Americans had committed no wrongs they needed no pardons. Howe was so downcast at the rejection of his efforts that he was half inclined to act on a suggestion by Dr. Franklin and relinquish his command, rather than proceed by force of arms against a people whose English privileges he respected and whose wrongs he desired to see redressed.

He had another reason for tarrying in his luxurious quarters at Staten Island. Like most English generals, he enjoyed "his glass, his lass, and his game of cards" better than fighting; and during the siege of Boston he had discovered a plump blue-eyed blonde named Mrs. Loring, who shared his taste for gambling and drinking and amorous pleasures. The unfortunate fact that Mrs. Loring's husband happened to be his own commissary adjutant was easily adjusted by offering Major Loring a more lucrative post as commissioner of prisoners; and Mrs. Loring, relishing the glamour of her new relationship, became Sir William's boudoir companion. Howe's dalliances were the subject of a satiric American ballad called "The Battle of the Kegs":

> Sir William, he, snug as a flea,
> Lay all this time a-snoring,
> Nor dreamed of harm as he lay warm
> In bed with Mrs. Loring.

August was already half gone; and the earlier tension in the American camp yielded to numb weariness, like a fist that has been held clenched for too long. Hale had suffered recurrent attacks of dysentery, and his confinement added to his own sense of frustration. He had seen no more action here in New York than at Boston, and he waited impatiently for the long-deferred British move so that he might prove himself in combat. No one knew whether that movement would be made against Long Island or the city itself. "Our situation has been such this fortnight or more as to scarce admit of writing," Hale said in a letter to his brother Enoch dated August 20th, the last he would ever send. "For about six or eight days the enemy have been expected hourly whenever the tide and wind in the least favored. We keep a particular look out for them this morning. The place and manner of attack time must determine. The event we leave to Heaven."

Two days later, on Thursday the 22nd, Howe removed his troops from Staten Island, doubtless to the relief of the harassed nymphs on that isle, and landed them with stately leisure at Gravesend and New Utrecht on the southwestern point of Long Island. Now that the British intent was clear, Washington hurried regiment after regiment from New York to bolster General Putnam's slim forces in Brooklyn. Captain Alexander Hamilton transported his cannon over the East River as part of General Charles Scott's brigade, and Lieutenant Tallmadge crossed with General Mifflin's regiment. To Hale's disgust, Webb's Nineteenth was ordered to remain in Manhattan for the defense of the city.

Putnam's selection as commander of the army on Long Island was a last-minute decision. Nathanael Greene, a conscientious and capable general, had been in command at Brooklyn for two months and was well acquainted with the topography of the island; but a week previous he was stricken with fever, and General Sullivan was put in temporary charge. On a tour of inspection, Washington found such a lack of discipline and military posture that Sullivan was reassigned to direct the troops outside the Brooklyn lines, and Putnam took his place. Sullivan's resentment at his demotion did nothing to improve his efficiency; and Old Put, though a fearless warrior, was a notoriously poor tactician. Most of his time was spent bouncing up and down the lines on horseback, a sleeveless waistcoat over his soiled shirt, bawling orders right and left without any clear purpose. Due to his ignorance of the terrain, he posted Lord Stirling at the Narrows Road near the shore, and Sullivan and Parsons at the passes leading from Flatbush to Brooklyn, but left the vital Jamaica Road to the east guarded only by a five-man patrol.

In his customary deliberate manner, Howe waited three more days before launching an assault. His strategy was based on information supplied two months before by a British spy, Sergeant Graham, who had sketched the very battle plan which Howe followed. The plan was simple and brilliantly successful. On the night of the 26th, shortly after Washington had returned to New York, the British feinted at the passes held by Sullivan and Stirling, and pinned them in their positions. Guided by local Tories, the main British force of ten thousand veterans, led by Generals Clinton and Cornwallis and accompanied by Howe himself, moved silently through the undefended Jamaica Pass, surprised the little patrol before it could sound an alarm, and at dawn took the American army in the flank and rear.

The troops in Manhattan were on the alert at the first sound of cannonading, and Hale paced restlessly before his Bowery Lane camp, watching the grayish cloud of smoke to the southeast. During the morning bits of news trickled back to New York, each report more discouraging than the last. Outmaneuvered, outnumbered three to one, the entire American left line had folded back, leaving Stirling's division exposed to the enemy on three sides with the wide Gowanus salt marsh and creek at their backs. Stirling was forced to surrender; Sullivan was captured during a furious engagement on the Flatbush plains; Parsons's brigade was wiped out, and he made his way back to the American lines with seven survivors. Within a few hours the army on Long Island had been totally defeated, two thousand men were killed or wounded or taken prisoner, and the rest had retreated to the main entrenchments at Brooklyn.

Only Howe's excessive caution had saved Putnam's forces from complete annihilation. As the British grenadiers pursued the fleeing soldiers to their own breastworks, Howe ordered them back with the bland remark: "Enough has been done for one day." His troops spread their tents less than a mile from the Continental front line, while American escapees and wounded continued to straggle in from surrounding camps and thickets to the temporary safety of the Brooklyn redoubts.

Washington had hurried to Long Island at the height of the battle to take belated command; and later that same afternoon Webb's Nineteenth was ordered to Brooklyn to reinforce the American position. A strong wind had sprung up out of the north, feathering the river with whitecaps as Hale and his men were rowed across in flat-bottomed boats, and the lashing rain drenched them to the skin. They landed at the Brooklyn ferry stairs and marched uphill to the American encampment on the plain. The entire army was crowded onto a small peninsula which jutted into the East River, south of Wallabout Bay. Across the neck of the peninsula from Vanbrunt's Mill to the river was the defensive perimeter, guarding an area barely two miles wide and a mile deep: the only territory in Long Island remaining in American hands.

The showers continued intermittently through the night. The scattered Dutch residences and the Brooklyn Church were taken over for billets by officers and such troops as could cram inside. There were no tents for the others, and they stretched out exhausted on the soaked ground, lying on top of their flintlocks to protect them with their bodies from the rain. Refugee farmers, driven from their homes during the battle, huddled with their families under wagons loaded with their few belongings. To add to the confusion, some fifteen hundred horned cattle had been rounded up in Flatbush, in order to deprive the enemy of supplies, and they roamed restlessly around the bivouac, the glow of the campfires picking out their eyes in the darkness. Now and then they stampeded through camp at a burst of gunfire from the picket guards, who stood waist-deep in water in the flooded trenches around the perimeter.

There was little sleep. Men sat with slack jaws and vacant eyes, stunned by the appalling extent of the catastrophe. Fully a fifth of their numbers were floating face down in the Gowanus marshes, or lying on the rain-soaked meadows of Flatbush, their racked bodies stiffening in death. The survivors were eager to talk, to purge their minds of the memory, and to forget the pangs of hunger; and Hale listened in silence as they lived the battle over.

The Hessian bayonets had been their greatest horror, some said. The British had craftily told their foreign mercenaries that the Americans were resolved to kill them on sight; and the credulous Germans, believing that they were facing implacable and savage warriors, had slaughtered them in self-defense. Soldiers recalled seeing groups of fifty or sixty fleeing Americans, their retreat barred by British dragoons, fling down their arms in surrender, only to have the Hessian troops rush them in a bayonet charge and never pause with thrust or shot until every man was slain. Others insisted that the wild Highlanders were even more sanguinary than the Hessian or Waldecker hirelings, each man of them armed with broadsword and dirk and pistol in addition to his musket and bayonet. Most of the Scottish troops spoke only Erse, and their unintelligible yells and the insane skirl of their bagpipes during the battle struck terror into the hearts of the Colonials.

Some who had stood on a conical hill overlooking the Gow-anus Road told Hale of the gallant stand of Lord Stirling and three hundred men of Smallwood's Maryland regiment. While the main body of retreating troops floundered across the Gow-anus meadows, flooded with a rising tide, Stirling and his Mary-

landers advanced toward the Cortelyou House which Cornwallis had turned into a redoubt. Artillery plowed into their
thinning ranks, infantry poured a constant volley of musket balls,
German jaegers picked them off with rifles from the surrounding
hills, the guns beside the Cortelyou House raked them with
canister and grape. Stirling, looking back, saw the remnants of
his troops still crossing the narrow causeway over Freeck's mill-
pond or swimming the tidal stream; and he led his little band
forward in a desperate charge that drove the gunners from their
batteries and sent Cornwallis fleeing through the back door.
British reinforcements ended the unequal engagement; within
a few moments 256 of the 300 Marylanders were dead, and
Stirling, scorning to yield himself to a Britisher, surrendered his
sword to the Hessian General von Heister. Their sacrifice had
given their comrades the precious time needed to escape.

Hale paused beside a group of Long Island militiamen who
were barbecuing a small pig they had caught. A barrel-chested
lieutenant was crouched over the fire, his fringed hunting shirt
soggy with rain. He wore his black hair braided in a sailor's
queue, and his leathery face was tanned with salt wind. He
talked in a deep rumble, like waves breaking on a rocky shore,
and brandished a great hairy fist for emphasis. "By God, I'd
like to see some of them orry-eyed politicians in White Plains
come down here and get their brains blowed out if they had
any. They're the reason we didn't get word in time to help
General Nate. Sat on their fat butts and waited till it was too
late." He lifted the spitted pig in one hand, sniffed it indignantly, and put it back on the coals. "I knowed the old man
real well, he lived in Mastic right near Setauket —"

Hale stepped into the circle of firelight. "Do you happen to
be acquainted with a Benjamin Tallmadge from Setauket?"

"Acquainted?" the lieutenant roared. "Hell, him and me

live practically next door. How'd you know about him?" He peered at the cockade on Hale's hat and added: "Sir."

"We were in college together."

"Well, I be go to hell. It's a small army, and God knows after today that's the truth." He ripped off a chunk of pork and handed it to Hale in his fingers. "Here, have something to eat, goddamit. I'm Caleb Brewster."

Hale squatted on his haunches beside the fire. "Where's Tallmadge now?"

"With Mifflin's outfit, way down the other end of the perimeter." Caleb Brewster bit off an enormous mouthful, and muttered as he chewed. "Wonder if Ben's heard his brother Will was took prisoner today. Hope they don't treat him like they done old General Nate."

"Nate?"

"Nathaniel Woodhull." Brewster swallowed and belched. "It's all the fault of them knuckleheads in the Provincial Congress, he was president of it, and they sent him to round up the cattle on the island so the British wouldn't get 'em. Hell, here's a great general like Washington, fought in the French and Indian wars, and they make him a goddam cowboy, but he's Long Island and they're his boss. That's why I'm transferring to the Continentals." He glared at Hale.

"What happened to General Woodhull?"

"That's what I'm trying to tell you. The old man done his job, took a detachment and herded up all the beef critters clear to Hempstead, but a couple of days ago he hears the British are getting closer, and he sends his brigade major to White Plains and asks for reinforcements from my regiment here, that is, Colonel Smith's regiment, and Colonel Remsen's. What do them rancified Congressmen do? They tell the major sorry, they're not meeting till the next day, and by the time they get around to issuing orders, the British has got him surrounded.

General Nate sends his men out of danger, about seventy of them, but he stays behind to meet the reinforcements that he still thinks is coming, and yesterday he's waiting at Increase Carpenter's Inn near Jamaica when a group of dragoons come looking for him. They're under this no-good Tory son of a goat Oliver de Lancey, that went over to the British and they made him a captain, and if I ever catch up with him I'll snap off his head and pull him inside out and use him for mackerel bait."

Brewster tore off another chunk of pork with his teeth.

"So they bust open the front door of the Inn, and the General runs out the rear door and across the yard to his horse, and he's almost in the saddle when the dragoons catch up with him. Captain De Lancey yells 'Surrender, you damned rebel,' and General Nate hands him his sword, and De Lancey starts slashing at his head with it, and the old man throws up an arm to protect himself and he hacks it nearly off, and they leave him bleeding there, seven sabre cuts in his arm and three on his head. Later they carry him to the Stone Church, and today I heard they moved him to prison in New Utrecht, tried to make him walk the whole way till he fell down in the road from loss of blood. Lady I know just come through the lines, she says he isn't expected to live. Well, mister, there's a lot of Britishers that ain't expected to live either, after I'm through." Brewster glanced at the sky, and wiped his mouth with the back of a greasy hand. "Getting on toward first light," he said, rising to his feet. "Best be at our posts in case they start coming."

The rain began again at dawn, and all that Wednesday a driving nor'easter drenched the hungry and dispirited troops, standing in the puddled trenches and maintaining a constant skirmishing fire. At any moment they expected that the overwhelmingly superior enemy forces would launch a general assault; but the British contented themselves with occasional heavy volleys at the American lines, and darkness fell without an attack. During the night the thud of pickaxes, loud in the still-ness, gave warning that the redcoats were establishing them-selves in a forward position. The gray rainswept morning of the 29th revealed the partly completed breastworks of a new re-doubt, only six hundred yards above Fort Putnam where Hale's company was stationed. Once the enemy cannons were mounted on this higher ground, their shot and shell would make the American situation untenable.

Hale realized that it was only a matter of time. The Con-tinental forces, including the reinforcements from Manhattan, numbered no more than five thousand men; against them was deployed the full strength of the British army, estimated at seventeen thousand. Zigzagging in long lines up the slopes of Brooklyn Heights before him, and massed in the clearing at the top, were the bright coats of Cornwallis's grenadiers and in-fantry, a solid field of scarlet; to his right above the Porte Road he could see the blue uniforms, faced with red, of von Heister's eight thousand Hessians; just beyond them were the kilted Highlanders of the dreaded Black Watch, with their strange plaid bonnets and goatskin sporrans and twelve-foot regimental tartans wrapped around their waists and draped over their left shoulders; on his far left were the ten artillery regiments under Lord Percy, completing the ring of steel around the besieged rebel army.

Still General Howe withheld his attack, hoping to avoid more bloodshed. He had no taste for this fratricidal war, and had been appalled at the carnage of Tuesday's battle. He had confidently expected the Americans to surrender at once when they found they were surrounded, since any professional mili-tary man could see that there was nothing to be gained by re-sisting; but the raw Continental troops, amateurs at war, knew no better than to contend every foot of ground as they fell back. Howe still felt that his prime mission was reconciliation, and any additional slaughter would unite the Colonies against his peace proposals. It was better to starve their army into bloodless submission. As soon as the nor'easter ended, his brother Admiral Howe would sail up the East River and seal off their rear, and sooner or later the trapped Americans would have sense enough to give up the fight.

The British fleet was already poised at the mouth of the river. During the afternoon of the 29th, a brief shift of wind lifted the rain clouds that obscured the upper bay; and American observers, standing on a high knoll at Red Hook, stared in dismay at an armada of four hundred men-of-war and transports riding at anchor in the Narrows. Small boats scurried back and forth from the Admiral's ship, indicating that a movement was contemplated as soon as the wind and tide were favorable. Washington heard the report, and at a council of general officers, held in the Pierrepont homestead late Thursday afternoon, it was decided to ignore the instructions of the Continental Congress and abandon the Long Island position that same night. An emergency request was sent to New York for all available small craft; and Colonel Glover's Marblehead regiment, stationed at the extreme left of the defense perimeter, was ordered to supply seven hundred of its ablest mariners to row the entire American army across the swift-running and treacherous river before tomorrow's dawn.

It was a desperate gamble. The short midsummer night would provide only eight hours of darkness to mask their retreat. Enemy pickets were within hearing distance of the American breastworks; the least sound, a careless oath or the rattle of a gun carriage, might betray their plan and bring the British forces pouring through the deserted front lines to annihilate the defenseless Americans at the waterfront. To insure against any chance slip, Washington kept the evacuation a secret from his own men. The regiments were notified that an attack against the British lines was being mounted, and were ordered to be in combat readiness.

Hale's company crouched behind the low dirt parapets of Fort Putnam, awaiting the drum call to advance. The night was deathly still, and Hale peered intently at the blackness that shrouded the British lines. Now at last he was to meet the unseen enemy, and he pictured himself leading his men, sword in hand, perhaps to "resign his life a sacrifice to his country's liberty." His ears, straining for any sound, detected a stealthy movement in the company to his left, the muffled tread of marching feet that faded away to the rear, and a whispered order told him to spread out his men to fill the gap so mysteriously left in the front lines. An hour passed, and one of Washington's aides hurried toward him, and he braced himself for the command to charge. Instead, he was instructed to withdraw his company, leaving only a couple of sentries to maintain a show of defense, and retreat in total silence to the Brooklyn ferry landing.

The waterfront was a scene of wild confusion. A motley flotilla of whaleboats, pettiaugers, flat-bottomed landing barges, scows, and dugout canoes were drawn up on the shore, manned by Glover's Marbleheaders. Scores of wounded had been carried down on litters from the field dressing stations, their heads wrapped in blood-soaked bandages and the stumps of severed arms or legs enclosed in canvas sacks. Piled ammunition, muskets, field guns, and horses were scattered along the beach, waiting for transportation. So impatient were the soldiers to board the boats that discipline cracked, and men in the rear ranks mounted on the shoulders of their comrades in front and clambered over their heads to be nearer the means of escape. A sharp command restored order to the panicky troops, and Hale, looking up in the direction of the voice, saw a tall austere figure on a gray horse at the top of the ferry stairs, directing the embarkation.

Hale and Sergeant Hempstead stepped into a crowded dory, and a Massachusetts sailor shoved off with an oar. A moment later they were lost in the solid blackness, their boat was yanked sideways by the swirling tidal currents, and the oarsmen struggled to hold them on course. They passed close by another scow, almost foundering under the weight of a brass cannon, and he recognized young Captain Hamilton crouched in the stern. A capsized canoe swept downstream past them, its occupants clinging to the gunwales and paddling desperately with their free hands as they were sucked out of sight in the darkness. The Marbleheaders pulled steadily against the racing tide, and incredibly they touched the New York shore at the precise spot designated. Hale and his men leapt out, and the dory started back at once across the river.

One by one the regiments were pulled out of the forward trenches so quietly that no enemy suspicion was aroused; though there were near mishaps. Once a cannon fired accidentally while the crew was spiking it, exploding the silence with a deafening roar, but the British did not investigate. Loyalist sympathizers within the American encampment presented a more serious hazard. A Tory named Mrs. Rapalye, whose house overlooked the point of embarkation, was awakened at midnight by the rattle of oarlocks and scrape of hulls on the beach, and she instructed her young Negro slave to slip through the lines and warn the British. The boy contacted a company of Hessians who did not speak English, and after a vain attempt to understand his babbling they threw him into a guardhouse until morning.

Despite the valiant efforts of the Marbleheaders, a number of regiments were still in position at the front lines when Friday dawned. Providentally a heavy ground fog settled over both encampments, so dense that it was impossible to make out a man a few yards away. Even in the final hours of the retreat, a mistake in orders threatened disaster. General Mifflin's regiment, to which Tallmadge's company was attached, received word from one of Washington's aides to march at once; they left their post exposed, and were almost at the waterfront when Washington met them, shaking with rage, and shouted: "Good God, General Mifflin, I am afraid you have ruined us." The error was explained, and Mifflin's troops did a hasty right about and returned to their station. Due to the fog that still hung over the area, the enemy had not noticed their absence; and two hours later the official order arrived for their withdrawal. "We very joyfully bid those trenches a long adieu," Tallmadge wrote in his Memoir. "When we reached Brooklyn ferry, the boats had not yet returned from their last trip, but they soon appeared and took the whole regiment over to New York; and I think I saw General Washington on the ferry stairs when I stepped into one of the last boats. I left my horse tied to a post at the ferry."

The thought of his favorite mount still preyed on Tallmadge's mind as he disembarked on Manhattan. The fog seemed as thick as ever, and he called for volunteers to return with him to Brooklyn. A hulking lieutenant shoved his way through the crowd. "Hell, Ben," Caleb Brewster rumbled, "there ain't no sense letting them lobsterbacks have a good horse like that." With two other Long Island militiamen, Brewster rowed the heavy scow back across the river, Tallmadge guiding it to the ferry slip. The morning sun was already struggling through the murky atmosphere as they landed, and enemy scouts, puzzled by the unnatural silence, were stealing through the abatis of felled trees and raising their heads cautiously above the parapets to stare at empty trenches. They sounded the alarm, and British light troops raced downhill toward the ferry landing, while others withdrew the spikes from abandoned American cannon and trained them on the water.

"I obtained my horse and got off some distance into the river before the enemy appeared," Tallmadge concluded. "As soon as they reached the ferry, we were saluted merrily from their muskets, and finally by their field pieces; but we returned in safety. In the history of warfare I do not recall a more fortunate retreat."

*   *   *

Just how fortunate was their retreat became abundantly clear on Friday morning. Less than an hour after the last boatload disembarked on Manhattan, the sun burned away the covering fog, the wind shifted to the south, and the East River was riffled by a brisk upstream breeze which would have moved the British fleet swiftly into position to cut off any escape.

Washington's beaten army was too downcast to appreciate its good fortune. Ammunition and field pieces lay where they had been unloaded on the New York waterfront, while weary soldiers carried their sick or wounded comrades to the city hospitals. Others wandered aimlessly through the streets in search of food, or stretched inert on the cobblestones, worn out by the strain of the past three days. Wet tarpaulins were spread on the sidewalks, and soggy clothing was draped over fences and doorsteps to dry in the sun. The officers were as exhausted as the men, and there was no effort to hold formation, no martial rhythm of fife and drum. The men straggled back in groups of two or three to their former stations, and silently counted the losses in their regiments, and appropriated the bunks and blankets of those who had not returned.

A black mood of despair had settled over the troops, and they began to drift away in increasing numbers, walking out of their camps singly or in squads or even whole companies. Some were farmers who had left their grain half cut in the fields at home; others were short-term recruits whose enlistments were nearly over; most of them had simply had enough of war. Within a week, the muster of thirteen Connecticut companies dropped from eight thousand to two thousand. The majority of deserters were Continental militiamen, the poorest soldiers in the army, but their defection tipped the scales even more heavily in favor of the overwhelming British forces, well supplied and flushed with victory. Morale dropped among those who re-remained, and they complained sullenly of their wretched living conditions and inadequate weapons and inefficient officers. Even General Washington came in for bitter criticism. He had blundered in trying to hold Long Island, they claimed, and now he was committing the same error in New York. The defense garrisons had been withdrawn from both Governor's Island and Red Hook, the night after the retreat, leaving the city exposed to a naval bombardment that could reduce it to rubble. The American army would be trapped on Manhattan, just as it had been surrounded at Gowanus Creek. The war was as good as lost.

Hale's company, back at its old quarters in the snuff mill on the Bowery Lane, was affected by the general despondency. Each day a few more faces were missing at roll call, and the rest grumbled at the daily drilling. "Why don't you train us to march backwards?" a soldier asked Sergeant Hempstead. "It's the only direction we ever go." Hale himself felt a numbing sense of defeat. He had come within six hundred yards of the British lines, only to turn tail and flee without meeting the enemy. He wondered if he would ever be as close again. Fourteen months in the army had gone by, and he had never fired a gun in combat. He would give his life to perform some signal service; and when Lieutenant Colonel Thomas Knowlton invited him to transfer to his newly formed Rangers, it seemed like a heaven-sent opportunity.

Knowlton's Rangers were all hand-picked volunteers, a unique detachment which called itself "Congress's Own" and was responsible directly to the Commander-in-Chief. Washington had realized the vital need of such a reconnaissance outfit when Howe made his night march undetected through the Jamaica Pass. Similar Ranger groups had been effective during the French and Indian War, one led by Colonel Israel Putnam and another by Major Robert Rogers; but Putnam was a major general now, and Rogers had switched his allegiance to the British side and was heading a party of Loyalist raiders on Long Island. Tom Knowlton had been a scout with Putnam, and Old Put called him without qualification the finest officer who had ever served under his command. Washington was impressed by his courage and natural leadership, and delegated him to organize and direct the special unit. Its mission was to supply forward reconnaissance, scout the enemy outposts, procure intelligence, and perform secret duties "either by water or land, by night or by day" which were too perilous to be entrusted to the regular troops.

The detachment was small, only a hundred and thirty men and twenty officers; and Knowlton, recalling his brief acquaintance with Hale during the Boston siege, offered him the captaincy of one of the Ranger companies. Hale accepted promptly, eager to be of greater usefulness, and Sergeant Hempstead and his personal striker, Asher Wright of Coventry, transferred at the same time. The men in his new company were veterans from Connecticut and Massachusetts: hard-shelled Yankees, short-spoken to the point of seeming hostile, skeptical of their young captain. Their salutes were perfunctory; he was still a stranger.

On the second afternoon after his arrival, he joined a group sprawled on the bank of Harlem Creek beside their encampment, cleaning their long rifles. There were only a few such weapons in the whole American army, all of them handmade by German and Swiss immigrants in Pennsylvania, but Washington had seen to it that his Rangers were equipped with the best. Hale borrowed a rifle from a white-haired corporal and inspected it with admiration; the heavy octagonal barrel was forty inches long, the stock made of polished maple and inlaid with brass. He hefted it a moment, and swung it to his shoulder

with an instinctive motion. The circle of Rangers observed him
in silence. "Hangs nice," he nodded, and handed it back.

"Uses a lighter bullet and less powder, and fits with a tighter
seal." The old corporal took a one-ounce ball from his bullet
pouch, and showed it to Hale. "Cuts down on the recoil."

"How fast does she fire?"

"A good rifleman can get off two shots a minute," the corporal
said, "because it loads so easy." He opened the hinged cover of
a small box embedded in the butt plate, removed a greased
leather patch, and placed the ball exactly in the center. "A
Brown Bess, now, it takes a heavy steel ramrod and sometimes
a mallet to drive the musket ball down the barrel so it fits snug.
A rifle, though, all you need is this."

He slid a light wooden ramrod from its compartment, and
shoved the lubricated patch and ball down the barrel onto the
powder charge. Uncapping his horn, he tipped some more
powder into the pan to prime it.

"A musket ball will spin eight different ways eight different
times, but a rifle ball always spins the same. Hits a redcoat every
time if you aim right. When you see red in your sights, just
squeeze slow and steady, and you'll bring down his meathouse."
He pointed to a black duck swimming among the reeds a little
way upstream, and handed the half-cocked rifle to Hale. "That
duck's about a hundred yards," he said laconically.

The other Rangers showed no change of expression, but Hale
knew they were watching him intently. He stretched full-length
on the grass, full-cocked the rifle, fitted the butt to his shoulder,
and laid his cheek against the stock. He took a deep breath and
let it half out, and his hand tightened around the small of the
stock. There was a click and a delayed explosion, and the cloud
of bluish smoke drifted away. The duck was lying on its back
in the water, floating down toward them.

The old corporal rubbed his chin. "You've shot before,
Captain."

"I used to hunt around Lake Wamgumbaug in Coventry."

"Coventry? Hell, I gunned there myself. I'm from Willimantic." One of the Rangers retrieved the duck, and the corporal grinned at Hale. "Let's roast this critter and see if it tastes as good as them ducks of ours back home."

Harlem was their patrol, and they were assigned to keep check of enemy movements across the river. There seemed to be increasing activity on the Long Island shore. The British were throwing up entrenchments from Brooklyn to Newtown Creek, just opposite Kip's Bay, and all the way north to Hell Gate and Flushing. While the American shore guns at Corlear's Hook blazed away without effect, the frigate *Rose* and a convoy of thirty vessels sailed nonchalantly up the East River and entered Turtle Bay; driven off by an artillery detachment, they moved a little upstream to Blackwell's Island and anchored in its shelter. Other warships appeared in the river, having circled Long Island and come down the Sound. Enemy forces had already established themselves on Montresor's Island near Hell Gate, so close that rebel scouting parties bandied insults across the water with the British picket guards. The noose was drawing tighter, Hale realized. Why didn't Washington set fire to New York and pull out before it was too late?

The fact was that the Commander-in-Chief found himself in a cruel dilemma. He realized that remaining on Manhattan was courting total disaster, but he feared that his demoralized army could not survive another humiliating retreat. His council of general officers was likewise of two minds. Putnam advised an immediate evacuation, since it was manifestly impossible for their depleted forces to defend sixteen miles of coastline. Heath and Spencer and Clinton were unwilling to abandon a city which had been fortified at such cost and labor. Others argued that there was a good precedent for destroying New York: the Virginians had laid Norfolk in ashes a few weeks before to prevent Lord Dunmore from using it as a base of operations. Even such staunch New Yorkers as John Jay advocated putting it to the torch; and General Nathanael Greene, from his sickbed, wrote Washington on September 5th: "There is no object to be obtained by holding any position below Kingsbridge. Two thirds of New York and its suburbs belong to the Tories. I would burn the city . . . to deprive the enemy of an opportunity of barracking their whole army together." With his habitual deference to civil authority, which even the debacle on Long Island had not shaken, Washington referred the question to the Continental Congress: "If we should be obliged to abandon the town, ought it to stand as winter quarters for the enemy?"

Ten days had gone by since the retreat from Brooklyn, and still there was no indication of a British assault; and Washington was at a loss to fathom Howe's plans. A ceaseless watch across the East River was not enough. Breastworks were in plain view, but what was going on behind them? When and where was the next blow to fall? Would the enemy land above Kingsbridge, at Morrisania or Westchester, and seal off the only exit from Manhattan? Would they attempt to establish a beachhead at Turtle or Kip's Bay, or strike at Bloomingdale on the Hudson shore? The General was desperate for any clue. "As everything in a way depends on obtaining intelligence of the enemy's motions," he wrote to his commanders, "leave no stone unturned, nor do not stick at expense, as I was never more uneasy than on account of my want of knowledge on this score." Led by General Clinton, a raiding party of one hundred men set out from New Rochelle for Long Island, in hopes of bringing off some Tory prisoners who might give information; but the British warship *Halifax* and three sloop tenders forced them to return. There was only one other recourse.

On the morning of Tuesday, September 10th, Lieutenant Colonel Knowlton summoned the twenty Ranger officers to a meeting at his headquarters. Captain Hale stood at the rear of the room, leaning against a table for support; he was just recovering from another attack of dysentery, and his face was drawn and colorless. Colonel Knowlton hesitated a moment, as though what he had to say were distasteful to him, and there was a hint of apology in his voice. His Excellency General Washington was most anxious to learn something of the enemy's battle plan, he explained, and he knew no other means of obtaining this intelligence than to send a spy into the British lines on Long Island. "By the rules of war," Knowlton said, "no soldier can be ordered on such duty, so the General has asked for a Ranger to volunteer for the mission."

His eyes moved over the silent faces, and Lieutenant James Sprague, a veteran of the French and Indian War, shifted uncomfortably under his gaze. "I think I can speak for everyone here, sir. I'm willing to fight the British and if need be to die a soldier's death in battle, but as far as going among them in disguise and being taken and hung up like a dog, I'll not do it."

Knowlton tried to argue. "I confess the office of a spy is as repugnant to me as to anyone else in the army," he admitted, "but the object is so important to the country, and so much desired by the Commander of her armies . . ." There was no response from the officers, and his voice trailed. "Think it over, gentlemen," he said, and dismissed the meeting.

Hale walked slowly from Ranger headquarters, the Commander's appeal still echoing in his troubled mind. The thought of spying offended every decent principle; but, offensive or not, here was the chance to serve that he had waited for. He wanted to talk to someone else, to express his own thoughts aloud and perhaps resolve his doubts. Benjamin Tallmadge was stationed on Harlem Heights with Mifflin's brigade, too far away to contact; but he knew where to find William Hull. Under the reorganization of the army after the retreat from Brooklyn, Webb's Nineteenth had been made a part of General Spencer's division, defending the East River from Horn's Hook to

Harlem. Hull, still aide to Colonel Webb, was billeted in Harlem Village, only a little distance from the Ranger encampment. His quarters were in a small stone farmhouse, recently vacated by a Dutch family; and that night Hale and his friend talked together in the quaint Flemish kitchen, the brick hearth inlaid with glazed tiles and the overhead beams painted in red and blue patterns. He told Hull of Washington's request, and added that he felt it was his duty to volunteer for the mission. Years later Hull set down his personal recollection of their conversation:

"He asked my candid opinion. I replied, that it was an action which involved serious consequences, and the propriety of it was doubtful; and though he viewed the business of a spy as a duty, yet . . . the employment was not in keeping with his character. His nature was too frank and open for deceit and disguise, and he was incapable of acting a part equally foreign to his feelings and habits. Admitting that he was successful, who would wish success at such a price? Did his country demand the moral degradation of her sons, to advance her interests? Stratagems are resorted to in war; they are feints and evasions, performed under no disguise . . . and, considered in a military view, lawful and advantageous. The tact with which they are executed exacts admiration from the enemy. But who respects the character of a spy, assuming the garb of friendship but to betray? The very death assigned him is expressive of the estimation in which he is held. As soldiers, let us do our duty in the field, and not stain our honour by the sacrifice of integrity . . . I ended by saying, that should he undertake the enterprise, his short, bright career, would close with an ignominious death.

"He replied, 'I am fully sensible of the consequences of discovery and capture in such a situation. But for a year I have been attached to the army, and have not rendered any material service, while receiving a compensation, for which I make no return. Yet,' he continued, 'I am not influenced by the expectation of promotion or pecuniary reward; I wish to be useful, and every kind of service, necessary to the public good, becomes honourable by being necessary. If the exigencies of my country demand a peculiar service, its claims to perform that service are imperious.'

"He spoke with warmth and decision. I replied, 'That such are your wishes, cannot be doubted. But is this the most effectual way of carrying them into execution? In the progress of the war, there will be ample opportunity to give your talents and your life, should it be so ordered, to the sacred cause to which we are pledged . . .' I urged him, for the love of kindred, to abandon an enterprise which would only end in the sacrifice of the dearest interests of both.

"He paused — then affectionately taking my hand, he said, 'I will reflect, and do nothing but what duty demands.'"

Wednesday's sun was just rising over the low hills of Long Island as Hale and Colonel Knowlton guided their horses over a boggy trail that crossed the Harlem Flats, and trotted briskly down the Post Road to the city. At the junction of the highway with the Bowery Lane, an auxiliary road cut west across the island to the Greenwich Road beside the Hudson. They followed the shore of the river south to the village of Greenwich, and turned into a boxwood-bordered driveway that led to the Richmond Hill House. Two guards in blue and buff coats braced their carbines in salute, and they dismounted and handed their reins to a couple of liveried servants, and climbed the broad front steps of the mansion.

Richmond Hill was celebrated as the most delightful country seat on Manhattan Island. It had been built by the Loyalist Abraham Mortier, now paymaster for the British army, and had been taken over in April as American command headquarters. Ancient oaks surrounded a lily pond in the center of the lawn; its gardens were brilliant with roses and gilliflowers and corn flags; and the checkerboard grounds, planted with grass and grain, reminded English visitors of Devonshire. The house was a massive frame building, its lofty portico supported by two Ionic columns and decorated with carved pilasters. Two balconies with wrought-iron railings looked west to the Hudson, and south to the city a mile and a half away.

Tench Tilghman, civilian aide to the Commander-in-Chief, greeted Knowlton cordially at the top of the steps, and ushered them into a cool high-ceilinged hallway. He disappeared, and was back in a moment, and signaled with a nod of his head. They followed him to a door at the rear of the hall, and he knocked once and opened it, and they stepped into a large hexagonal room, richly furnished. The tall figure at the desk looked up from his writing, and Hale and Knowlton stiffened at attention. His impassive gaze had a way of freezing men into silence, and it crossed Hale's mind that he would not like to give the General cause to be angry.

Washington returned their salute and motioned them to be seated, and Hale fumbled behind him for a chair, unable to take his eyes from the General's face. It was long and rather full, peppered with smallpox scars and curiously pallid, and the blue eyes were set wide apart in deep sockets. His reddish-brown hair, carefully powdered, was drawn back tightly, accenting his high forehead, and there was a curled puff above each ear. The lips were compressed in a thin line; though Hale did not know it, his false teeth were ill-fitting, and he kept his mouth closed habitually so they would not slip. His expression seemed to Hale stern and forbidding.

"Your Excellency," Knowlton said, "Captain Hale has volunteered to undertake the mission you requested."

General Washington looked at Hale in swift appraisal. His

voice was husky, roughened by shouting orders, but a polite Virginia accent softened his speech. "You're aware of the dangers of this mission, Captain?"

"I'm aware of the importance you attach to its execution, sir."

The General half smiled without parting his lips, and an unexpected warmth reached out to Hale and made his throat unaccountably tighten. Now he understood how this one man could hold an underpaid and disheartened army together. "Do you have a particular plan in mind?"

"Sir, I served a month on Long Island early this summer, and I'm reasonably well acquainted with the countryside. I propose to cross the Sound to Huntington Harbor, which would provide a safe landing at night, and also put me near some people in Oyster Bay whom I know to be trustworthy. I'm confident they would give me cover."

"Who are they?"

Hale paused a moment. "I'd prefer not to mention their names unless your Excellency insists."

Washington's eyes were opaque, and it was a moment before Hale realized they were amused. "I admire your discretion, Captain. What disguise will you assume?"

"I hadn't given it much thought, sir. Perhaps a farmer."

"No." The General shook his head. "No, a farmer is too attached to his soil to be apt to wander." He was obviously taking a small boy's delight in plotting the deception. "What's your peacetime calling?"

"I was a Latin teacher in New London."

"Good. There's your answer. Pose as a Tory schoolmaster who has fled from Connecticut to seek employment on the Island. That would permit you to ask intelligent questions and to move about at will. Find yourself some clothing that would be in character. Do you have any evidence of your profession?"

"My college diploma, sir."

"Carry it with you." The General nodded, satisfied. "Colonel Knowlton will brief you on the particular information I desire." He rang a table bell, and his aide appeared in the doorway. "Mr. Tilghman, will you write an order to the captains of all armed craft to convey Captain Hale — " He paused and turned to Hale. "Will anyone go with you?"

"I'd like to bring my first sergeant, Stephen Hempstead, as far as the place where I disembark. From then on I'll be alone."

" — and party to any point he may designate. Prepare the order at once and bring it to me to sign." He explained to Hale: "Our need is urgent, Captain. How soon can you start?"

"Tomorrow, sir. At dawn."

* * *

At British command headquarters in the Billopp homestead on Staten Island, that same Wednesday noon, Admiral Lord Howe was entertaining some distinguished guests from Philadelphia. The front drawing room of the manor house had been decorated with a bower of cedar boughs and vines and moss, and a bountiful collation of claret and cold ham and tongue and mutton was spread on the table. To ensure a harmonious atmosphere, General Sir William Howe had discreetly moved elsewhere with the blonde Mrs. Loring, so that her presence would not embarrass the visitors.

The brothers Howe had planned this meeting with great care. A week ago General Sullivan, a prisoner since the Long Island battle, was exchanged for Governor Franklin of New Jersey, Tory son of Benjamin Franklin, who had been jailed by the patriots for his treasonable activities. The credulous New Hampshire general was convinced by the Howes that King George was ready to forgive the Americans and grant all the Colonies had ever asked. He agreed, upon his release, to carry this momentous news to the Continental Congress, and persuade a delegation of its members to visit Staten Island and learn the peace proposals. John Adams called Sullivan "a decoy duck, whom Lord Howe has sent among us to seduce us into a renunciation of our independence"; but Congress, after a heated debate, decided to send a committee consisting of Adams and Edward Rutledge and the seventy-year-old Dr. Franklin to attend the conference.

It was a two-day journey from Philadelphia, since the aging Franklin had to be borne the whole distance in a chair, and the inns were crowded with troops on their way to the defense of New York. In New Brunswick, space was so limited that Adams and Franklin had to share a double bed in a garret chamber with one small window. Here an impasse developed, as difficult to solve as the peace negotiations. Adams, a semi-invalid, was deathly afraid of the night air and insisted on keeping the window closed; Franklin complained that they would suffocate by morning and wanted it left open. "I cannot run the risk of a cold," Adams announced, lowering the sash with a determined bang. "But the air within the chamber is more dangerous than that without doors," Franklin argued, opening the window again. "Come to bed, and I will explain my theory of colds." "I've read some of your theories, which are inconsistent with my own experience," Adams replied dubiously, crawling beneath the covers. Franklin climbed into bed beside him and embarked on a lengthy scientific discourse in order to lull his bedfellow to sleep, describing the amount of air per minute which the human body destroys through respiration and proving, by a devious chain of reasoning, that the danger of colds is increased by breathing an impure atmosphere. So detailed was his argument that Franklin himself dozed off in the midst of it. When he awoke in the morning, he found the window tight shut.

At Perth Amboy, the Admiral's red-and-gilt barge was waiting to transport the envoys to Staten Island. Lord Howe, standing on shore to greet them, exclaimed: "Gentlemen, you make me a very high compliment." He escorted them to the

Billopp house through a double line of Hessian grenadier guards
with bayonets fixed, who Adams thought "looked as fierce as
ten Furies," and they sat down immediately to luncheon. Lord
Howe opened the discussion with an eloquent expression of his
attachment to the Colonies, and declared that "should America
fall, I should feel and lament it like the loss of a brother." Dr.
Franklin bowed with bland courtesy.

"My Lord," he assured him, "we will do our utmost endeavors to save your lordship that mortification."

Lord Howe, sipping a glass of claret while he regained his
composure, stated that he had long believed the difficulties between England and the Colonies could be ironed out, though he
mentioned that the Declaration of Independence, unless it were
withdrawn, would preclude all treaty-making. He said he would
like to outline a plan to avert the calamities of war, but that he
was unable to confer with them as official members of Congress,
since the King did not recognize that body. He could negotiate
with them only as private citizens.

"Your Lordship may consider me in what light you please,"
Adams said tartly, "except that of a British subject."

Lord Howe turned to Franklin and Rutledge. "Mr. Adams
is a very decided character," he observed.

The conference went on until the claret was consumed; but
since Howe had no authority to treat with the Colonies as independent states, and the Congressional committee was not
authorized to make any promises, it ended in total failure. "I
can only lament that it is not within my power to bring about
the accommodation I wish," Lord Howe said sadly as he saw
them aboard the barge to Perth Amboy. "I am sorry, gentlemen, that you have had the trouble of coming so far for so little
purpose." He bade them adieu, heaved a heavy sigh, and sent
word to General Howe to mount the assault on Manhattan.

The following day, September 12th, Washington called a
council of his generals at the Richmond Hill House, and read

to them a dispatch he had just received from Congress in reply
to his query. The lawmakers in Philadelphia, buoyed by a com-
placent optimism, had ordered that "no damage should be done
to New York, as it could undoubtedly be recovered even should
the enemy obtain possession for a time," but left the question of
abandoning the city to Washington's discretion. By a vote of ten
to three, the Council of War resolved to evacuate New York at
once.

Friday morning, the 13th, saw the town in a ferment. Horse-
drawn vehicles and water craft began transporting military supplies and equipment to Kingsbridge. Carts laden with sick and
wounded were driven hurriedly over the country roads to
points as far north as Dobb's Ferry. Forts were dismantled and
defenses torn down; bells were removed from all the city
churches and public buildings; even the brass knockers were
taken from private doorways, weighed and valued, and deposited for safekeeping in Newark. Washington made preparations to move his headquarters to Roger Morris's mansion on
Harlem Heights. Civilians packed their household effects in
panic, spurred to haste by the steady cannonading of four enemy
ships-of-war which sailed past the American batteries and
dropped anchor in the East River. By nightfall, nineteen-twen-
tieths of the population had fled. The busy garrison town was
once more a ghost city.

Mifflin's reserve brigade had been ordered down from Harlem
Heights to aid in the evacuation; and late Friday afternoon
Tallmadge rode in haste to William Hull's quarters in Harlem
Village. He had just visited the Ranger encampment, Tallmadge reported, and learned that yesterday at dawn — a few
hours before the decision was made to abandon the city — Hale
and Sergeant Hempstead had departed on an undisclosed mission. Asher Wright, Hale's striker, had told Tallmadge that
Hale took with him some civilian clothes and a round school-

master's hat, and he suspected the Captain was planning to pass in disguise into the enemy camp. Did Hull know anything about it?

Hull nodded unhappily. "I feared his mind was resolved when I talked with him Tuesday. We shook hands at the door, and he asked me if I recalled a drama we studied at Yale called *Cato*. 'In the fourth act,' he said, 'you may remember a scene where Cato views the body of his dead son Marcus.' Nathan then quoted me a couple of lines:

> " *'How beautiful is death when earned by virtue.*
> *Who would not be that youth? What pity it is*
> *That we can die but once to serve our country.'* "

*   *   *

For all the weary months of entrenching and barricading the city, General Howe won New York virtually by default. The American army had been caught off balance. Washington was still in the process of evacuating his troops; more than half had already been moved to Harlem Heights, and the rest were awaiting transfer. A skeleton force maintained a show of defense in lower Manhattan. Others were busy loading the remaining military supplies on carts, or dismantling fortifications, or were strung out in a thin and highly vulnerable line guarding the East River.

Early Sunday morning, September 15th, five British frigates with an armament of eighty-six guns anchored bow to stern directly in front of Kip's Bay. They lay only two hundred yards offshore, so close that the Americans in the forward trenches could see the cannon protruding through their gun ports in firing position, and even read the names on their round hulls. Their rigging swayed against the sky, studded with small swivel guns which could fire from the higher elevation directly into the ditches where the militiamen crouched behind piles of loose dirt. At seven that morning the first British assault wave

of light infantry and Hessian grenadiers and chasseurs boarded
a flotilla of sixteen-oared landing barges, which had been concealed in the mouth of Newtown Creek on Long Island, and
rowed out into the river. They took their places beside the warships, while the outnumbered Continental recruits, some less
than a week in the army, watched wide-eyed from the Manhattan shore.

Promptly at eleven o'clock the rowboats started pulling for
Kip's Bay, the soldiers in their gaudy scarlet coats standing erect
with muskets shouldered, until the broad surface of the river
reminded a young Connecticut private of "a clover-field in full
bloom." At the same moment, the warships let go with a thun-
dering broadside. Dust and smoke and flying clods of turf filled
the air, smothering the Americans and obscuring their vision
of the oncoming flotilla. Though the cannonballs landed in
Jacobus Kip's pasture behind them and almost no one was hit,
the ear-shattering din was too much for the raw levies, and they
broke and ran in terror up the sloping meadow and sought cover
in the woods. The panic spread up and down the line, abetted by
a false rumor that a general withdrawal had been ordered, and
the supporting units scattered in disorder. By the time the assault
force landed, the American defenders were in full retreat up
the island.

Washington had left his newly established headquarters at
the Morris Mansion on Harlem Heights, and was on his way
to the city when the booming of cannon warned him that the
battle had begun. As he galloped down the Post Road to take
personal command, he met his runaway troops in frantic flight,
discarding muskets and knapsacks and even hats and coats in
their haste to escape the British. In vain he and his staff cursed
and waved swords and slashed right and left with riding crops
to halt the stampede. "Take the walls! Take the cornfield!" the
Commander-in-Chief shouted, urging his horse into the midst
of the milling men. The tide swept irresistibly around and past

him and continued north toward Harlem Heights; and Washington, his head bowed in dejection, sat motionless in the saddle as a small enemy detachment came over the crest of Inclenberg Mount and moved toward him. The General seemed in a kind of trance, oblivious to their approach. They were almost within musket range when an aide grasped the dangling reins and led him out of danger.

The successful landing at Kip's Bay had cut the Post Road in the middle of the island, and left the 3500 troops on lower Manhattan in imminent peril of being sealed off completely. Seeing the danger, General Putnam spurred his horse down the Bowery Lane to rescue them before the trap was sprung. Precious supplies and ammunition and fieldpieces, numbering more than half of all the artillery which Washington possessed, had to be abandoned. Within an incredibly short space of time, Putnam and his aides managed to round up three thousand of his scattered forces, and at four in the afternoon he started them on a twelve-mile forced march up the Greenwich Road on the west side of the island, hugging the woods so they would not be spotted by enemy warships in the Hudson.

During the confusion, part of one American brigade failed to receive the order to retreat. They were under General Knox, the portly bookseller who had brought the cannon from Ticonderoga during the Boston siege; he had heard the bombardment that signaled the enemy landing, and had taken refuge in the earth redoubt on Bayard's Mount near the Bowery Lane. Captain Alexander Hamilton, in charge of artillery, loaded his cannon and prepared for a last-ditch defense. As their chances of escape grew less by the minute, one of Putnam's aides, Major Aaron Burr, raced uphill to the fort and gave Knox the delayed order. "I know the back roads, I can guide you to safety," Burr offered. The terrified Knox could picture his tiny force trying to fight its way through the entire British army, and replied that retreat was impossible. Burr turned to the troops and, in an impassioned speech, urged them to disregard Knox and come with him. Ignoring the red-faced and huffing general, Burr assumed command and ordered Captain Hamilton to follow with his artillery company.

It was the first meeting between Hamilton and Burr, and their lifelong enmity may have been born of that moment. They were oddly alike: Burr was twenty, less than a year older than Hamilton, with the same slight physique and delicate feminine features, the same arrogance, the same driving ambition. It galled Hamilton to see this rival officer steal the spotlight, and his resentment was intensified when he was told to leave his personal baggage and treasured cannon behind. He trudged sullenly at the rear of the procession as Burr led them through unfrequented country lanes and footpaths. They caught up with Putnam's main column just as it reached the Bloomingdale Road.

The retreating soldiers were near exhaustion. Sweat poured down their faces in the stifling afternoon heat, their canteens were empty, but there was no time to halt at a stream. Old Put galloped up and down the long plodding line, shouting encouragement to his men, urging stragglers to keep up with the rest, sending flanking guards across the farmlands to scout for signs of the expected British attack. They were halfway up the island, almost abreast of Kip's Bay, and at any moment Putnam expected to find Howe's advance guard blocking his path. He could not understand why the enemy failed to appear.

General Howe was not to be hurried. His battle plan, based on Captain Montresor's maps, called for the establishment of a secure beachhead before extending his forces across the island; and the unexpected collapse of the American defense did not alter his original concept. With orthodox military caution, he waited until the nine thousand men of his second division were ferried across the East River. Meanwhile Sir William and General Henry Clinton and Governor Tryon passed their time at the

Murray Mansion, enjoying cake and wine with their charming Quaker hostess. Not until five o'clock that afternoon did Howe embark on the next phase of his carefully worked-out attack, sending a brigade of Hessians south to raise the Union Jack over the abandoned city, and dispatching his main body of troops, led by the light artillery, up the Post Road toward Harlem.

As Howe's forces marched north along the East River side of the island, Putnam's column was progressing at about the same rate of speed on a parallel course up the Hudson side, less than a mile away. Neither army was aware of the other; and it was not until Smallwood's Marylanders made a stand at McGown's Pass, and inadvertently deflected the British troops west to the Bloomingdale Road, that any contact was made. By the time the leading company of enemy artillery reached the highway, the bulk of Putnam's column had already passed. There was a brief skirmish with the last regiment in the line; a determined rear-guard action held off the British until the American troops were safely out of range, whereupon they broke off the engagement and followed their comrades across the Hollow Way to Harlem Heights.

The sultry day ended at dusk with a hard rain shower, followed by a chill wind out of the north that cut to the bone. The shivering soldiers on Harlem Heights lay on their arms on the wet ground, tired and hungry and ashamed. Tents and blankets had been abandoned in New York, and they had tossed away most of their outer clothing in their panicky retreat. Still worse, they had lost all confidence in themselves. Their pride was gone. Even the miraculous escape of Putnam's column failed to cheer them. It was useless to argue that the evacuation of the city had been planned for days; the fact remained that they had been driven from New York in cowardly flight, whole regiments had stampeded without firing a gun, and their Commander-in-Chief had denounced their conduct as "disgraceful" and "dastardly."

"Are these the men with which I am to defend America?" Washington asked in despair.

All that night, while his army slept, the General and his staff sat around guttering candles in the Morris Mansion, drawing up plans to dispose the forces on the Heights in a defensive posture, and preparing orders for the troops to dig fortifications along the bluffs as soon as the sun rose. Washington was counting heavily on the military advantage of defending high ground. Should the British attack, he might be able to score a victory, however small. Some token success was needed to keep his demoralized army from fading away altogether. If the Americans could make the redcoats turn and run, if they could demonstrate just once that Howe's mighty regiments could be driven from the field, then perhaps the war was not yet lost.

Well before first light on Monday, September 16th, Lieutenant Colonel Knowlton and his hundred and twenty Rangers crept across the Hollow Way and climbed the heights above the Hudson to reconnoiter the enemy disposition for General Washington. British pickets guarding the Bloomingdale Road sounded an alarm, and the Rangers took cover behind a stone wall and maintained a steady fire for half an hour against four hundred of General Leslie's light infantry. The squeal of bagpipes warned them that heavy reinforcements from the Royal Highland Regiment of Foot were on the way, and Knowlton staged a skillful withdrawal, keeping the British at a respectful distance. As the Rangers climbed back up the Harlem bluff, a red-coated bugler stood on the heights in full view and blew in derision the fox-hunter's call for the end of the chase: "The fox has gone to his hole."

The insulting implication was not lost on the Americans, and Washington decided on a strategic counterattack. While one of General Greene's brigades made a feint at the British front, hoping to draw the enemy down into the Hollow Way, Knowlton's Rangers and three Virginia companies formed a flanking party and stole around them to cut off their rear. Through some error, the Virginians opened fire too soon, while Knowlton's group was still exposed at the right of Leslie's infantry. The British swung around to protect their flank, and Major Leitch, commanding the Virginians, was mortally wounded on the first volley. Colonel Knowlton leapt onto the ledge where Leitch had been standing, turned to order his Rangers forward, and a musket ball severed his backbone. A Ranger captain caught him as he fell. "I do not value my life," he heard Knowlton whisper, "if we do but get the day." He died within an hour.

Despite the loss of their leader, the Rangers and the rest of the flanking party continued to press the attack; other American units joined the growing battle, including several New England regiments who had disgraced themselves the previous day; and the British retreated across the Hoaglandt buckwheat field, showing the backs of their uniforms to the Americans for the first time. The fighting continued for four hours, and the enemy was forced back with heavy losses as far south as Stryker's Bay. When the guns of the British frigates in the Hudson opened fire, Washington prudently sent an order by Tench Tilghman to break off the engagement. The troops shouted a loud "Huzza!" and returned in orderly ranks to Harlem Heights.

No ground had been gained or lost by the battle, the two armies remained in the same positions, but an unbelievable change had taken place in the American camp. The untrained Continentals had put some of the best soldiers in the British army to rout, they had atoned for the shame of Kip's Bay, they had won new pride and new hope which would carry the little army through seven more years of war. Knowlton's Rangers had turned the tide with a victory which, from the standpoint of morale, was one of the most important engagements of the Revolution. Washington stated that the day's success had "inspirited our troops prodigiously," and his Adjutant General,

Colonel Reed, wrote his wife: "The men have recovered their spirits and feel a confidence which before they had quite lost." A ration of rum was issued to the soldiers, and they clicked their tin cups together to the defiant toast: "Rather death and jack boots than dishonor and wooden shoes."

Only one Ranger officer missed the action. At the moment that Kowlton's detachment was mounting its predawn foray, Captain Nathan Hale was making his way across Long Island Sound toward the dark shore of Huntington Bay.

***

V

The Inglorious Tree

A SOLID overcast hid the moon, and the coastline of Long Island was a low shadow on the horizon, broken by a gap of lighter gray that marked the entrance to Huntington Bay. A triangular sail moved across the gap, and was lost behind the point. The sloop glided ghostlike over the dark waters of the bay, every light extinguished. The only sound was the chuckle and slap of little waves at its bow and an occasional groan of the boom's jaws grinding on the downhaul.

Hale stood in the forepeak, impatient to be on his mission. For four days he and Sergeant Hempstead had traveled north through Westchester and Connecticut in a vain search for transportation across the Sound. The British 10-gun brig *Halifax*, commanded by Captain Quarme, was patrolling the Long Island shore, and the smaller American vessels were afraid to risk an encounter; but on Sunday the 15th, by rare luck, he had encountered Captain Charles Pond in Norwalk. Pond was a fellow officer in Webb's Nineteenth, detached on special duty as skipper of the privateer *Schuyler* to prey on enemy coastal shipping. He read Washington's order, and nodded. "Sure, I'll take you across the Devil's Belt." Pond cast a mariner's glance at the lowery sky. "Making up for weather. Tonight should be good for a moon-curser."

"How soon can we start?"

"Not till full dark. I'll have the *Montgomery* give us escort, in case we run afoul of Quarme's brig."

A little before midnight the *Schuyler* and her sister sloop crept out of Norwalk inlet, and as soon as they were under way Hale went below to Pond's cabin to change clothing. The portholes were shrouded, and the only illumination was a swinging whale-oil lamp. He stripped off his Ranger uniform coat and buckskin breeches, and donned a white linen frock and plain civilian suit of brown Holland cloth, and set a round broadbrimmed hat on his head. As an extra precaution, he removed the silver buckles from his shoes. "They'd scarcely comport with the character of a poor schoolmaster," he remarked, giving them to Sergeant Hempstead for safekeeping.

Hempstead's brow was furrowed, and his deep voice dropped to a whisper. "Let me come with you, sir."

"One's enough, Steve. Wait for me in Norwalk. I'll send word when I'm ready to return." Hale stuffed a loaf of bread and a sausage into his knapsack, folded his Yale diploma and tucked it inside, and hastened back on deck.

The *Montgomery* had paused in the Sound outside Huntington Bay, ready to give warning if the enemy brig were sighted, and the *Schuyler* felt its way cautiously through the pitch blackness of the inner harbor. Captain Pond stood at the helm, snuffing the air for a scent of land. He grunted "Ready about!" and Hale heard the slosh of the quarter wake rolling off, and the creak of rigging as the canvas went slack. The sloop came up into the breeze and drifted to a halt, as motionless as a loon on the water. A small boat was put over the side, making a faint splash as it settled, and two sailors took their places at the oars. Hale shook hands quickly with Pond and Hempstead. The Sergeant's big worried face loomed out of the shadows as he stepped over the rail.

He dropped lightly into the bow of the small boat, and the sailors pulled with muffled oars toward shore. A startled water

bird scuttled ahead of them, the thrashing of its wings unnaturally loud in the stillness, and an owl tolled somewhere in
the surrounding hills. They were getting near land; Hale could
smell the dank iodine odor of seaweed, and strands of salt grass
hissed along the sides of the boat. Its bow grated on sand, and
he leapt out and shoved the boat off again, and it was promptly
lost to sight.

On the other side of the narrow spit was a marsh, and he
waded ankle-deep around the curving shore toward higher
ground. He could hear the soft pop of canvas filling with wind,
and he turned and looked back as the *Schuyler* ghosted out of
the harbor. Its mast and sails were outlined clearly in the first
glow of Monday's dawn, and he realized that the night was
receding like an outgoing tide, and hummocks and boulders
were emerging from the murk and taking shape. He bent low
and hurried across the exposed marsh toward a stand of jack
pine, silhouetted against the eastern sky, and his crouching
form was swallowed in the darkness.

The *Schuyler* and *Montgomery* had not gone undetected.
Lookouts on the hills had spotted the activity in the harbor, and
their signal fires sped a warning to Captain Quarme. "AM at
4 came too Huntington Bay," the log of the *Halifax* noted.
"Sent the Tenders and Boats Armd to search the Bay for two
Rebel Privateers haveing Interlagence of them . . ."

*   *   *

The darkness that enveloped Hale that morning has shrouded
him in mystery ever since. No letter, no personal diary note
throws light on his movements from the start of his mission to
his execution in front of the Artillery Park a week later. The
date of his capture is fixed by the British Headquarters Order
of September 22nd, stating that he was "apprehended last
night," but the place and circumstances have been argued for
two centuries. Some historians say that he had returned from

New York to Huntington and was betrayed by a Tory relative at a local tavern kept by a widow named Chichester; though there is no record of any such tavern or proprietor, and the distance would scarcely have permitted him to be brought back to the city that same night. Others claim that he made his way up the east shore of Manhattan Island almost to Harlem, and by mistake hailed an approaching barge from the enemy brig *Halifax* under the impression that it was manned by Americans. Still others insist that he crossed the East River and was seized at Flushing by none other than the turncoat Robert Rogers, in command of the Queen's Rangers on Long Island.

Even his contemporaries disagreed. British Captain Frederick Mackenzie, stationed in lower New York at the time of Hale's hanging, wrote in his diary on September 22nd: "A person named Nathaniel Hales, a Lieutenant in the Rebel Army and a native of Connecticut, was apprehended as a Spy, last night upon Long Island." Another British officer, Captain William Bamford, noted the same day: "Nathan Hales, a Capt in ye Rebel Army & a spy was taken by Maj^r Rogers & this m^g hang'd." Evidently Bamford referred to Lieutenant Colonel Rogers, who was frequently stationed aboard the *Halifax* and may have been ashore on patrol duty at Flushing. Both diary notes misspell Hale's name, and one misstates his rank, and in all likelihood the authors relied on campfire gossip heard in the city.

More dependable, it would seem, is Sergeant Hempstead's own statement that Hale "was passing the British piquet guards between the lines of the two armies within a mile and a half of his quarters" (Harlem Heights) "when he was stopped at a tavern, at a place called the Cedars." Hale's personal striker, Asher Wright of Coventry, also told an interviewer years later that he "passed all their guards on Long Island, went over to New York in a ferryboat & got by all the guards but the last. They stopped him, searched & found drawings of the works, with descriptions in Latin, under the inner soles of the pumps which he wore. Some say his cousin, Samuel Hale, a tory, betrayed him. I don't know; guess he did." Wright was eighty-two at the time, and his memory of the details may have been faulty. Enoch Hale, Nathan's favorite brother, made a careful investigation of the circumstances and wrote that "being suspected by his movements that he wanted to get out of N York was taken up & examined." The Coventry town records contain a specific entry by Enoch that his brother "was taken up in the City of New York."

All their statements are based on hearsay, and there is no scrap of firsthand evidence. The section of the dinosaur is missing, we can only guess its shape and structure by fitting together the few fragments which exist. Selecting the bits of testimony that are most convincing, and putting myself in Hale's place — knowledge combined with imagination — I have tried to reconstruct what seems to me his logical procedure during the unrecorded seven days. This, I suggest, is the probable course of Hale's movements after he was set down on the shore of Huntington Bay, shortly before dawn on September 17th . . .

He lay concealed for a time under the jack pines, breakfasting on bread and sausage and waiting until the sun was a little higher. It might arouse suspicion if he were seen abroad too early. Travelers were beginning to move along the Old Post Road, a farmhand herding a drove of pigs, a girl with a leather milk bucket balanced on her shoulder. Stealthily he worked his way through the pines, stepped onto the highway, and set out at a brisk pace for Oyster Bay. Passers-by exchanged a casual "Mornin'" with him as they met, and he breathed more easily, relieved to find that he attracted no undue attention.

A cart rattled past him, loaded with purple cabbages, and an elderly farmer reined his horse and beckoned. "Want a ride?" Hale swung himself up into the cart, and sat on the plank seat beside the driver. His patched homespuns were streaked with tobacco stains, but he sported a jaunty red bow on his hat. He flicked the reins against the horse's back, and the cart jolted forward. "What's your line o' work?"

"I'm a teacher."

"Preacher, eh? That's what I thought when I seen you." The driver's voice had the hollow toneless quality of the deaf. "You ain't got a ribbon on, Parson."

"Ribbon?"

"Don't do to be without your Tory badge. Folks might think you was the other party."

"I must have lost it somehow."

"Here, cut an end off mine." The driver handed his hat to Hale. "Can't nobody take chances these days. Some folks even paint a black ring around their chimbleys so's everybody will know they're loyal." He shifted a wad of tobacco to his other cheek. "You f'm around these parts?"

"I'm looking for employment," Hale said, fastening a section of ribbon to his hat. "I thought perhaps in Oyster Bay — "

"Oyster Bay? That's where I'm taking this load. The market boat leaves for New York tomorrow."

"How will it get by the British?" The driver cupped an ear, and he raised his voice and repeated: "How about the British?"

"Ain't you heard? They landed in New York yest'day morning. Drove them rebels clear to Harlem."

Hale made an effort to conceal his surprise. "Did the rebels fire the city?"

"Hell, no, they run so fast they didn' have time to." The driver spat tobacco juice over the side of the cart, and wiped his grizzled chin with a sleeve. "I reckon the war's about finished, don't you, Parson?"

Hale nodded absently, trying to adjust himself to this abrupt change in his plans. Obviously military intelligence from Long

Island was no longer of any value. Should he abandon the mission, and go back to his Ranger company? Or should he continue into New York, in hopes of gleaning information about the present British strength and disposition? The danger of discovery was far greater than here on the island; but the Commander-in-Chief would be more anxious than ever for knowledge of Howe's plans. Then, too, some patriots might have remained in the city. Perhaps he could make contact with them. If they could do what the fleeing American army had neglected to do, if they could destroy the enemy's winter quarters . . .

The sound of hoofbeats startled him out of his thoughts. A party of light dragoons was coming down the highway, smartly clad in green coatees faced with blue, chain shoulder straps, and black canvas spatterdashes. Their tall leather caps were crested with black bearskin, and on the front of each hat was a white metal crescent engraved: *Queen's Rangers*. Hale sat rigid on the front seat as a bull-necked officer, wearing the insignia of a lieutenant colonel, held up a hand to halt the cart. His face was battle-scarred, with thick lips and puffy bags beneath his gray eyes, and he spoke in a growl. "Where you from?"

The driver tilted his head to hear. "What say?"

"I asked you where you've been."

"Pretty well, thank you," the driver said genially. "Meet the new preacher over to Oyster Bay."

The colonel gave Hale a brief glance, and turned back to the driver. "A rebel privateer was reported in the harbor this morning. Have you seen anybody suspicious on the road to Huntington?"

"Yes, this is the road. Just keep going the way you're headed. You can't miss it."

One of the younger officers murmured to the colonel: "He's deaf as a post, sir. I know him, he's all right. He's a King's man."

"Better check the cart to make sure."

A soldier dismounted, and jabbed his bayonet blade several times into the load of cabbages. He shook his head, and swung back into the saddle, and at a command from their leader the horsemen trotted down the road. The driver slapped his horse with the reins.

"Good thing you had your badge, Parson. Colonel Rogers is real ornery about rebels. Used to be one himself, till they threw him in jail. Guess that's why he don't like 'em much."

They were coming into the village of Oyster Bay, and Hale thanked his benefactor and jumped to the ground. He waited until the cart had rumbled around a corner to the waterfront, and strode quickly up the main street toward Raynham Hall. He had a good memory; there was no trouble finding the white clapboard house again. He rapped the brass knocker, and the front door was opened by a dark-haired and rather grave young man, only a couple of years older than Hale. "Is Mr. Samuel Townsend at home?"

"Come in, sir." The young man led the way across the hall to the dining room. "Father, a gentleman to see you."

The dining room of Raynham Hall doubled as a magistrate's office and retail merchandising shop. Boxes of foodstuffs and spices stood on display around the oak floor, and spelling books and quires of paper were stacked high against the blue paneled walls. An open pine chest held layers of imported fabrics, Dutch lace and shalloon and calimanco. Every shelf of the triangular corner cupboard was crowded with items for sale: a set of cream-colored plates, cards for combing wool, pewter porringers, horn buttons, sconces, hatchels for hackling flax. On the other side of the hall, Hale saw, the downstairs bedroom served as a storehouse for barrels of molasses and cider, salt pork, pickled oysters, sacks of flaxseed, calfskins taken in trade. The whole house had an aromatic country-store smell of nutmeg and apples and brine.

Samuel Townsend was seated at the round dining table, entering some figures in a ledger. He was dressed Quaker-fashion in a severely simple snuff-colored suit and white shirt of cambric lawn, gathered in plaits and fastened behind with a paste buckle. His face was distinguished by a prominent nose and deeply cleft chin, and he wore his gray hair unpowdered. He rose courteously as Hale entered, but there was no sign of recognition.

"You don't remember me, sir, but you were kind enough to assist me last May, when I was here with a regiment rounding up Tories." He hesitated a moment. "I'm Captain Hale."

Townsend gave a quick glance at the door, and his son closed it. His eyes moved slowly over Hale's civilian clothes, and down to the red ribbon on the hat he was holding. "You've changed your allegiance since then?"

"No more than you have, sir. That's why I've come to you for help."

The older man sank back in his chair, and shook his head. "No. No, don't ask me. It's too dangerous." He spread his hands in appeal. "Please understand, Captain. Last week a troop of Light Horse seized me here as a rebel, smashed my Queen's Arm musket hanging over the mantel, and carried me off to Jericho for trial. They may have suspected I named some neighbors to you as King's men. Fortunately my niece Almy is married to a wealthy New York Loyalist, Thomas Buchanan, who posted my bond; but I had to take the Oath of Allegiance before Judge Hicks next day, and my son did the same . . ." Hale was looking at him steadily. "So you can see why . . ." He faltered and dropped his hands in resignation. "What help do you need?"

"I must get to New York."

"It's impossible, Captain. All the ferries are watched, and everyone is stopped and questioned on the highway. If you don't have a pass —"

His son interrupted. "The market boat's sailing in the morning, sir. Perhaps he could sign on as one of the crew."

Samuel Townsend sighed and nodded. "Take him down to the dock, Robert. See Captain Klaas. He'd do a favor for me."

The barge made slow progress down the Sound, its sails straining to pull the heavy load. Captain Klaas sat in an armchair before the mast, his seaboots stretched out comfortably, a stubby clay pipe gripped in his teeth. His pale eyes, all but hidden in the fat folds of his face, darted here and there around the deck, missing nothing, and he grunted orders in a heavy Dutch accent. "Is coming Whitestone Landing. Make ready for unload."

It was stifling in the hold. Hale had stripped to the waist, and sweat puddled at the small of his back as he handed up barrels and boxes of fresh farm produce: red and green cabbages, paler green watermelons, golden squash; early apples and pears and plums; beef carcasses, slaughtered hogs, chickens tied together by their feet in feathery clusters. A couple of British commissary officers came aboard at Whitestone to purchase their quota of supplies, and Hale listened as they chatted with Captain Klaas. "We'll need all the cabbages you can spare. A thousand Hessians in camp, they eat cabbage morning, noon and night." Hale moved past them slowly, a sack of onions on his back, his face smeared with grime. The officers ignored him. "Could you let us have extra beef, Captain? Two more artillery companies due here tomorrow for the big move against Throg's Neck."

They put in at Flushing, and again at Montresor's Island, and late that afternoon the barge moved through Hell Gate channel, on its way to Brooklyn. Hale stood on deck, letting the cool wind dry his perspiring body. On the opposite shore he could see the mouth of the Harlem, but the Ranger encampment was gone; his company had pulled back to join the main army dug in on the Heights. The East River bristled with enemy ships-of-war, and the market boat sailed almost under their guns, close enough for him to make mental notes of their names and firepower. A flotilla of transports and landing boats lay in Turtle Bay, ready for action, and a British headquarters flag was flying over the Beekman Mansion on the crest of the hill. They passed Newtown Creek, and Bushwick Inlet, and the broad indentation of Wallabout Bay. A battered hulk was riding at anchor in the center of the bay, its masts and sails removed and its decks stripped of guns. Captain Klaas pointed at it with his pipestem.

"Prison ship *Jersey*. Is no room in the city jails for hold all them rebels they took at Brooklyn." The offshore breeze brought a sickening stench, and he wrinkled his nose in disgust. "Og heden, how it makes the stink, them prisoners below."

Hale thought of the men crowded together without air in the putrid hold. "Do they ever try to escape?"

"But sure, the devils. Two nights ago I hear was an officer and four men steal a small boat and row over to the city. Is hiding there now for make trouble, I bet you."

The sun was setting as they tied up at the Brooklyn ferry landing. Several rusting fieldpieces lay half buried in the mud, and strips of rotting canvas and abandoned items of equipment had been washed high on shore by the tides. It was dark before the crew finished unloading, and Hale slept that night in a hammock slung in the hold, and early on the morning of Wednesday, the 18th, the market boat crossed the East River to Whitehall Slip, its final destination. Hale was paid off by Captain Klaas, and the British guards on the pier took no notice as he strolled past them with the rest of the crew, and entered New York.

A week ago he had walked these streets freely in uniform. Now he slunk up Dock Street with head lowered, hoping the broad brim of his hat would conceal him from the prying eyes of some Negro slave or hungry urchin who might turn him in

for a half-joe reward. Four days of British occupation had
wrought a drastic change in the city. The door of every patriot
residence was painted with a black *G. R.* to signify that it had
been taken over for His Majesty's service. Bedding and uniforms hung out of dormer windows to air, and polished jack
boots stood on the sills. Now and then a bright-painted feminine
face would appear in a window, to be hauled back into the bedroom amid shouts of hoarse male laughter. Shops had been
looted along the waterfront, broken bottles littered the gutters,
and books stolen from the King's College library were being
hawked by soldiers for a shilling apiece. Some Royal Grenadiers,
staggering out of a tavern, jostled Hale rudely off the curb.
"Walk on the cobblestones, civilian."

He crossed to Queen Street, and hurried up the block to
Number 23. A metal cutout sign was suspended from a hori-
zontal rod, displaying a Golden Thimble and Shears. Over the
door was a small wooden plaque lettered: *H. Mulligan,
Clothier*. He gave a quick glance up and down the street, and
ducked inside.

*   *   *

There had been no rain in New York since last Sunday, the
night of the British landing, and by Friday the city was parched
and choked with dust. The drought had begun to lower the
water level in the wells, and the cedar-shingled roofs, baked by
the sun, were tinder-dry. A hot breeze sprang up out of the
south on Friday afternoon, building to a near gale as darkness
fell.

Shortly before midnight, a fire broke out in a small public
house and brothel on the wharf near Whitehall Slip, at the
lower end of Manhattan. It raced through the flimsy wooden
structure, feeding on combustible materials strewn on the floor,
and in a matter of minutes the entire building was a torch,
scattering sparks onto the cedar roofs of the adjoining dwell-

ings. At the same moment, another blaze was discovered in the old Fighting Cocks tavern at the Battery; over on Broadway an inn called the White Hall was suddenly engulfed in flames; three or four more fires started simultaneously at scattered points around the city.

There were no church bells to sound the alarm, and the conflagration was already out of control when the civilian firefighters arrived. Their companies were undermanned, some of the engines had been dismantled, their hand pumps were out of order. They watched helplessly as the separate blazes leapt from roof to roof, fanned by the wind, and united in a single wall of fire that moved irresistibly up the island. From Dock Street it crossed to Bridge Street and Stone and Field Market. Rickety tenements went up like matchwood, sending a shower of flying embers to kindle the next block. "If one was in one street and looked about," Pastor Shewkirk of the Moravian Church reported, "it broke out already again in another street above." Flames sucked the air from the narrow lanes and alleys, and half-naked men and women with children in their arms fled panic-stricken through the smoke and falling brands. Some took refuge in houses well in advance of the blaze, only to have them smolder and catch in the intense heat. Others raced barefoot before the pursuing fire, beating out sparks that ignited their scanty garments, and flung themselves face down on the Commons and covered their heads with their clothing, gasping for breath.

Now the fire torrent seemed to fork. One branch progressed up Broad Street, destroying prim Dutch houses and stately Georgian residences alike. Another river of flame swept north along Broadway, searing the beeches and lime trees along the fashionable Mall, and flowed down the side streets to the Hudson, consuming all the buildings west of the avenue. An ammunition dump blew up near Stone Street, turning the center of the town into an inferno. The midnight sky was blood-red, and the decks of ships five miles away were as bright as noonday. Watchers in Brooklyn and Paulus Hook could hear the solid roar, punctuated by the occasional long sigh and rifle-shot reports of exploding pitch-pine timbers, the rumble of a toppling brick wall, the screams of residents pinned in the wreckage. Wild hogs ran squealing through the streets, adding to the pandemonium; horses kicked in terror at the locked doors of stables; some gamecocks scattered from a burning pen, their feathers in flames, and set a series of new blazes in their flight.

From Beaver Street the fire moved northwest up New Street, heading toward Trinity Church. Long before it reached the ancient edifice, the whole interior was seen to be ablaze. Red tongues licked up the sides of the wooden steeple, transforming it into a lofty pyramid of flame. As the shingles burned away, the skeleton of the spire appeared for a transcendent moment, each separate piece of timber blazing, and then collapsed with a thunderous roar into the blackened and empty stone shell. So fierce was the heat that the Rector's House and the old Lutheran Church nearby had to be abandoned. St. Paul's Chapel, a few blocks north, was in the direct path of the flames; members of the congregation mounted ladders brought from the burying ground and stood on the roof with buckets of water, drenching sparks as fast as they fell.

Two regiments of the Fifth Brigade had been ordered into town by Major General Robertson, in command of the city, as soon as he was notified of the emergency. Troops manned litters and carried the sick out of burning hospitals, while other patients screamed from upper-story windows to be rescued. American prisoners, evacuated from the city jails, were marched north under heavy guard; some broke for freedom, and several were shot as they fled. Soldiers with carts helped merchants remove their wares from stores menaced by the fire. Looters took advantage of the confusion; a wine-shop proprietor transferred the contents of his shelves to a wagon in desperate haste, and a

forever. More than its buildings, the neighborly character of lower Manhattan had been erased in a few hours. New York would never be a town again.

The American army on Harlem Heights had watched the great column of smoke and flame during the night, and New Englanders made no secret of their joy at the destruction of the Tory city. General Washington, awakened shortly after midnight by Tench Tilghman, stood calmly on the upper balcony of the Morris Mansion, observing the spreading glow in the sky and the points of flame like candles along the southern horizon. His face was impassive as he said to Tilghman: "Providence, or some good honest fellow, has done more for us than we were disposed to do for ourselves."

*   *   *

Eight miles down the island, General Howe had also been aroused from his slumbers at midnight, and watched the fire from the veranda of the Beekman Mansion; but, unlike Washington, he was far from calm. Sir William was a pettish man in his latter forties, tall and rather ungainly, with narrow shoulders and broad hips and a pronounced paunch which sagged over the sash around his middle, the result of overindulgence in rich foods and wines. His features bore a remarkable resemblance to those of George III, a fact which London gossip whispered was more than coincidental. The eyes were set a little too close to the bridge of his large nose, and he had a sulky full-lipped mouth which pouted when he was annoyed.

He was annoyed now. There was little doubt in his mind that the fire had been set willfully by some villains who had concealed themselves in the city for that express purpose. The fact that it had broken out at so many widely separated points, that the fire equipment was out of order, and that his soldiers had caught arsonists setting fire to empty houses at a distance from the blaze was proof enough that it had been a deliberate plot; and he was privately convinced that the New England people were at the bottom of it. He wrote Lord George Germain in London: "A most horrid attempt was made by a number of wretches to burn the town, in which they succeeded too well, having set it on fire with matches and combustibles that had been prepared with great art and ingenuity. Many were detected in the act, and some killed upon the spot by the enraged troops in garrison."

All that Saturday he paced the terraced gardens of the Beekman estate, scowling at the dense pall of smoke that hung over the stricken city. He took the fire as a personal affront. Such a dastardly act was small return for the gentlemanly way in which he had conducted the war up to now. He had shown the rebels the greatest indulgence, allowing Washington to retrieve his army from Brooklyn and again delaying his attack on New York until the Continental forces were largely withdrawn. The least they could have done, he felt, was to return the courtesy by leaving his army's winter quarters unharmed.

His temper was not improved when, shortly after he and Mrs. Loring had retired to their bedchamber late Saturday evening, he was aroused again by an aide. Shouldering into a dressing gown and cramming his wig back on his head, he listened with increasing annoyance as the aide explained the emergency. An American officer in civilian clothes had been apprehended by one of the patrol parties earlier in the evening, attempting to escape through the lines to Harlem. Brought before General Robertson, he had insisted he was a refugee schoolteacher from Connecticut, and had shown a Yale diploma in proof. Robertson had been struck by the similarity between his name and that of Samuel Hale, deputy commissary of prisoners under Major Loring; and Samuel Hale, summoned by Robertson, had identified the culprit by a birthmark on his neck as his own cousin, Captain Nathan Hale of the Continental Army. The prisoner had been stripped and searched, and minutes were found inside his shoes, including sketches of British fortifications and notes on military strength and position. He had made a full confession.

Howe inspected the evidence, his lower lip protruding. "Where is he now?"

"Downstairs, sir."

The General cast a regretful glance at the chamber door, gathered his dressing gown about him, and descended the stairs in grumpy silence. He scowled at the prisoner who had caused him to be torn from Mrs. Loring's warm embrace. "Did Washington tell you to burn the city?"

"I cannot disclose the orders of my Commander, sir."

Sir William's rosebud mouth pursed, and he turned to his aide. "Lock him in the greenhouse," he said. "Have the Provost hang him in the morning. And don't disturb me again tonight," he snapped over his shoulder, hitching the skirts of his dressing gown and hurrying back upstairs.

*　　*　　*

Toward evening of Sunday, the 22nd, American outposts in Harlem Lane sent word to headquarters that an enemy flag of truce was at the lines, with a communication for General Washington. Colonel Reed, the Adjutant General, accompanied by Major General Israel Putnam and Captain Alexander Hamilton, rode down from the Heights to meet the flag. The waiting officer identified himself as Captain Montresor, aide to General Sir William Howe, and presented a letter from the British commander. It was a routine message, complaining of an illegal weapon, a musket ball cut and fixed to the end of a nail, one of a number found in the encampments quitted by the American troops. The letter made no mention of the fire, and Old Put was unable to contain his curiosity. "We were sorry to see New York ablaze yesterday."

Captain Montresor's sharp chin elevated, and his eyes were

mocking. "I can well imagine the distress it occasioned in your camp, sir," he said thinly. "It was a most unfortunate fire. Not only was the entire lower portion of the city destroyed, but it pains me to inform you that a number of Americans were caught spreading the blaze, and tossed into the flames or otherwise punished." He added: "One of your officers, a Captain Hale, was arrested yesterday night within our lines, and hanged this morning."

William Hull learned of Hale's execution from Hamilton at the Harlem Heights camp that night. Stunned by the news, he secured permission to accompany Tench Tilghman and another of Washington's aides when they delivered General Washington's reply, a formal note apologizing for the "wicked and infamous weapon" about which General Howe had protested. Like Howe, he made no reference in his letter to the fire or to the reported hanging of Hale. Captain Montresor met the party by appointment at the front lines on Tuesday morning, and Hull recalled the scene vividly half a century later:

"I learned the melancholy particulars from this officer, who was present at his execution, and seemed touched by the circumstances attending it. He said that Captain Hale had passed through their army, both of Long Island and York Island. That he had procured sketches of the fortifications, and made memoranda of their number and different positions. When apprehended, he . . . at once declared his name, his rank in the American army, and his object in coming within the British lines.

"Sir William Howe, without the form of a trial, gave orders for his execution the following morning. He was placed in the custody of the Provost Marshal, who was a Refugee, and hardened to human suffering and every softening sentiment of the heart. Captain Hale, alone, without sympathy or support, save that from above, on the near approach of death asked for a clergyman to attend him. It was refused. He then requested a Bible; that too was refused by his inhuman jailer.

" 'On the morning of his execution,' continued the officer, 'my station was near the fatal spot, and I requested the Provost Marshal to permit the prisoner to sit in my marquee, while he was making the necessary arrangements. Captain Hale entered: he was calm, and bore himself with gentle dignity, in the consciousness of rectitude and high intentions. He asked for writing materials, which I furnished him: he wrote two letters . . . He was shortly after summoned to the gallows.' But a few persons were around him, yet his characteristic dying words were remembered. He said, 'I only regret that I have but one life to lose for my country.' "

By order of Marshal Cunningham, his body was left hanging for three days, as a warning to others. Some guardsmen removed the sign from the Dove Tavern, a painted Colonial gentleman, and hung it in jest on a limb of the apple tree beside him, labeled *G. Washington.*

Hale's family was prostrated with grief at the news. "Betra'd he doutles wass by Somebody," Deacon Hale mourned. "A Child I sot much by but he is gone." The Reverend Enoch Hale, a country preacher, made several visits to the American camp to learn at first hand about his brother; and in December he met Major John Wyllys, a member of Hale's college class and salutatorian at his Commencement, who had just been exchanged by the British. Wyllys, brigade major to General Wadsworth, had been captured at Kip's Bay during the American retreat, and was a prisoner in New York at the time of the execution. Enoch noted in his diary: "Wyllys saw my Brother's Diploma, which the Provo' Marshal showed him who also had two letters of his one to me the other to his Commanding Officer, written after he was sentenced." Since the letters were never delivered, it can be assumed that Cunningham destroyed them.

Sergeant Stephen Hempstead waited in Norwalk long after there was no more need to wait. At the end of September, he gave up his hopeless vigil and returned to the Ranger camp, where he was told the fate of the Captain he worshiped. "He died upon the 'inglorious tree,' " he wrote, "not the death of the soldier, but for his country's sake."

*   *   *

Hale's mission had ended in failure, but the lesson that it taught was still fresh in Washington's mind two years later. In May of 1778, General Howe relinquished his command, and General Sir Henry Clinton, who succeeded him, evacuated Philadelphia and brought his army back to New York. Once more Manhattan was the British command center; and once more Washington found himself in urgent need of intelligence concerning the enemy plans. From his Miller House headquarters near the White Plains — named for the fields of white daisies which grew in profusion — he sent a message to Benjamin Tallmadge, ordering him to report to the Commander-in-Chief.

Tallmadge had risen rapidly in the service. He had been made brigade major under Wadsworth after Wyllys was captured; later that same year he was offered a captaincy in the Second Regiment of Connecticut Light Dragoons; and early in 1777, at the age of twenty-five, he was promoted to major. His new duties involved an increasing amount of reconnaissance work. During the campaign around Philadelphia, the cavalry was used to scout British positions and gather information about their movements. When Washington returned to the Hudson Valley, after Clinton re-established himself in New York, Tallmadge's dragoons were placed directly under General Charles Scott, Washington's intelligence chief, with orders to patrol the Neutral Ground between the opposing camps, and locate reliable correspondents behind the enemy lines.

Washington's level blue eyes scanned Major Tallmadge as

he entered the room and saluted trimly. Clasped under one arm
was his metal dragoon hat, shaped to protect both eyes and neck
from a saber stroke, and decorated with a white horsehair plume
flowing from its peak. Tallmadge's patrician features showed
culture and breeding, and his natural courtesy impressed the
Virginia aristocrat, who did not always hold Yankee manners
in esteem. It occurred to the Commander-in-Chief that here was
a young officer who came close to fulfilling his own stern quali-
fications. He motioned Tallmadge to a chair. "General Scott informs me that you have means of obtaining information from
Long Island."

"There's a Lieutenant Caleb Brewster at Fairfield, your Excellency, operating a fleet of whaleboats which are raiding the
other shore. He is in a position to bring back such intelligence as
you desire."

"You can depend on him?"

"We grew up together in Setauket, sir. My father was pastor
of the church there until he was forced to take refuge in Connecticut last year."

Washington studied him for a moment. "Would you be able
to organize an intelligence unit among your friends in Setauket
to procure knowledge of the enemy, not only on Long Island
but in New York?"

"I'm confident it could be done, sir."

"Bear in mind that you must be convinced of the absolute integrity of anyone you employ. I'll see that sufficient funds are
available, and to avoid any slip you will report directly to me.
It will not be necessary to inform General Scott of this operation,
nor divulge the names of those involved. Everything depends
on secrecy and careful organization." The General's expression
softened. "Two years ago I sent a captain into New York without adequate preparation or cover, and he was caught and
hanged."

"I know, sir. He was a friend of mine."

Tallmadge's *Memoir* states tersely: "This year (1778) I opened a private correspondence with some persons in New York . . . How beneficial it was to the Commander-in-Chief is evidenced by his continuing the same to the close of the war. I kept one or more boats constantly employed in crossing the Sound on this business." It is the only public reference to the Culper Ring that Tallmadge ever made.

BOOK TWO

❀❀

Conscience Bay

I am perfectly acquainted with a full year's anxiety,
which no one can scarcely have an idea of, but those that
experience. Not long since, there was not the breadth of
your finger betwixt me and death. But so long as I reside
here my faithful endeavours shall never be wanting.
— SAML. CULPER

I

The Devil's Belt

THE north shore of Long Island, honeycombed with se-
cluded inlets and hidden harbors, offered a natural haven
for rebel privateers. Oyster Bay coils around Rocky Point peninsula so tightly that a sloop lying at its tip would be concealed
both from the mainland and the sea. Cold Spring Harbor adjoining it bites deep enough into the island to be a tidal river, a
convenient hideout for small craft. A few miles down the coast,
stretching from Lloyd's Neck to Eaton Neck, is the complex
known as Huntington Bay, a tortuous labyrinth of coves and
estuaries where marauding parties could lurk undetected by the
enemy. Further to the east, the coast is indented again by a
sheltered inlet called Crane Neck Bend, and a little beyond it
is the narrow passageway, between Old Field Point and Mt.
Misery, that leads to Setauket Harbor and Conscience Bay.
Three miles east of Setauket is still another arm of the Sound
called Old Man's Bay, with an entrance so small and treacherous that unwary vessels often foundered on the sandbar at its
mouth.

All these clandestine coves were used as hideouts by the
whaleboat fleet which crossed the Devil's Belt from Westchester
or Connecticut to harass the enemy; but Conscience Bay had a
unique advantage over the rest. The bay is separated from the

Sound itself by a long low sandspit, only a couple of hundred yards across, which extends eastward from Old Field Point to the harbor entrance. The deep-draft schooners and sloops were blocked by this barrier; but a whaleboat crew could disembark and drag their light craft across the spit to the head of Conscience Bay without being observed by enemy lookouts on Mt. Misery, guarding the main channel.

America's rowboat navy, virtually its only sea power, was employed to prey on British commercial shipping and to destroy their stores of food and hay on Long Island. The whaleboats were thirty feet or more in length, manned by eight or ten pairs of oars, and sometimes carrying sail. Their bows and sterns were sharp-pointed to make them swifter and more maneuverable. They would tag after an enemy merchantman like a school of blackfish stalking a lumbering sperm whale, waiting until it was vulnerable. As the ship completed its starboard tack and came about, momentarily in irons with its bow dead into the wind, the small boats would come hard alongside for the kill.

Their success depended on quick action and quicker thinking. A Captain Ebenezer Jones, leading his whaleboats out of Stamford on a foggy night, ran onto an enemy ship-of-war directly in his path. With great presence of mind, Captain Jones bellowed through cupped hands that he was an inspector sent by the British naval commander, and denounced the skipper for allowing a strange boat to get so near him unchallenged. Still berating the British captain for his carelessness, Jones and his crew boarded the vessel, while the other whaleboats circled it in the fog. At a signal, the boats closed in on their victim, the surprised skipper surrendered without a struggle, and the warship was brought back to Stamford in triumph.

It was the kind of bold derring-do which Caleb Brewster relished. He had spent several years on a whaler off Greenland, and his seagoing experience was combined with reckless audacity

and a lust for battle. Although he came from a long line of
ministers, there was nothing of the cleric about him; he was a
swashbuckling young giant with a shaggy chest and fists like
cannon balls, profane and hard-drinking and reveling in danger.
Early in the war he had been put in command of a fleet of whaleboats operating out of Penfield's tide mill in Fairfield, Connecticut; and he and Joshua Davis, also of Setauket, had made a
number of hit-and-run raids on their home town, slipping
through the shortcut into Conscience Bay and plundering the
enemy garrison entrenched in the village.

Setauket had been a British outpost since the fall of Long Island. The Reverend James Lyon, an ardent Tory, had wel-
comed the troops to his Caroline Episcopal Church; and the
Reverend Tallmadge's Presbyterian Church across the park had
been taken over as a fortified barrack. Breastworks were thrown
up around the house of worship, gravestones were ripped from
the cemetery to build a stockade, and the mouths of four swivel
guns protruded from its shattered stained-glass windows. On
August 22, 1777, Lieutenant Brewster's whaleboats accompanied
an expedition of five hundred men, under General Parsons, sent
to attack Setauket. They landed at Crane Neck Bend, marched
overland with their muskets and a brass six-pounder, and
surrounded the church, demanding the surrender of its garrison.
A lively skirmish ensued for several hours, but the arrival of
British warships in Setauket Harbor forced the raiders to retreat,
carrying off some horses and a quantity of military supplies.
Later that same year another raid was attempted by the *Schuyler*, the sloop which had ferried Nathan Hale across the Sound,
but an enemy frigate ran her aground on Old Man's Point, and
the entire party was killed or taken prisoner.

On a late evening in August of 1778, a year after the Battle
of Setauket, Caleb Brewster set out once more for Conscience
Bay, carrying Benjamin Tallmadge on his secret mission for
General Washington. . . .

The Devil's Belt was dead calm in the breathless summer twilight, and each bite of the oars sent a swirl of moonlight-green bubbles down through the phosphorescent water. Brewster held the tiller firm for Old Field Point, sweeping the horizon with his eyes. A limp sail stood against the faded sunset, and he gave it a hungry glance. "Enemy prize, Ben. We could take her as easy as grabbing a hen off a nest."

Major Tallmadge shook his head. "Not this time, Cale."

"Aw hell, it wouldn't be only a few minutes, and me and Josh here been hankering for a good boat fight." He saw that his pleas were futile. "Feller's got to get a little excitement out of this war," he grumbled.

Tallmadge peered ahead at the Long Island shore, looming out of the dusk. Only two years had passed since he had visited his father here on his way to New York to report for duty; it seemed a lifetime ago. His older brother William, captured during the fighting around Brooklyn, had died of mistreatment in a British prison. The Reverend Tallmadge and his family had fled to Connecticut, troops were quartered in the old rectory, and the Presbyterian Church, as a final desecration, had been stripped of its pews and pulpit and converted into a stable for the British horses. Most of his boyhood friends had left Setauket for the service, but Abraham Woodhull and Austin Roe had remained with their families, living resignedly under the enemy occupation.

Brewster guided the whaleboat past Old Field Point, and swung in toward a low place in the sandspit. The boat grounded with the sloshy sound of reeds, and the crew leapt out and hauled it quickly through a flooded marsh, their boots sucking and splashing in water. On the other side of the spit, Conscience Bay was a flat shadow, with the darker shape of Strong's Neck marking its far shore. They climbed aboard again, and rowed silently across the bay to the Neck, and secreted the whaleboat in a clump of willows. While Joshua Davis and the crew remained on guard, Brewster and Tallmadge followed a trail through the oak woods to Judge Selah Strong's homestead on the other side of the peninsula.

Strong's Neck juts north to bisect Setauket Harbor, separating Little Bay on the east from the shallower waters of Conscience Bay on the west. The peninsula is shaped like a crookneck squash, attached to the mainland by a slender stem but swelling to a round point of land more than a square mile in area. The body of the squash curves east and then south, so that its butt is actually lower than the stem. The Strong Manor House was situated on a hill at this southern end, looking across Little Bay to the Woodhull farm on the narrow part of the neck. Behind the farmhouse, Woodhull's back pasture ran down to the shore of Conscience Bay.

The Manor House at first glance seemed deserted, but a candle glowed behind the drawn shutters. Tallmadge hurried across the yard, overgrown with weeds, and mounted the sagging front steps. It was like coming home; Judge Selah Strong's sister Zipporah was the Reverend Tallmadge's second wife, and the two families had always been very close. There was no answer to his knock, and he rapped on the door again, and gave his name in a low voice. The lighted candle rose and moved past the shutters, and floated spectrally down the front hall toward him, and he heard a heavy bolt slide. Judge Strong's wife opened the door.

Anna Strong was stooped and gaunt, and the candle held in her hand accented the hollows of her cheeks and her sunken eyes. Tallmadge embraced her without speaking, and he and Brewster entered, and Anna Strong bolted the door securely behind them. She led them into the musty-smelling front room, emptied of most of its furnishings, and set the candle on a bare table. "The Rangers have plundered me twice," she said, "and when I heard your knock . . ."

Her tired voice had a way of fading off into nothing, and

Tallmadge looked at her more closely in the candlelight. He remembered her as a beautiful woman, delicate as a cameo, but now she wore rough homespuns and heavy square-toed shoes, and her hands were calloused. She had been doing all the farm work, she explained, since the British arrested Judge Strong last January and put him on the *Jersey* prison ship. "Rivington's *Gazette* printed a story that he'd been corresponding with the rebels. Perhaps he was; I never knew. I went to see Colonel Benjamin Floyd in Brookhaven, he's an influential King's man, you know, and he arranged for me to visit the *Jersey* several times and bring Selah food. You can't believe what those prison ships are like . . ." Her voice died again.

"You're all alone here?"

Anna Strong nodded. "The children are in Connecticut with your father and Zipporah. Even the slaves have run away."

"We'd be glad to take you across to the main, ma'am," Brewster offered.

"Thank you, Caleb. I want to stay here until Selah . . . Colonel Floyd thinks he might be able to arrange a parole." She collected herself, and tucked a gray strand of hair under her mobcap. "Why are you here, Ben?"

Talmadge hesitated. "I want to talk to Abe Woodhull and Austin Roe. Would you let us meet here tonight?"

"Of course. If I can be of any . . ."

"I'll go fetch them," Brewster said. "Abe ought to be at his father's now, and I'll most likely find Austin at the tavern."

"It's full of Britishers, Caleb," Anna Strong warned. "They might know who you are."

"Hell, ma'am, that's nothing to worry about. They known who I am for two years, and they ain't caught me yet."

The guttering candle had melted down to its pewter holder by midnight, and the group in the front room listened in silence as Tallmadge outlined his proposal. Woodhull would gather intelligence in New York, and Roe would pick up his messages and bring them out to Setauket and give them to Brewster when he arrived. A black petticoat, hung on Anna Strong's clothesline and clearly visible across the bay, would be the signal that the whaleboat was waiting. Austin Roe scratched his head. "S'pose you can't get into Conscience Bay?"

Brewster thought a moment. "Count the handkerchiefs hanging on the line beside the petticoat. One handkerchief means I'm here in the little willow cove where the whaleboat is now. Two handkerchiefs mean, say, I'm up at the north end of Strong's Neck by the big oak that was struck by lightning. Know where I mean? All right, then, three is Crane Neck Bend, and four is Setauket Harbor down by John Willse's shipyard, and five is Drowned Meadow, and six is Old Man's Bay if there's enemy craft around and I have to put in there."

Tallmadge was leaning back in his chair, waiting for an answer. Austin Roe rested an elbow nonchalantly on the mantel. "Sure, Ben, I wouldn't mind riding into the city now and then. I can claim I'm buying goods for the tavern, or shopping for some neighbors here."

Tallmadge inquired: "Abe?"

Abraham Woodhull was sunk in a corner chair, almost lost in the shadows. His face was colorless, and the knuckles cracked audibly as he locked his fingers in a torment of indecision. His father Richard was in his late sixties, too feeble to work the farm alone; Abraham had resigned his commission in the militia to aid him. He did not want to bring any more suffering to his parents. "The lobsterbacks watch every move we make," he murmured. "They'd be bound to wonder what I was doing in New York."

"What about your sister Mary?" Austin Roe suggested. "She and Amos Underhill still run that boardinghouse of theirs on Queen Street. You could visit her without anybody asking questions."

Woodhull moistened his dry lips. "They might find the messages. They might know who wrote them."

"We have a debt to our country, Abe." Tallmadge added: "Remember General Nate."

Abraham Woodhull's voice was so low that they had to strain to hear him. "I'll try it."

Tallmadge submitted his plan in a letter to the Commander-in-Chief, and suggested an interview with Woodhull. On August 25th the General replied from his White Plains headquarters: "I shall be glad to see you upon the business mentioned in yours of this date . . . You should be perfectly convinced of the Integrity of W —— previous to his imbarking in the business proposed — this being done I shall be happy in employing him — but there will be an impropriety in his coming with you to head Quarters, as a knowledge of the circumstances in the enemy might blast the whole design. You will let me see you this afternoon — if you can come to Dinner at three oClock I shall be glad of yr Company. I am Sir yr very Hble Servt, Go. Washington."

Final details of the operation were worked out at their meeting that afternoon. For purposes of security, it was decided to use code names. Major Tallmadge would assume the alias of "John Bolton" and Woodhull would be "Samuel Culper," and thenceforth the General mentioned him in correspondence only as "S —— C ——." So closely was the secret kept that even General Scott, chief of intelligence, was not aware of their identity. In a letter to Washington on November 8th, Scott spoke of "John Bolton the person whom Majr. Tallmadge recommended to Your Excellency some time ago. there will be no Dainger of his being discovered. I do not know his Propper Name my self."

General Scott had been in failing health, and that November he requested to be relieved of his duties. On November 18,

Benjamin Tallmadge succeeded Scott as deputy intelligence chief under Washington, and sole liaison with the Setauket agents. "You will be pleased to observe the strictest silence with respect to C——," the General cautioned him, "as you are to be the only person entrusted with the knowledge or conveyance of his letters."

Horses for Austin Roe's use, paid for by Washington, were stabled at relay points along the express route between New York and Conscience Bay; Brewster was assigned to transport the dispatches at regular intervals across the Devil's Belt to Tallmadge in Connecticut; and American's infant intelligence service began its secret business in the heart of the enemy-held city.

* * *

New York in 1778 was overcrowded, squalid, ugly. There had been no effort to rebuild since the American evacuation and the great fire. Two years afterward the trenches dug by the rebels remained untouched, gradually filling with "stagnant water and spoiled sauerkraut and filth." The gutted area between upper Broadway and the Hudson, and east of lower Broadway to Whitehall, was still a wasteland of rubble and empty cellar holes, with stark chimneys standing to mark the ruins. Now and then a charred foundation would cave in with a ghostly rumble, or a brick wall, weakened by wind and eroding rain, would topple and crush the children playing at its base.

The scant population left behind in 1776, when the colonial army fled, had multiplied ten times to a present census of thirty thousand; and the destruction of more than a quarter of the city's buildings made the housing problem acute. British officers had taken over the best remaining residences for their quarters. Troops filled the bleak wooden barracks north of the Commons, and spilled over into private dwellings deserted by their patriot owners. Every transport from England brought more wives of British soldiers to join their husbands, and Loyalists were summarily evicted from their homes to make room for the visitors. Runaway slaves were pouring into the city in a steady stream from the surrounding countryside, lured by General Clinton's promise of freedom, and more liberated Negroes followed north when the Royal army returned from Philadelphia. Hundreds of Tories from Westchester, fearing the lawless raiders who prowled the Neutral Ground between the two armies, arrived with families and household effects to seek protection under the British flag. There was no way to accommodate all the refugees. Most of New York's public buildings and churches had already been commandeered for hospitals or prisons, and wood was too scarce to be spared for erecting new billets for the homeless and destitute.

In despair, the poor sought refuge in the abandoned ruins. Half-burned beams were placed across the cellar holes, and covered with mildewed tents left by the American army or sections of sailcloth stolen from the shipyards. Block after flattened block was spread with gray canvas, stretched like cobwebs between the foundations. Beneath these flimsy shelters, the squatter families lived in dank underground ghettos without flooring or walls, sleeping on cinders, separated from their neighbors only by piles of refuse and human waste. Women suckled babies at bared breasts as they squatted over open fires, choking in the smoke that filled the windowless catacombs. Children emerged to roam the city in wolf packs, stealing fuel and food. The garbage from an officers' mess was no sooner tossed into the gutter than it was snatched up and brought home to the slums to be cooked again. Starving dogs lurked in the shadows, waiting to pounce on what scraps were left.

This was Canvas Town, the Wapping and St. Giles' of the desolated city, a sordid plague spot where every kind of vice and depravity flourished. The prostitution district called the

Holy Ground had been leveled in the fire, but its former occupants still plied their trade in the cellars of the old bawdyhouses. The sound of amorous brawls echoed all night, and girls staggered down the dark passageways with eyes blackened and dresses ripped from their shoulders. Rouged perverts in Macaroni wigs loitered in ruined doorways, soliciting sailors from the fleet. Robberies were so common that no citizen of New York dared venture out after sunset without an armed guard. Each morning the bodies of a few drunken soldiers would be found lying in the alleys of Canvas Town, their skulls crushed and their pockets emptied of cash.

The stench of the slums and the noxious odor of sewage in the open trenches mingled with an overpowering death-smell that permeated every corner of New York, the effluvia of American prisoners-of-war crammed in the city jails. In Bridewell on the Commons and the Livingston Sugar House at Crown Street, the inmates were wedged so tightly that, when they desired to change position on the hard plank floor at night, a command would be given and the whole human mass would turn at once. William Dunlap recalled as a boy walking past Bridewell and seeing "every window filled with heads, thrust one above another to the top of the scanty aperture, to catch a portion of the blessed air which could not find place to circulate within the massive walls and among the throng of victims." As Bridewell and Livingston filled to overflowing, other gloomy sugarhouses were converted into jails; the French Church and the North Dutch Church, which had been used as a riding school for the British dragoons, were pressed into service as added prisons; and the remaining unfortunates were confined aboard the *Jersey* and other prison ships in Wallabout Bay, from whose pestilential holds an estimated eleven thousand dead were removed during the war and buried in the mud banks of the East River.

Even the misery of Canvas Town was preferable to the wretched existence of these captive Americans, hobbled with leg irons or chained to walls, given polluted water to drink, exposed to bitter winter weather without adequate clothing or fuel. There was no glass in the windows, nothing but iron bars to keep out the cold. In the crowded French Church, only half the prisoners could lie down at a time, and a survivor testified: "They never received a stick of wood, and for the most part they ate their pork raw when the pews and doors and window-facings failed them for fuel." A prisoner in Bridewell wrote his wife, through a bribed attendant, that "at nine of the clock at evening the Hessian guards would put out the fires and lay on the victims with heavy clubs for sitting around the embers." The cells were never cleansed, men were covered with filth and vermin, and medical aid was denied them when contagious diseases spread. The prisoners "began to die like rotten sheep with cold, hunger and dirt," and ten or twenty bodies were carted out of Bridewell daily and thrown into pits without any rite of burial.

Total rations per man for three days consisted of six biscuits, half a pound of pork, often tainted, and a gill of rice. Two days a week they were defrauded even of this meager fare by the prison commissaries. Judge Thomas Jones wrote that the enterprising Joshua Loring, who had sold his plump wife to Sir William Howe in exchange for an appointment as Commissary of Prisoners, fattened his income by "appropriating to his own use nearly two-thirds of the rations allowed to the prisoners" and "actually starved to death about 300 of the poor wretches."

Even more inhumane was William Cunningham, the Provost Marshal who hanged Nathan Hale. Cunningham's headquarters were in the New Gaol, commonly called the Provost, a square stone building on the upper side of Chambers Street which held mostly American officers. Here the Provost Marshal amused himself by dosing his captives' food with arsenic "for the sake of cheating his King and country by continuing for a time to draw their nominal rations." He would sit in his quarters opposite the guardroom on the right of the main door, "drinking punch until his brain was on fire, and then stagger out into the corridors — usually followed by the mulatto Richmond, the common hangman — and pour forth volleys of abuse on the sufferers, driving the rebel spawn back to their holes and kicking over vessels of soup which the charitable sometimes placed there." After the war, Cunningham admitted that, due to his maltreatment, more than two thousand prisoners starved to death.

Many of the inmates had been in jail for better than two years, some captured in the Battle of Long Island, another two thousand taken prisoner late in 1776 when Fort Washington was betrayed by Lieutenant Demont and its entire garrison was forced to surrender. They had followed the course of the war through chance remarks dropped by the guards, or accounts of engagements told by newer captives. White Plains; Trenton; Ticonderoga. They listened avidly to the growing roll of battlefields. Oriskany; Brandywine; Bennington. Late in 1777, Colonel Ethan Allen, imprisoned in the Provost, received the first report of Burgoyne's surrender at Saratoga, smuggled to him in a loaf of bread. "Cheer, you rebels!" he shouted to his fellow inmates; the uproar brought Cunningham running, and he cursed the rumor as "a damned lie." In the spring of 1778, news that France had entered the war to aid the Colonies brought another salvo of cheers. And when General Sir Henry Clinton evacuated Philadelphia for fear of the French fleet, all but lost his army at Monmouth on his march north, and scuttled back to New York in inglorious retreat, the emaciated prisoners lined the windows of Bridewell and chanted "Yankee Doodle" until the Hessian guards clubbed them into silence.

Impervious to the poverty and suffering around them, the British high command remained as aloof as the Union Jack which fluttered high above headquarters. The city bristled with military pomp and display. Officers and their mistresses promenaded past the charred stumps along the Mall, or paused to watch the parade of guards from City Hall up Wall Street to Broadway, where they stood for daily inspection in front of the ruins of Trinity Church. Hessians with towering brass-fronted caps, their mustaches colored with the same paste as their boots, their hair plastered with tallow and flour and bound in a long queue that reached to the waist. Tall Highlanders with checkered bonnets cocked at a jaunty angle, knobby knees bare above their varicolored stockings, tasseled sporrans dangling before their kilts. Fierce Anspach grenadiers with black bearskin hats and cross-belts festooned with cartouche boxes and bayonets and brass-hilted swords. Gaudy Waldeckers, their cocked hats edged with yellow scallops, their matching yellow breeches met at the knee by black gaiters. Stolid British guardsmen with muskets held stiffly at attention as they braced themselves to receive the command or cane from the inspecting officer.

General Clinton had established his town residence in the Kennedy House at Number One Broadway, undamaged by the fire. Each morning he and his entourage would ride at full gallop up the avenue to one of the only two public houses left standing north of St. Paul's, a notorious gaming establishment with billiard tables in the front apartment and a five-alley at the rear. After a few hours spent at bowling or other pleasures, Sir Henry would remount and race back down Broadway "like a sportsman at a fox-chase." There was little applause from the citizens as he passed; the egotistical and intolerant British Commander-in-Chief was feared and hated by the Tories as well as his own staff. Judge Jones, whose contemporary history of New York is a classic in invective, described him as "haughty, morose, churlish, stupid, and scarcely ever to be spoken with." Clinton's only friend and confidante was his young aide, Major John André.

Over on Queen Street, a couple of blocks from Clinton's headquarters, was the little boardinghouse run by Amos and Mary

Underhill. It was a dingy brick building, with raised stoop and brownstone lintels in the old Georgian style. A creaking staircase led to the upstairs sleeping chambers, mostly rented by company-grade British officers. They paid no attention to the eccentric occupant of the top attic bedroom. Each morning he would set out for a brief stroll around the city, and return to his room and occupy himself with writing letters. His only caller was a lanky neighbor from Long Island who would drop in occasionally to visit him. Mary Underhill's brother, so the officers understood. A homeless derelict, one of the victims of the war. There were thousands like him in New York.

⚜ ⚜

II

Samuel Culper

T HE congestion of the city provided perfect cover for
Samuel Culper. New Yorkers were too preoccupied with
their own problems of food shortage and exorbitant rents to
notice the slight hollow-chested figure, bundled in an oversized
greatcoat, who drifted like a wraith through the busy streets,
quaking as he rubbed elbows with British soldiers and Tory
civilians. He had crossed on the Brooklyn ferry and slipped
unchallenged into town, early in October, and taken residence
in the Underhill boardinghouse. From this safe refuge, he
moved furtively around Manhattan, mingling with the crowds
at the marketplaces or tarrying in the coffeehouses in hopes of
picking up bits of military gossip from incautious officers at the
adjoining tables.

Abraham Woodhull's appearance was his best protection. No
one could have seemed more unlikely as a spy. His ashen face
and thin trembling hands, his frightened voice which seldom
rose above a whisper, were the very opposite of the conventional
cloak-and-dagger operator. He lived in constant terror of discovery, his stomach knotting whenever a stranger looked at him
twice. Only by sheer force of will could he bring himself to visit
enemy encampments on the island and observe their strength
and position. A sharp glance, a routine challenge by a sentry
was enough to send him into a nervous decline and he would

take to his bed with a chill. The Culper correspondence with Tallmadge fairly shivered with anxiety. "I have to request that you will destroy every letter instantly after reading," he pleaded, "for fear of some unforseen accident that may befall you and the letters get into the enemies hands and probably find me out and take me before I have any warning. I desire you to be particularly cairfull."

His apprehension that the letters might betray him was relieved by a Sympathetic Stain developed in London by Sir James Jay, brother of John Jay, according to a formula of his own that has never been solved. The secret ink consisted of a fluid which would disappear immediately when applied to the whitest paper, and a counterpart which could be brushed over the paper to make the writing visible again. By this means, Sir James wrote Thomas Jefferson, he had been able to transmit from England "the first authentic account which Congress received of the determination of the British Ministry to reduce the Colonies to unconditional submission; the ministry at the time concealing this design, and holding out conciliatory measures. My method of communication was this," he explained. "To prevent the suspicion which might arise were I to write my brother John only, who was a member of Congress, I writ with black ink a short letter to him, and likewise to 1 or 2 other persons of the family, none exceeding 3 or 4 lines. The residue of the blank paper I filled up, invisibly, with such intelligence and matters as I thought useful to the American Cause." He had also furnished some of his ink to Silas Deane when the Colonies' confidential envoy first arrived in France, and "in this invisible writing I sent to Franklin and Deane, by the mail from London to Paris, a plan of the intended Expedition under Burgoyne from Canada."

Even the use of Jay's Sympathetic Stain did not wholly allay Woodhull's jitters. The presence of British officers in adjoining chambers at the Underhill boardinghouse kept his nerves on edge, and his conversations with Austin Roe were conducted in whispers lest the enemy should overhear him through the thin walls. On one occasion, while he was sitting alone in his attic bedroom preparing a dispatch in secret ink, the door burst open behind him. In panic he leapt to his feet, upsetting the table and spilling the precious bottle on the floor, only to find that the intruder was his sister Mary. Tallmadge reported the incident to Washington, explaining soberly that the temporary lapse in Woodhull's correspondence was because "an excessive fright and turbulence of passions so wrought on poor Culper that he has hardly been in tolerable health since."

Slowly and cautiously the Culper Ring expanded that fall. Woodhull confided his mission — though not his code name of Samuel Culper — to his brother-in-law Amos Underhill, who was in a good position to gather information from his British boarders. William T. Robinson, a prominent local merchant who was accepted as a Loyalist, passed bits of intelligence to him, and occasionally prepared a letter, written in Tory style, which contained news of military interest. Joseph Lawrence of Bayside, a friend of Robinson and also of Caleb Brewster, cooperated in sending him word of enemy movements on Long Island.

He was more hesitant about allying himself with Hercules Mulligan, whose clothing store at 23 Queen Street was near the Underhill house. The genial Irishman had smooth-talked himself out of jail, after being apprehended fleeing from the great fire, and was popular with the British officers who patronized his fashionable tailor shop. Through the influence of his protégé Alexander Hamilton, Mulligan had been engaged as a confidential correspondent by General Washington, and in April of 1777 had sent warning of Howe's intended expedition to Delaware; but Woodhull, always discreet, preferred not to involve the ring too closely. Although their secret activities were known to each other, Mulligan continued to operate as a lone agent.

Woodhull realized that his prolonged absence from home might arouse enemy suspicion in Setauket, and he made every effort to enlist a trustworthy confederate who would gather information in New York while he returned to Long Island. He found his answer in a quiet and highly respected young Quaker merchant from Oyster Bay named Robert Townsend. On October 31, 1778, Woodhull sent a relieved message from Setauket to Tallmadge:

"Since my last have explored Long Island, City of New York and island unto the ten mile stone to Tryons Quarters where I received his threats for comeing their that made me almost tremble knowing my situation and business but blessed be God have been prospered and particularly successful in ingaging a faithful friend and one of the first characters in the City to make it his business and keep his eyes upon every movement and assist me in all respects and meet and consult weekly in or near the city. I have the most sanguine hopes of great advantage will accrue by his assistance . . . Hoping this may arrive safe and be able to serve you better in my next is the earnest desire of your most obedient Hbl. Servt., Samuel Culper."

Woodhull had struck up an acquaintance with Robert Townsend before the war, when he traveled to Oyster Bay with produce from his Conscience Bay farm to be shipped by market boat to Manhattan. They became good friends, and on his recommendation Townsend boarded with the Underhills on business trips to the city for his father. Lately the trips had been growing more frequent; Old Samuel Townsend had been in poor health since the shock of his arrest by the British, and he preferred to remain at Raynham Hall while his son acted as purchasing agent for the Oyster Bay store. Since much of Robert Townsend's business was conducted along the waterfront, he was in a good position to observe British shipping activity.

Townsend had another means of access to advance enemy intelligence. He had always had a taste for journalism, and as a sideline he had contributed occasional social items to James Rivington's *Gazette*. By 1778 he had become one of the Tory paper's regular reporters, and a favorite of its enigmatic publisher.

*   *   *

The *Royal Gazette*, formerly called the *New-York Gazetteer*, was Manhattan's most popular newspaper, at least with Loyalist readers. It outdid even its rival, Hugh Gaine's *Mercury*, in slanting the news against the patriot cause. Rivington filled every issue with calculated falsehoods about patriot defeats and bald-faced lies about British victories, aimed to please his Tory audience. He refused for several weeks to print the fact of Burgoyne's surrender. Instead, he published an apocryphal story that England had concluded a treaty with Russia and shortly would send thirty-six thousand Cossacks to strengthen the British forces. His paper featured reports that Major General Mifflin had resigned from the American army, that Roger Morris had quit Congress in a huff, that Benjamin Franklin had been mortally wounded and was not expected to live. In January of 1778 he ran a series of forged letters, purporting to be by George Washington, which indicated that the General was trying to effect a reconciliation with Great Britain. The patriots burned his paper whenever it fell into their hands, and denounced him as a "Pensioned Servile Wretch who is daily insulting, reviling, and Counteracting this Whole Continent in a most Malevolent and Rancorous Manner"; but Rivington acknowledged their abuse with an urbane shrug, satisfied that the more the rebels attacked him, the more Tory subscriptions he would sell.

Nothing ever ruffled his serene poise. He was a slim dapper man in his middle fifties, impeccably attired in cut velvet and neatly folded white stock. His curled wig framed an oval face with a long fox-nose and sly blue eyes. When he was amused, his lips formed a small tight triangle. An extant portrait, copied from a lost original by Gilbert Stuart, accents the lean well-shaped hands clasped unctuously together, the devious three-cornered smile, the fleshy bags under his eyes and slight tendency toward a double chin which were the penalties of dissipation and high living.

All his life he had been in and out of debt, due to an incurable weakness for betting on the horses. He had made a fortune in London as publisher of Smollett's *History of England*, and lost it all at the track; and he had come to America in 1760 at the suggestion of Dr. Samuel Johnson, who advised him that there were no booksellers of note in the backward Colonies. Jemmy Rivington was a born opportunist. Having married a widow with a large inheritance, he opened a bookshop at the northeast corner of Wall and Queen Streets, where he added to his profits by offering a variety of other items for sale: sealing wax, fiddle strings, jars of pickled sturgeon, slates, violins, gamecocks which he raised in a pen behind his shop, and even patent medicines, including a new remedy called "Dr. Keyser's Pills, which infallibly Cure a Disease not to be mentioned in a Newspaper, without the Knowledge of the most Intimate Friend. They are also wonderfully efficacious in curing the Rheumatism."

His book business prospered, due to his wholesale piracy of foreign editions — he brought out an unauthorized edition of *Robinson Crusoe* under the imprint of his Boston bookseller friend Henry Knox — and in 1773 he installed a printing press and started his own newspaper. It was a four-page folder, only seven by nine inches, and bore the ambitious title: *Rivington's New-York Gazetteer; or, the Connecticut, Hudson's River, New-Jersey and Quebec Weekly Advertiser*. Though he promised his readers an impartial editorial policy, the newspaper became more and more Loyalist in sentiment; and after the skirmish at Lexington — which he neglected to mention — he no longer pretended to be unbiased. When New York came under the temporary mob rule of Isaac Sears in 1775, Rivington was proscribed as one of the "Odious Six" marked for punishment. He replied in his best satiric style with a personal attack on "King" Sears, mocking him as a "tool of the lowest order, a political Cracker, sent abroad to alarm and terrify, and finishing his career in an explosion that bespatters his friends."

The explosion was prompt and violent. Led by Sears, a group of Liberty Boys surrounded Rivington's shop, and two of them, dressed as sailors, knocked on the door. When Rivington opened it, they grabbed him and wrestled him to the floor. His shouts alarmed some neighbors, who secreted him in a chimney for the night, and the following morning, slightly sooty but otherwise intact, he rowed out to the British man-of-war *Kingfisher* in the harbor. A month later, having apologized profusely to the patriots, he resumed publication of the *Gazetteer* and reverted to his old calumnies; and "King" Sears determined to finish the job.

On a cold November morning in 1775, Sears and a party of Connecticut raiders clattered down the cobbles of Queen Street toward the Tory print shop. While Rivington hid in the Merchants' Coffee House on the other side of Wall Street, the raiders went to work. Methodically they removed the devil's-tail from the press and used the curved iron handle as a sledge to batter the delicately rifled screw into uselessness, smashed the marble type bed, and shattered the stone of the imposing table. All the lead type and copper engravings were gathered in sacks and carried back to Connecticut. With his printing plant in ruins, Rivington suspended publication of the *Gazetteer* and shortly after sailed for England.

Jemmy Rivington was not a man to be suppressed. In September of 1777 he returned to New York in triumph as "Printer to the King's Most Excellent Majesty," with a new press and promise of a substantial subsidy from the British government. His print shop had escaped the fire, and he cleared out the wreckage left by Sears's raid, and in October produced the first issue of *Rivington's New York Loyal Gazette*, later changed to *The Royal Gazette*, which led off with an ecstatic account of Washington's defeat at Germantown. His crusade against the patriot cause was more violent than ever, stimulated by the memory of his previous misfortunes; and once he tasted the wrath his paper aroused among the rebels. Colonel Ethan Allen, exchanged in May of 1778 and released from the Provost on parole, hastened to Rivington's shop to chastise the hated Tory printer. Rivington himself described the interview later:

"I was sitting alone, after a good dinner, with a bottle of Madeira before me, when I heard an unusual noise in the street . . . and stepping to the window saw a tall figure in tarnished regimentals, with a large cocked hat and an enormous sword . . . I was certain the hour of reckoning had come . . . I heard him on the stairs, his long sword clanking at every step. In he stalked. 'Is your name James Rivington?' It is, sir, and no man could be more happy to see Colonel Ethan Allen. 'Sir, I have come — ' Not another word, my dear Colonel, until you have taken a seat and a glass of old Madeira. 'But, sir, I don't think it proper — ' Not another word, Colonel; taste this wine, I have had it in glass for ten years. He swallowed the wine, smacked his lips, and shook his head approvingly. 'Sir, I come — ' Not another word until you have taken another glass, and then, my dear Colonel, we will talk of old affairs . . . We finished two bottles of Madeira, and parted as good friends as if we had never had Cause to be otherwise."

His polished aplomb concealed a growing concern over the progress of the war, coupled with a mounting anxiety about his personal finances. The decline in British fortunes had been matched by a simultaneous decline in his own. The Royal government had failed to pay him the subsidy they had prom-

ised, and in November he wrote a friend in London, urging
him to use his influence with Lord George Germain. "His
Majesty has honoured me with a Commission, under the Royal
Sign Manual, to be his Printer, and the Lords of the Treasury
have given me an establishment for my salary, but alas! it is
to be paid out of the quit-rents in this Country, so that there
is no fund for the purpose . . . I humbly hope I may be
thought worthy of some farther indulgences, by my ever gracious and noble benefactor Lord Germain." All his spare cash
had been squandered at the Hempstead race track; competitors
were pressing him; and Jemmy Rivington began to cast about
quietly for other ways to bolster his income.

Still his newspaper exercised great influence; and Robert
Townsend, supplying bits and squibs of society news, was cultivated by ambitious British officers who hoped to see their names
in the *Gazette*. They fawned over him, entertained him at the
best taverns, and in their cups they talked to him freely of
military matters. He had a good memory, and reported the information to Abraham Woodhull when they met each week in
Underhill's boardinghouse or at the Joseph Lawrence home in
Jamaica. Inevitably his newspaper writing was neglected, and
James Rivington commented on the fact in his usual oblique
manner. "I notice, Robert, that you've gathered very few
gossip items of late."

"I'm sorry, but I've found no social information of interest."

"Perhaps, dear boy," Rivington murmured, "you find other
information of more interest."

His smile was disarming, and Townsend could not be sure
what lay behind it.

Another talented young man in New York had become an
occasional contributor to Rivington's *Gazette*. During the summer and fall of 1778, Major John André published several
satiric poems ridiculing the rebels, including a parody account
of the British raid on New Bedford entitled "Yankee Doodle's

Expedition to Rhode Island." Townsend considered his new associate somewhat affected, but witty and entertaining and altogether pleasant company.

*   *   *

War was as seasonal with the British as cricket, and all hostilities ceased during the inclement winter weather; but as spring burgeoned so did American speculation about the enemy's coming 1779 campaign. Washington, who had never abandoned the hope of regaining Manhattan someday, was anxious to learn of any unusual shipping or troop movements which might indicate that Clinton would leave New York vulnerable to attack. This meant constant spy surveillance in the city itself. From his headquarters at Middlebrook, New Jersey, he wrote Tallmadge on March 21, 1779: "As all great movements and the fountain of all intelligence must originate at, and proceed from the Head Quarters of the enemy's camp, C —— had better reside at New York — mix with and put on the airs of a tory, to cover his real character and avoid suspicion . . ."

Late in March, Abraham Woodhull set out again for the city with dark foreboding. Everywhere along the road were signs that the British were stirring from their winter hibernation. A regiment of Queen's Rangers was encamped in Oyster Bay, he saw as he passed, and the fine apple orchard behind Raynham Hall had been felled to build an abatis around their new redoubt on Fort Hill, commanding the village. He encountered more troops in Jamaica and Brooklyn, and a Hessian guard challenged him at the ferry stairs. His hand shook as he produced his pass; his nerves were taut, and only a sense of duty persuaded him to resume the role of Samuel Culper.

The past six months of suspense had left their mark. His face was pallid, his frail body given to uncontrollable fits of shuddering, and what little confidence he had was gone. Naturally diffident and self-effacing, he had convinced himself that

he was unfitted for the task. A letter to Tallmadge on April
12th revealed his own deep feeling of inadequacy. It was addressed to John Bolton, sent from "No. 10," and began with an
acknowledgement of Tallmadge's previous communication,
which had forwarded some money and a bottle of Sympathetic
Stain, and also conveyed a personal word of praise from His
Excellency General Washington. "Your No. 6 came to hand,
together with a Vial for a purpose which gives me great satisfaction, and twenty guineas. It is a great satisfaction to me to hear
that his —— is well pleased with my letters."

Here the mood shifted abruptly to one of apology and intro-
spection. "Whenever I sit down I always feel and know my inability to write a good Letter. As my calling in life never required it — Nor led me to consider how necessary a qualification
it was for a man — and much less did I think it would ever fall
to my lot to serve in such a publick and important business as
this, and my letters perused by one of the worthiest men on
earth. But I trust he will overlook any imperfections he may
discover in the dress of my words, and rest assured that I in-
deavor to collect and convey the most accurate and explicit intelligence that I possibly can; and hope it may be some service
toward alleviating the misery of our distressed Country, nothing
but that could have induced me to undertake it, for you must
readily think it is a life of anxiety to be within (on such business) the lines of a cruel and mistrustful Enemy."

Having unburdened himself of his doubts, the rest of the
letter presented an excellent account of recent British ship movements, including names and exact number of guns, and added
that "all transports laying in the East or North River are completely victualed and waterd for sixty five days for their compliment of troops." He concluded with a note of warning: "You
must be every where on your guard, and be more assiduous than
ever . . . The Enemy seem to be in high spirits, and say now
that Great Britain is Roused and will support them and carry

on the war at all events . . . The Torys have not the least
doubt but that they shall succeed and enjoy their possessions
yet." A postscript explained the substitution of numbers for
names, the first use of code in the Culper correspondence:
"N.B. — No. 10 represents New York, 20 Setauket, and 30 and
40 two Post Riders," Jonas Hawkins and Austin Roe.

His apprehension was not without foundation. On April 16th,
after Woodhull made a quick trip to Setauket, Tallmadge reported to Washington that "Cr. was the other day robbed of all
his money near Huntington, and was glad to escape with his
life." Though the highwaymen were local banditti, taking advantage of the disordered times to plunder any traveler they
met, Woodhull knew that if they had discovered the secret
papers hidden in his saddle they would have turned him over
to the British for a reward. A week later he had an even
narrower escape. "On the 24 of April," he wrote Tallmadge
from the city, "John Wolsey returned from Connecticut being
Paroled by the Company of Prisoners (although taken in a
Privateer) and Lodged information against me before Coll.
Simcoe of the Queens Rangers who thinking of finding me at
Setauket came down but happily I set out for N. York the day
before his arrival, and to make some compensation for his voige
he fell upon my father and plundered him in a most shocking
manner."

Lieutenant Colonel John Graves Simcoe, who had succeeded
Robert Rogers as commander of the Rangers, had established
his Oyster Bay headquarters in Samuel Townsend's home on
West Main Street. He was an Oxford graduate, supercilious and
sullen, with a powerful body capable of great cruelty. During
Howe's occupation of Philadelphia, he had become intimate with
Major John André, and they had painted scenery and acted in
theatrical presentations together. Simcoe, like André, fancied
himself as an artist and writer of light verse. Always with an eye
for the fair sex, he became enamored of the youngest Town-

send daughter Sarah, and on Valentine's Day he wrote her a fatuous love poem which concluded: " 'Fond youth,' the God of Love replies, 'your answer lies in Sarah's eyes.' " Simcoe did not suspect the patriot sentiment that Sarah's eyes concealed.

Abraham Woodhull was with Robert Townsend in New York when he received word that the Conscience Bay farmhouse had been ransacked, and the aged Richard Woodhull knocked about and abused when he refused to reveal his son's whereabouts. Townsend knew Simcoe; he had met him on several visits to Raynham Hall. He also knew of Simcoe's friendship with General Clinton's aide.

"I've done some small favors for André on the *Gazette*," he said thoughtfully. "Perhaps I could persuade him to intervene."

Woodhull's letter of June 5th to Tallmadge mentioned only that Colonel Simcoe's designs had been defeated "by a friend of mine makeing interest with the Genl Aid and only that saved me. But I am very obnoxious to them and think I am in perpetual danger." In a second letter, also dated June 5th, he came to the reluctant conclusion that the British threat "hath rendered me almost unservicable to you. I purpose quitting 10 and residing at 20. As I am now a suspected person I cannot frequent their camp as heretofore . . . shall anxiously await your directions Weather I shall endeavor to establish a confidential friend to step into my place. I remain your most obet. H. Servt., Samuel Culper."

Washington replied on June 13th that Culper should "by all means employ some person of whose attachment and abilities he entertains the best opinion"; and early the following morning Woodhull started back once more to New York. Robert Townsend was not at Underhill's boardinghouse when he arrived; and Woodhull, unwilling to tarry in the city any longer than necessary, hurried up Queen Street in hope of finding him at Rivington's print shop.

The office of the *Gazette* was a two-story brick building on the northeast corner of Queen and Wall, marked by a wrought-iron silhouette of a printing press hanging beside the door. The walls of the composing room were covered with old broadsides and sample advertisements and charts of type sizes, and the room gave off a mingled sour smell of wet paper, sheepskin-covered inking balls soaking in slop buckets, acrid printer's ink in salt-glaze jars, an open vat of lye for cleaning type. Pages of tomorrow's edition, already printed on one side, hung from the drying-racks in overlapping quires. The type for the next run was framed in a wooden chase, locked by quoins on the marble bed of the press. Aloof from the bustle around him, James Rivington stood before a schoolmaster's desk at the rear of the room, and his quill pen made meticulous corrections in the hand-written manuscript of an editorial.

Woodhull managed to catch the attention of Robert Townsend, who was reading proof on a galley of social notes, and he gestured toward the door. Townsend glanced around quickly, clipped the galley on the visorum above the type boxes, and took his hat from a peg. Rivington's sharp eyes followed him across the shop, and his lips formed an inscrutable triangle as Townsend and Woodhull departed together.

They climbed the steps of the Coffee House Bridge, and forced their way through the noonday throng of traders before the Merchants' Exchange. Vendue masters were auctioning their wares, and a news-hawker peddled copies of the *Gazette* with the repeated cry: "Bloody news — bloody news — where are the rebels now?" Skirting the piles of produce on the bridge, they strolled past the Merchants' Coffee House, crossed Water Street, and sauntered down Murray's Wharf toward the thicket of tall rocking masts at the foot of Wall Street.

Woodhull waited to speak until they were alone at the end of the pier. It was safer talking here than at Underhill's, where they might be overheard by British officers in the next room.

His low murmur was barely audible above the creak of rigging and suck of water at the pilings below them, the screaming of sea gulls, the steady chant of British tars scrubbing the deck of a man-of-war at anchor in the river. Townsend listened to his friend's appeal, and his face grew troubled, and he shook his head regretfully.

It was not the danger; he did not suffer Woodhull's neurotic fears. No, the reason for his refusal lay deeper. It was his Quaker upbringing which cringed at the thought of lying and deceit. His religious belief had kept him out of uniform; his moral scruples were equally opposed to the degrading character of a spy. Even the passing of occasional bits of oral intelligence to Woodhull during the past few months had been against his code of honor. He would have nothing but contempt for himself if he undertook this task, he told Woodhull. The stigma would be with him all his life.

"But you're in the ideal situation here. Your merchant business explains your residence in New York, you have the full confidence of the enemy, your work on the newspaper gives you added opportunity to pick up information." Woodhull's voice faded to a whisper. "You too have a debt to your country."

Townsend did not answer and they fell silent, gazing across the East River toward the opposite shoreline of Brooklyn. To the north, just around the curving point, was Wallabout Bay where the prison ships lay. Townsend thought of his fellow Americans dying below decks; they had discharged their debt. Out of the past came the memory of a young Connecticut captain who had come to Raynham Hall one September day. Hale had not hesitated to give his life in the same service.

He asked: "Will you give me your word that no one — not even General Washington — will ever know my name?"

From Setauket on June 20th Woodhull wrote Tallmadge: "I have communicated my business to an intimate friend and

disclosed every secret and laid before him every instruction that
hath been handed to me; it was with great difficulty that I
gained his complyance . . . He is a person that hath the interest of our country at heart and of good reputation, character
and family as any of my acquaintance. I am under the most
solemn obligation never to disclose his name to any but the
Post who unavoidably must know it. I have reason to think his
advantages for serving you and abilities are far superior to
mine . . . As long as I am here I shall be an assistant and do
all that I can. In the interim I remain Your Most Obt. HumL
Servt., Samuel Culper."

III

Culper Junior

EVERY pleasant afternoon, during the spring and summer of 1779, the military Band of Music gave an outdoor concert before the blackened ruins of Trinity Church. The slabs in the cemetery had been uprooted and laid flat for paving, and young British subalterns and their sweethearts strolled hand in hand or danced on the gravestones. Some uneasy Loyalists saw it as symbolic of England's waning hopes in the war.

Things had not been going well for His Majesty's forces in America. The vast reaches of the continent made it impossible to pin down as sly and elusive a foe as Washington. General Pattison, relieving the doddering Robertson as commandant of New York, wrote his brother in London: "We have not only armies to combat with, but a whole country . . . One Royal Army has already been obliged to do what is not in our history to be met with — to lay down their arms and surrender as prisoners of war." Burgoyne's disastrous failure to sever the Colonies had been a rude jolt to the Ministry. Howe had let victory slip through his fingers so often that he was at last recalled to England. Now Clinton seemed content to remain inactive on Manhattan Island, with the excuse that he must protect it from a rebel invasion. "I do not know whether our generals frighten the Americans," Lord North, the Prime Minister, observed dryly, "but they certainly frighten me."

The truth was that the British high command in New York had no desire for another rugged campaign. Life in the garrison city was leisurely and gay. Never had the debutantes of Manhattan been offered such an abundance of eligible young males, with time on their hands and money to spend. The galaxy of titled noblemen and marquises and heirs to dukedoms set feminine fans aflutter. Manners and morals were relaxed, and the onetime proper and Puritanical town took on the gala atmosphere of a European capital. There were flirtations and marriages, elopements and scandals, challenges and duels with pistol or sword. Provincial society was introduced to the sophisticated custom of dinner at four in the afternoon, with blinds drawn and candles glowing. Gold coins clinked on the gaming tables, and drinking bouts went on until morning. Staid citizens like Judge Thomas Jones frowned at "the mistresses, the little misses, and dulcineas" who flaunted themselves brazenly on the arms of ranking officers; but Clinton and his generals, separated by a convenient ocean from their wives, escorted their doxies to an endless round of parties and balls and dancing assemblies, drenching themselves with perfume to offset the charnel-house odors that emanated from Canvas Town and the crowded prisons.

Long Island had become the haven of the sporting set. Just across the river, in the village of Brooklyn, the popular Ferry House Inn offered fresh lobsters taken out of the East River, clams and oysters dug along the Brooklyn waterfront, plover netted in the Gowanus marshes, passenger pigeon and quail and heath hen from the wild countryside around Flatbush and Jamaica. Local promoters put on cockfights, bullbaiting and bearbaiting exhibits in which the animals were chained in pits and set upon by savage dogs, cricket matches, even golf tournaments for which James Rivington furnished clubs and "genuine Caledonian balls." Crowds flocked to the New Market race course on Hempstead Plains, or the smaller Brooklyn track

above Beaver Pond, which featured a "ladies' subscription purse
of £50," and also a race by women — quarter-mile heats — in
which the winner received "a Holland smock and chintz gown,
fully trimmed." As an added attraction, the spectators could
listen to "God Save the King, played every hour."

Boxing bouts were staged weekly behind the Ferry House
Inn, and Negro slaves and sailors from the fleet would don
knee-length tights and battle each other with bare knuckles for
a hatful of coins tossed by the onlookers. One of the favorite
pugilists was fifteen-year-old Bill Richmond, the mulatto hangman who had adjusted the noose around the neck of Nathan
Hale. In 1777, young Richmond had been attacked in a New
York tavern by three drunken guardsmen and had knocked his
assailants senseless with his fists. General Lord Percy, who
chanced to observe the fight, had been impressed by the boy's
magnificently muscled body and had taken him on as a protégé,
billing him as "The Black Terror" and pitting him against all
comers. Later Richmond would accompany Lord Percy to England and knock out the top heavyweight Jack Carter to become
first of the great Negro ringmen from America, predecessor to
Molyneux.

For those with more aesthetic tastes, the little theater on
John Street, which had been closed by Congress in 1776 because
the Boston representatives feared that the morals of the American army might be impaired by play-acting, was reopened as the
Theatre Royal. All proceeds were donated to charity, and the
benefit shows were patronized by a glittering audience of the
elite, led by General Clinton who bought a season ticket. Regimental bands furnished the orchestra; Surgeon General Beau-
mont served as stage manager; and British officers acted in a
repertoire which ranged from *Tom Thumb* to Shakespeare.
Females who had "followed the drum" were engaged for three
or four guineas a performance, and an advertisement in the
Gazette announced: "Theatre Royal. Such ladies as are duly

qualified, and inclined to perform on the stage, will please to send in their proposals, to be left at Mr. Rivington's." When feminine talent was unavailable, the women's characters were played by junior officers, who donned rouge and petticoats in the cause of art. The lurid scenery, depicting palace chambers and wildwood glens, was painted by Captain Oliver de Lancey, Jr., and Major John André, who also took an occasional female role.

Clinton's handsome young aide had become the pampered pet of New York society. Born of a Swiss father and French mother, he had a Gallic charm and vivacious wit which made him the center of any social circle. His features were delicately modeled, and his long dark eyelashes and curling locks would have adorned a girl. He had been trained to follow his father in the mercantile business in London, but his talents ran rather to belles-lettres, and he had a natural flair for sketching and painting and composing light verse. He was also skillful at needlepoint and embroidery.

Although women swooned over him wherever he went, John André's romances never seemed to prosper. In his youth in England he was said to have been engaged to one Honora Sneyd, member of a literary salon which he frequented, but somehow her ardor cooled and she married a wealthy Irish widower instead. André did not seem unduly crushed by the blow. His mother and three doting sisters had spoiled him as a boy, and his interest in the opposite sex was more fraternal than physical. He was a dilettante, not a lover, and a military career suited his vanity to perfection: he could strut in his gaudy uniform, enjoy the adulation of the ladies, and move on to his next post with a sigh, perhaps a poem, but no serious regrets.

During the British occupation of Philadelphia, he was the star of the glittering Meschianza given in honor of the departing General Howe. His gallant manners captivated the local belles; and Peggy Shippen, youngest daughter of the Loyalist Judge

Edward Shippen, was deeply smitten. Peggy was a seductive blonde, accustomed to having her way with men, but André was not to be seduced. He parried her advances with urbane amusement, and remained unmoved either by her tender caresses or her hysterical tears. Never blinded by passion, he could see that her coquettish smile masked a nature as vain and self-centered and ambitious as his own. He left for New York without any deep involvement; and less than a year later, in April of 1779, Peggy became the wife of the middle-aged American commandant in the city, General Benedict Arnold.

On May 10th, a month after their marriage, a Philadelphia china merchant named Joseph Stansbury arrived in New York with a confidential message for the British Commander-in-Chief; and Major André, as Clinton's aide, met him in private. Stansbury brought overtures from an American general, known only as "Monk," who offered his services to the Royal cause "either by immediately joining the British army or cooperating on some concealed plan with Sir Henry Clinton." André recalled Peggy Shippen's shrewd smile, and guessed from the outset that she was the Lady Macbeth of the conspiracy. He was so sure of the identity of "Monk" that in the first draft of his reply he inadvertently wrote *Arnold* and then scratched it out. Having assured his anonymous correspondent that "in the very first instance of receiving the tidings or good offices we expect, our liberality will be evinced," he arranged for Stansbury to be taken by armed vessel to Perth Amboy for his return journey to Philadelphia; and André and Clinton waited patiently for Arnold's next move.

*   *   *

That same spring Robert Townsend entered into partnership with Henry Oakman, and opened a dry-goods business at 18 Smith Street, a block from his boardinghouse. It was a good precaution. Austin Roe's frequent calls at the Underhill home were bound to provoke enemy questions in time; but the courier could visit the Oakman & Townsend store without arousing suspicion, on the pretext of purchasing goods for his Setauket neighbors, and deliver a message from Tallmadge or pick up a dispatch from Samuel Culper Junior.

Townsend had entered into his new role with reluctance, torn between a deep sense of guilt and a deeper sense of duty. His upright Quaker conscience rebelled against his shameful occupation, but the same conscience would not let him go back on his promise to Woodhull. He was a grave and introspective young man, not yet twenty-five, simply dressed in Quaker style, his chestnut hair cut short and drawn back in a club. His features were rugged rather than handsome; he had the prominent Townsend nose and cleft chin, and there was a dark pigmentation around his eyes, the result of sleepless nights. They were soft brooding eyes, not coldly estimating like André's or glazed with fanatic conviction like those of Nathan Hale. His rare smile was shy and sensitive, and women found it irresistible.

Austin Roe shared none of Townsend's self-doubts or Woodhull's fears. He possessed a serene indifference to danger, and his lackadaisical drawl disarmed any sentry who challenged him. His feats of horsemanship outshone those of Paul Revere; on innumerable occasions he rode the 110-mile round trip between Setauket and New York, through a countryside infested with bandits and regularly patrolled by Royal dragoons. Once his wife Catherine asked him on his return if he had run into any trouble on the road. "Nothin' to speak of, dear," he replied casually. "Just these couple of little holes in my hat."

He would leave his horse at the hitching-post in front of Oakman & Townsend's and saunter into the store, covered with dust from his long morning ride, and hand Robert Townsend a written order from John Bolton: "You will be pleased to send by bearer ½ ream letter paper, same as last shipment." Townsend would wrap and seal the ream, and Roe would pay for his purchase and leave the store. As soon as his partner's back was turned, Townsend would slip out a rear door and hurry to the boardinghouse where Roe would be waiting. They would climb the stairs to his chamber, and he would take a vial of Sympathetic Stain from his closet and brush John Bolton's order with the restorative fluid, bringing out the message from Tallmadge inscribed between the lines. Carefully unwrapping the ream of paper so it could be sealed again, Townsend would remove a single page and write in invisible ink his answers to General Washington's questions. He would count the sheets in the ream until he reached a number agreed upon with Roe, insert the apparently blank page, and replace the wrapping; and Roe would stow the package with the other purchases in his saddlebag, and set out on his perilous ride back to Setauket.

Roe had arranged to pasture his cattle in Abraham Woodhull's rear meadow which sloped down to Conscience Bay. On his return to the tavern that evening, he would pull out the blank sheet from the ream, conceal it in his shirt, and stroll over to the Woodhull farm to attend his cows. Since it might have attracted attention if they were seen to meet, a wooden box was buried in a corner of the meadow. Roe would drop the paper in this box, and shortly afterward Woodhull would go to the pasture and retrieve it.

Locking the door of his bedroom, Culper Senior would develop Townsend's reply with the restorative, and either transcribe it or enclose it in an added letter of his own. A black petticoat on Anna Strong's clothesline across the bay would tell him that Caleb Brewster had arrived, and the number of handkerchiefs hanging beside it would direct him to the particular cove where the whaleboat was hidden. Shortly after dark, Woodhull would follow the back lanes to the rendezvous point and deliver the message, and Brewster would row back across the Devil's Belt to Connecticut, fighting down the temptation to tackle an enemy merchant sloop on the way. In Fairfield he would hand the message to Tallmadge, and a series of mounted dragoons, posted every fifteen miles, would forward Culper's dispatch to Washington's headquarters over by the Hudson.

The circuitous route was necessarily slow, and sometimes the delay proved costly. On June 29th, Culper Junior wrote Tallmadge from New York: "I was this day informed that 2 British Regt. of Col. Fanning's Corps & the associated loyalists, is now at white Stone, where they arrived yesterday from Rhode-Island — This I have no doubt of, as it was told me by a person who came passenger with them — He thinks they are to make excursions into Connecticut — and from what I can collect I believe they are, and very soon." Woodhull forwarded the message with a warning of his own. "Enclosed you have Mr. Saml. Culper Junr's letter . . . He hath hinted to you the prospect of their making excursions in to Connecticut soon. Very probably the war will be carried on in that manner, as free liberty is granted to the Refugees to plunder as much as they can. You must keep a very good look out or your shores will be destroyed."

The Culper warning arrived too late. Colonel Sheldon's Second Regiment of Dragoons was stationed at Poundridge, near Bedford, New York, and Major Tallmadge and some ninety troops occupied an advance post near the Poundridge Church. In a dawn attack, Lord Rawdon's Light Horse and a body of light infantry charged the forward position. The outnumbered Americans fought with clashing cavalry sabers until Tallmadge ordered a retreat. Much of the regiment's equipment fell into the enemy's hands, and Tallmadge lost not only a fine horse and most of his field baggage, but, far more serious, some money and confidential papers which Washington had sent him to be delivered to the Culpers. One captured letter from the General mentioned S —— C —— and "his successor (whose name I have no desire to be informed of)," and also "a man on York Island living at or near the North River of the name of George Higday, who I am told hath given signal proof of his attachment to us . . . his name and business should be kept profoundly secret, otherwise we not only lose the benefits derived from it, but may subject him to some unhappy fate." Washington promised that "when I can procure some more of the Liquid C —— r writes for, it shall be sent."

Tallmadge reported the loss of his papers, and Washington rebuked him in exceedingly mild terms, pointing out that the unlucky accident "shows how dangerous it is to keep papers of any consequence at an advanced post," and offering to replace the guineas and also Tallmadge's personal effects which had been abandoned in his hasty flight. The General added: "The person who is most endangered by the acquisition of your letters is Higday . . . I wish you could endeavor to give him the speediest notice of what has happened. My anxiety on his account is great."

The raid had given British counterintelligence some valuable information. Now they knew the existence of a secret ink, the route of the messages by way of Connecticut, the initials of two spies, S —— C —— and C —— r, and the name and location of another. Though George Higday was promptly seized, he had been alerted in time to destroy any incriminating evidence. He escaped being hanged, but his usefulness to the Culper Ring was ended.

There was another aftermath to the raid. Robert Townsend visited Rivington's print shop a week later to deliver some social items he had written, and paused to glance at an advance copy of the *Gazette* for July 10th. His eyes fell on a small news item: "As it is confessed, without the least reserve, there are many Sons of Liberty in New-York that hold a constant intercourse with the Commander-in-Chief of the Rebel Army, from whom he is supplied with accurate information of all arrivals and departures, and of everything daily carrying on here, both in the military and civil branches. The rebels on Long-Island (notwithstanding being indulged with their paroles) and the whitewashed inhabitants, are in constant communication with the inhabitants of Connecticut."

James Rivington, composing an editorial at his tall schoolmaster's desk, observed Townsend's involuntary start, and his eyes twinkled. "Does the paragraph surprise you, Robert?"

Townsend sought to cover his confusion. "I'm shocked to read that the rebels are descending to such meanness."

"I don't doubt they'll be equally shocked to read it." Rivington laid down his quill pen, and strolled across the room. "I have a confession, dear boy." He rested a confidential hand on Townsend's shoulder." "It so happens I'm in rather straitened circumstances at the moment, and if some financial offer were made," he purred, "I might be persuaded not to publish such items in the future." His smile was bland. "Pity the idea can't be broached to the other side, isn't it, Robert?"

He went back to his desk, dipped the quill in an inkpot, and resumed writing.

Since British intelligence had learned that the Americans were using a Sympathetic Stain, Washington was fearful that they might intercept a secret letter and find a way to develop it. Late in July, as an added measure of security, Major Tallmadge was ordered to work out a cipher and numerical code to be used by the Culpers in future correspondence. Only four code books were prepared, for General Washington and Townsend and Woodhull and Tallmadge himself. These were zealously guarded by the Culpers, for their discovery would mean certain conviction and death on the gallows.

The code was simple enough. On a double sheet of foolscap, Tallmadge listed in alphabetical order the words most apt to be employed in the Culper messages, taken from a copy of Entick's *Dictionary*, and opposite each word he wrote a corresponding number. In addition to the standard vocabulary, certain important geographical names had special designations — New York was 727, Long Island 728, Setauket 729 — and the key personnel were likewise assigned numbers. General Washington was 711, and the leading members of the espionage ring followed in sequence. 721 was John Bolton; 722 was Culper Saml.; 723 was Culper Junr.; 724 was Austin Roe; 725 was C. Brewster.

726 was Rivington.

*   *   *

Culper Junior's prediction of enemy excursions into Connecticut proved all too accurate. The raid on Poundridge was part of a new and vicious turn that the war had taken. Unwilling to face the American army in battle, after his near disaster at Monmouth, Sir Henry Clinton resorted to a campaign of terrorism, burning defenseless coastal towns and looting the civilian population. During the summer of 1779, the air of Westchester and Connecticut was heavy with the pungent odor of smoldering farmhouses and barns and scorched grainfields. Blazing settlements turned the sky blood-red at night, and homeless victims, roused from their sleep by crackling flames, fled down the country roads carrying babies and bundles of household goods.

There was no distinct or decisive object to the wanton pillaging, save to inflict as much misery as possible on the Americans. General Tryon, once the respected Royal Governor of New York, staged a savage hit-and-run raid on Connecticut, and left Danbury and Ridgefield in ashes. In retaliation, Lieutenant Colonel Return Jonathan Meigs, a hard-bitten Yankee with a wizened face like a winter apple, led a fleet of whaleboats across the Sound and attacked the British fort at Sag Harbor on eastern Long Island, destroyed twelve brigs and sloops, a hun-

dred tons of hay, and ten hogsheads of rum, and returned to
Connecticut without the loss of a man. Tryon and his second
in command, Brigadier General Oliver de Lancey, struck back
at the lower Hudson valley, sacking Tarrytown and Dobbs
Ferry and leaving a trail of desolation across Westchester. The
villages of Greenwich, just across the Connecticut line, and
Rye were ravaged, and the already legendary General Israel
Putnam contributed still another fable to American mythology
by claiming that he rode his horse down the steep rocks of "Put's
Hill" to escape capture. A small band of Jersey patriots avenged
themselves by crossing the Hudson to Bloomingdale, north of
New York City, and putting General De Lancey's beautiful
mansion to the torch. De Lancey's wife and daughters fled in
their nightclothes to take cover in a Manhattan swamp until
morning.

Any last hope of a reconciliation with the mother country was
lost in the mounting bitterness and hate which united the
Colonies against the enemy. Even staunch Loyalists like Judge
Thomas Jones deplored such British atrocities as the slaughter of
Lieutenant Colonel Baylor's body of Virginia Light Horse,
called "Mrs. Washington's Own," who were stationed near
Tappan, New York. Surrounding the camp at night, Judge
Jones wrote, the Royal troops "seized the sentinels and with
fixed bayonets entered the houses and barns where the rebels
were sleeping, and before they could have recourse to their arms,
the whole corps was massacred in cold blood, and to the disgrace of Britons many of them were stabbed while upon their
knees humbly imploring for mercy . . . An act inconsistent
with the dignity or honour of a British General, and disgraceful to the name of a soldier."

Clinton was determined to punish both the Connecticut and
Long Island patriots for their collaboration in transmitting intelligence across the Devil's Belt. Foraging parties scoured the
northern shore of the island, stealing everything of value and

confiscating cattle which they branded *G.R.* and left to fatten up over the summer. On the first of July a fleet of forty-six sail, manned by two thousand sailors, carried General Tryon — "Judas Tryon," Woodhull termed him in a letter — across Long Island Sound to Connecticut "to execute vengeance upon rebellious women and formidable hosts of boys and girls." Poundridge was attacked on July 2nd. Three days later, Tryon landed with three divisions at New Haven.

It was not yet daylight when alarm guns and the ringing of church bells aroused the inhabitants of the college town. A group of Yale students rallied on the green, and Colonel Aaron Burr, who happened to be visiting in New Haven, offered to lead them to the attack. Crouched behind earthworks thrown up on Bridge Street and Beacon Hill, they held off the invaders for several hours. As they fell back, the venerable Reverend Naphtali Daggett, retired president of Yale, seized his fowling piece and rode into the face of the enemy, discharging and reloading as the British column surrounded him. "What are you doing, you old fool?" asked an officer, puzzled at the spectacle of a lone individual in clerical clothes fighting an entire regiment. "Exercising the rights of war, sir," replied the president, and touched off his musket again. The officer brandished a sword and demanded: "If I let you go, will you ever fire at the King's troops again?" "Nothing more likely," the Reverend Daggett retorted, and the officer's saber descended on his skull. Gashed and bleeding from a dozen wounds, he was forced to escort the regiment to the heart of New Haven, where he collapsed and died shortly afterward. A number of houses were ransacked and their cellars plundered of rum, and by nightfall Tryon's army was so drunk that many had to be carried back to the harbor in carts or wheelbarrows. After setting fire to the warehouses and shipping at Long Wharf, the divisions re-embarked and sailed down the Sound toward Fairfield.

Early the following morning, Tryon's forces descended on the peaceful fishing village, which had no troops and was totally defenseless. Three churches, two schools, the courthouse, and over two hundred residences and shops were set ablaze. Threatened by the approach of some Connecticut militia, the British left Fairfield in ruins and crossed the Sound to Huntington Bay to rest and mount their next attack. On Sunday morning the armada headed once more for the Connecticut coast and struck at Norwalk, also without any defense. Tryon climbed a small hill and seated himself in a comfortable chair, gazing down from his Olympic height at the methodical destruction of the city. Only six houses were left standing when his ships hoisted sail and returned to New York in triumph.

Tryon's raid on Fairfield did not deter Caleb Brewster. His whaleboat fleet had scurried for safety when the enemy was sighted, and concealed themselves in tiny creeks and sloughs along the marshy shore. As soon as Tryon departed, they returned to their former anchorage; and a couple of days later, while the smoke of burning Norwalk smudged the western sky, Brewster set out for Conscience Bay with another message to the Culpers from General Washington.

* * *

For all his reputation as a paragon of truth, the General was revealing a remarkable talent for duplicity and intrigue. The machinations of military espionage fascinated him, and he took keen personal pleasure in plotting subterfuges to outwit the enemy. Although he had delegated Major Tallmadge to coordinate the activities of the Culper Ring, the Commander-in-Chief remained its real director. Washington, and Washington alone, was the head of American secret intelligence.

No detail was so small that it escaped his attention. Lest the repeated use of a sheet of blank stationery might provoke suspicion, he recommended that Culper Junior should write his messages in invisible ink "on the leaves of a pamphlet, on the first, second, and other pages of a common pocket book, or on the blank leaves at each end of registers, almanacks, or any new publication of small value." A further deception, he suggested artfully, would be to send "a familiar letter on domestic matters to his friend in Setauket, interlining with the Stain his secret intelligence," and "fold it up in a particular manner" to distinguish it from other correspondence. In a lengthy memorandum, dictated to Tench Tilghman at his West Point headquarters, Washington prepared a list of "Instructions for C—— Senior and C—— Junior," which specified precisely how his Manhattan spies should operate:

> C—— Junr. to remain in the City, to collect all the useful information he can — to do this he should mix as much as possible among the officers and Refugees, visit the Coffee Houses, and all public places. He is to pay particular attention to the movements by land and water in and about the city especially.
>
> How their transports are secured against attempt to destroy them — whether by armed vessels upon the flanks, or by chains, Booms, or any contrivances to keep off fire Rafts.
>
> The number of men destined for the defence of the City and Environs, endeavoring to designate the particular corps, and where each is posted.
>
> To be particular in describing the place where the works cross the Island in the Rear of the City — how many Redoubts are upon the line from River to River, how many Cannon in each, and of what weight and whether the Redoubts are closed or open next the city. To be very particular to find out whether any works are thrown up on Harlem River, near Harlem Town, and whether Horn's Hook is fortifyed.
>
> To enquire whether they have dug Pits within and in front of the line and works in general, three or four feet deep, in which sharp pointed stakes are fixed. These are intended to receive and wound men who attempt a surprise at night.

The state of the provisions, Forage and Fuel to be attended to, as also the Health and Spirits of the Army, Navy and City.

These are the principal matters to be observed within the Island and about the City of New York. Many more may occur to a person of C. Junr's penetration which he will note and communicate. C —— Senior's station to be upon Long Island to receive and transmit the intelligence of C —— Junior.

There can be scarcely any need of recommending the greatest Caution and secrecy in a Business so critical and dangerous. The following seem to be the best general rules: To intrust none but the persons fixed upon to transmit the Business. To deliver the dispatches to none upon our side but those who shall be pitched upon for the purpose of receiving them and to transmit them and any intelligence that may be obtained to no one but the Commander-in-Chief.

In line with Washington's instructions, Culper Junior developed another lucrative source of information during the summer. The enterprising James Rivington, who never neglected an opportunity to augment his income, opened a small Coffee Shop on Wall Street, near his printing plant. It was usually crowded with military personnel, who were given to understand that their patronage would insure favorable mention in the *Gazette;* and Townsend spent much of his time visiting from table to table. No one, not even Abraham Woodhull, knew that Townsend himself had supplied most of the funds for the new venture.

The quiet young merchant was learning to be crafty. His conscience still shied at the thought of betraying the confidences of the British officers with whom he fraternized, but he forced himself to shed his drab Quaker garb and assume the polished appearance and airs of a Tory gentleman. He spent hours before a dressing table spread with essences and pomatums, awkwardly twisting his chestnut locks on curling tongs, fluffing the curls above his ears, dusting his hair with fashionable blue powder and tying the knot with a velvet solitaire. Holding a hand mirror before him, he practiced the foppish mannerisms of the young subalterns, trying to ape their gestures and affecting a superior social sneer. At Hercules Mulligan's tailor shop he purchased a plum-colored sateen coat and embroidered waistcoat, and Mulligan chatted casually as he draped the garment over Townsend's shoulders and fitted it to his tapering back and narrow waist. "Would ye ever be guessing who was here only a few moments ago? Lord Rawdon himself. He'll be sailing south with his whole corps shortly, so he told me."

Swinging an ebony walking stick, he strolled up Queen Street to the Coffee Shop and joined the afternoon throng, gossiping with the guests over a comradely glass of Madeira and listening for any chance remark that might have military significance. A ship's pilot from Cape Fear, Carolina, paused at his table to bid him farewell; he would be leaving for home shortly, he said, with the Fifty-fourth Regiment. A Loyalist merchant, swollen with self-importance, confided that the *Greyhound* with Lord Cornwallis had just arrived, and it was claimed by those in the know — he gave Townsend an intimate wink — that a sizable fleet had sailed a few days previously, carrying a couple of thousand troops to the Carolinas. Don't ever mention it, of course.

Townsend sauntered across the room, and a group of officers invited him to join them for a spot of wine. They were toasting the popular General Vaughan, they explained, who was being recalled to England. He ordered another bottle for the table, and asked innocently whether Vaughan's departure meant that New York's defenses were to be weakened. "Quite the contrary, ol' chap," a colonel assured him, his speech a little slurred. "We're preparing at this moment to for'fy Governor's Island and the Narrows and repair the works at Paulus Hook. City'll be in best possible state of defense, don' fret." He raised his glass. "By the by, Rob, I've just been promoted, y'know. Thought you might like to put it in the paper."

Back in his room at Underhill's that night, Townsend wrote a hurried note to Tallmadge: "July 29, 1779. The 54th Regt. and Lord Rawdon's Corps bound southward . . . The Greyhound frigate, with Lord Cornwallis, arrived the 21st inst . . . It is generally believed by the Torys that the Fleet said to have on board 2000 for Carolina, sailed . . . General Vaughan is positively going home . . . Preparations are being made to Fortify Governor's Island, the Narrows at Staten Island, repair the Fortifications at Paulus Hook & the Battery at New York; all of which places to be put in the best state of defense . . . I am, Sir, your Hbl. Servant, Samuel Culper, Junr."

So highly did Washington value Culper's intelligence that on August 2nd the General dispatched a communication to John Jay, the President of Congress in Philadelphia: "Sir, I do myself the honor to transmit to Your Excellency an Extract of a letter from a confidential correspondent in New York. It contains the latest advices I have had from thence . . . with respect to an embarkation and the Enemy's intentions to repair and erect Fortifications."

Robert Townsend had developed other contacts in the city, but their identity was his own secret, and he guarded their names scrupulously until his death. Only Townsend knew how much information Jemmy Rivington peddled to the Americans. Rivington was well acquainted with General Clinton, and Major André admitted that the canny publisher was privy to some of the inner workings of the British intelligence service; but he was never an active member of the Culper Ring. Townsend realized that his partner in the Coffee Shop was an unscrupulous opportunist, quite capable of shifting sides whenever a better offer was made, and he was careful not to reveal any code names or methods.

Rivington was just as careful to maintain his reputation as a devoted Tory. He continued to publish slanderous attacks on Washington and other patriot leaders in his *Gazette*, and as added proof of his loyalty he christened his new son in honor of General Clinton. "Permit me to creep still a little further into debt," he wrote André obsequiously, "by begging the favor of you to present my humble duty to his Excellency the Commander in chief, with an entreaty that I may be suffered to honor an unbaptised son, two months old (a comelier hardly existing in the Universe) by naming him after the General, a Liberty I cannot help blushing at the idea of solliciting while I write this application." André replied that the General was "highly flattered."

Equally obscure to this day is the contribution of Alexander Hamilton's friend Hercules Mulligan; though the popular Irishman was in a good position to pick up items of intelligence from British officers who patronized his fashionable tailor shop. Early in 1779, so Alexander Hamilton's son John C. Hamilton wrote years later, an officer "called at the shop of Mulligan late in the evening to obtain a watch-coat. The hour awakened curiosity, and after some enquiries, the officer vauntingly boasted that before another day they would have the Rebel general in their hands." Mulligan foiled the attempt to kidnap Washington by "giving information of the design." Now and then Mulligan furnished the Culpers with advance news of troops arrivals and departures. On August 12th, Woodhull wrote Tallmadge: "I received a message from a person that I intimated in my last was an acquaintance of Hamiltons, that 4 or 5 Regts. were embarking, generally said for Quebeck had taken altogether thick clothing, yet nevertheless he thought most likely for Georgia." Mulligan's tip could have come from officers who visited his shop to purchase clothes for the expedition.

Some of Culper Junior's assistants were members of his own family or related by marriage. Sarah Townsend in Oyster Bay kept her ears open for any tidbits to pass along to her brother. The helpful Joseph Lawrence of Bayside was married to the former Phebe Townsend. In an effort to shorten the spy route, a young cousin, James Townsend, was employed once to carry a secret message directly across the Hudson to Washington's headquarters in New Jersey; but the boy was captured by some overzealous patriots, and it taxed all the General's ingenuity to set him free without revealing the Culper Ring. Another confidant may have been the wealthy Tory importer Thomas Buchanan, husband of Robert Townsend's cousin Almy, who had gone bail for old Samuel Townsend when he was arrested by British dragoons. The Buchanan town house was at 41 Wall Street, just west of Rivington's, and Townsend was a frequent visitor. While Buchanan's name does not appear in the Culper correspondence, his value to the American cause is indicated by the fact that his Wall Street property was not confiscated by the patriots at the end of the war.

Colonel Benjamin Floyd of Brookhaven, Tory brother of William Floyd who signed the Declaration of Independence, seems also to have cooperated secretly with the Culpers. He had befriended Mrs. Anna Strong, and later arranged for Judge Selah Strong's release from the prison ship. Captured by a patriot raiding party and carried off to Connecticut, Colonel Floyd was returned to Long Island on parole in 1779, and Woodhull wrote Tallmadge an urgent letter asking for Floyd's complete discharge. "I repeat it again, I anxiously desire you would not forget it. I am most likely to stand in need of his services." Tallmadge forwarded the request to Washington with a personal endorsement: "From a long and intimate acquaintance with this gentleman, I believe him to be of more service to the Whig interest in Setauket than every other man in it."

Abraham Woodhull still served as Setauket link in the chain, though his thin frame was emaciated from constant worry, and his hair had turned a dusty gray. Never a well man, he was subject to increasing nervous disorders, and he became fretful and cranky and sometimes erratic. One letter to Tallmadge complained querulously that the firm of Oakman & Townsend consumed too much of Culper Junior's time and "interfereth with the important business he hath undertaken." In another letter he stated: "Nothing could induce me to be here but the earnest desire of C —— Jnr."

Each new brush with the enemy brought him nearer a state of mental collapse. In August he forwarded a Culper message with a shaky postscript: "I this day just saved my life. Soon after I left Hempstead Plains and got into the woods I was attacked by four armed men, one of whom I had frequently seen in New York. They searched every pocket and lining of my clothes, shoes, and also my saddle, which the enclosed was in, but thank kind Providence they did not find it." A week later, on his way to keep an appointment with Townsend at Oyster Bay, he "suddenly met a foraging party of 40 horse and 200 foot . . . but after answering a few questions passed them unmolested."

Adding to Woodhull's alarms, a detachment of British troops came to Setauket in the fall, and some soldiers were billeted in the Conscience Bay farmhouse. "Their coming was like death to me," he assured Tallmadge. He was distraught with fear, and daily growing more despondent. "I am tired of this business, it gives me a great deal of trouble, especially when disappointment happens. I am perfectly acquainted with a full year's anxiety, which no one can scarcely have an idea of, but those that experience. Not long since, there was not the breadth of your finger betwixt me and death." He summoned up his courage to add: "But so long as I reside here my faithful endeavours shall never be wanting."

The Culpers had still another accomplice in New York. In a cipher letter, using the code book supplied by Tallmadge, Woodhull wrote on August 15th: "Every 356 [letter] is opened at the entrance of 727 [New York], and every one is searched. They have some 345 [knowledge] of the route our 356 [letter] takes . . . I intend to visit 727 [New York] be-for long and think by the assistance of a 355 of my acquantance, shall be able to out wit them all."

355 was the code number for "lady." Although she became one of the most important agents of the American secret service, and the mother of Robert Townsend's child, 355 was never known by any other name.

Three Five Five

IN October of 1779 Major André was promoted to be Clinton's deputy adjutant general. Robert Townsend knew that, in this new position, André was in command of all British intelligence; but André never guessed that his unassuming Quaker acquaintance was his own opposite number in the New York secret service. The personal relationship between the two rival espionage chiefs is probably without parallel in intelligence annals. They met casually in Rivington's Coffee Shop or in the office of the *Gazette,* and on several occasions the unsuspecting André paid a weekend visit to his friend Lieutenant Colonel Simcoe, at his quarters in Townsend's family home at Oyster Bay.

As Adjutant General, André assumed full charge of the smuggled letters from Philadelphia signed "Monk," later "Mr. Moore," and finally "Gustavus." The correspondence had been desultory during the summer, while "Gustavus" haggled over the price he would be paid for selling out to the British, and by fall their discussion had reached a stalemate. André had no doubt that his correspondent was General Arnold; and in an effort to revive the negotiations he sent a cryptic letter to Peggy Shippen Arnold, assuring her that "my respect for you and the fair circle in which I had the honour of becoming acquainted with you remains unimpaired by distance or political broils. It would make me very happy to become useful to you here. You know the Meschianza made me a complete milliner. Should you not have received supplies for your fullest equipment in that department, I shall be glad to enter into the whole detail of cap-wire, needles, gauze, etc., and, to the best of my ability, render you in these trifles services from which I hope you would infer a zeal to be further employed." He was sure that Lady Macbeth could guess his meaning.

Toward the close of the year, as cold weather closed in, General Sir Henry Clinton decided to move the war south for the winter. Georgia had fallen to the British a year ago, and Clinton hoped to restore his somewhat tarnished prestige by reducing the adjoining province of South Carolina. On the day after Christmas, a formidable armada of ninety transports, under Admiral Arbuthnot, carried 8500 troops and sailors for a full-scale attack on the capital city of Charleston. Amiable old General Knyphausen, commander-in-chief of the German auxiliaries, was placed in temporary charge of New York; Major André deputized him to handle the Gustavus correspondence in his absence; and Sir Henry disengaged himself from the clinging embrace of Mistress Blundell, the daughter of his butler, and he and André left the city's bitter climate for the balmier land of Spanish moss and magnolias.

Clinton sailed south none too soon. That winter of 1779–1780 was the severest ever known in the middle colonies. Snow started falling as early as the beginning of November, and continued almost daily until March. By New Year's Day it lay four feet deep in the woods of Manhattan, and giant drifts blocked all the roads. So intense was the cold that every river and harbor froze solid. The ice on the Hudson was reported to be eighteen feet thick, and there was no open water south of Albany. Residents of New York and Brooklyn visited back and forth over the hard surface of the East River. In January three Tory refugees crossed Long Island Sound on foot from Saybrook, Connecticut, to Oyster Bay, a distance of twenty miles.

Despite the strong tidal currents of the Narrows, New York Bay was completely icebound, a sight which no man living had seen before. Two hundred loaded sleighs, each drawn by a pair of horses, were hauled in a body over ten miles of ice between New York and Staten Island, escorted by a regiment of mounted dragoons. Taking advantage of the opportunity, a number of captive Americans slid through the portholes of the prison ships locked in Wallabout Bay, and walked ashore to freedom. One party of thirteen escapees, under cover of a blizzard, made their way undetected up the middle of the East River and across the Sound to Stamford.

As the sub-zero weather kept up month after month, the city's provisions and fuel grew critically short. The snow was so deep that forest trees could not be dragged out of the woods after they were felled, and in desperation the residents leveled the remaining orchards and ornamental trees which had survived war and fire. Judge Thomas Jones, who spent that winter in the city, recorded that by March "all the wood on New York Island was cut down." Wall Street lost its beautiful oaks, some over a century old, and the elm-shaded Bowery Lane was left denuded and bare. Old hulks were chopped up at the piers where they lay, and one seagoing vessel ready for a voyage was unloaded and cut up for fuel. In Canvas Town the poor burned fat to cook their soupaan. There was no heat in the city jails and sugarhouses, and prisoners who lay down in the numbing cold were found stiffened in death in the morning. Their frozen bodies were stacked in the snow behind Bridewell and the Provost, to be buried when the ground thawed.

The scarcity of food sent prices out of reach of even the well-to-do families. British garrison troops were on starvation rations in their frigid barracks. When the surrounding countryside refused Knyphausen's appeal for help, he sent foraging parties over the winter roads of Westchester and Long Island to seize what they could. Some farmers outwitted them by burying their meat and grain and vegetables in deep drifts and carrying off their cattle and poultry to the hills; and the foragers, angry at the emptied barns and granaries, revenged themselves by firing the buildings. Such supplies as they brought back were plundered in turn by corrupt barrack masters, who set aside a quarter of each load of firewood, called a "barrack-master's cord," which they sold privately for enormous profit. Judge Jones recalled that wood normally worth 16 shillings a cord was priced at £4 for oak and £5 for hickory nut. The dwindling supply was further exhausted by conniving officers, the caustic Judge claimed, who appropriated a sizable portion to be "lavished away among strumpets, panderers, and pretty little misses." There was similar profiteering in grain and meat by the Commissary of Forage and the Cattle Commissary, "as cunning, artful and hypocritical as the devil himself," who not only stole their share but billed the British government for the rest. Judge Jones estimated that during the war these "blood-sucking harpies did not swallow up less than twenty millions sterling" in illicit gain.

The extreme weather brought other hardships. Mounted raiders from both armies took advantage of the frozen coastline to strike at exposed outposts and isolated towns. In mid-January Lord Stirling led an American expedition with five hundred sleds over the ice from Elizabeth, New Jersey, to attack a British encampment on Staten Island; but the enemy troops entrenched themselves behind a ten-foot snow fort, and Stirling was forced to withdraw. A few days later some British horsemen crossed the lower bay from Staten Island to Newark, burned a number of buildings including the Newark Academy, destroyed the courthouse and Presbyterian Church in Elizabeth, and carried off several prominent citizens as prisoners. In another midnight raid, a group of Tories descended on Rahway, where an American lieutenant and eight men "were found at a fandango, or merry-meeting, with a party of lasses, who became planet-struck at this sudden separation from their damons." The planet-struck lasses were robbed of their jewelry, and the hapless damons, together with three handsome sleighs and ten good horses, were taken across the Hudson to New York. Many of the raiders were no more than common thieves, ravaging the countryside under cover of British protection and the pretense of serving the King; but the small American army in Morristown could not guard the whole Jersey shore, and the looting continued as long as the ice lasted.

To the Continental troops, shivering in their crude log huts in the swirling snow, the winter at Morristown was even more cruel than that at Valley Forge. They were often without meat and bread, their uniforms had worn threadbare and many were shoeless, and several regiments were on the verge of mutiny. General Washington, who insisted on enduring the rigors with his men, had established his headquarters in the drafty Ford homestead; and in January Martha Washington left the comforts of Mount Vernon to join her husband, riding sidesaddle through a two-day blizzard with an escort of Virginia dragoons. The headquarters stood several miles away from the main camp, and elaborate precautions were taken against a surprise raid by the enemy. Pickets were thrown out toward the Hudson and the Raritan, and at the firing of a distant alarm gun Washington's life guard would rush to the house, barricade the doors, throw up all the sashes, and stand with primed muskets at the open windows. Mrs. Washington was often obliged to lie in bed for hours, her chamber filled with guards and a wintry gale blowing through the room, until the alert ended.

General Knyphausen was just as fearful of an assault on New York. The surrounding waterways, which were Manhattan's best protection, had become highways of ice which made the island highly vulnerable. All the British men-of-war were frozen in the lower harbor, unable to bring their cannon to bear on an enemy approach from New Jersey. To make Knyphausen's problem more acute, Clinton withdrew another four thousand troops from the New York garrison to complete his investment of Charleston. Not realizing that the American army was far too weak to mount an attack, the worried German general envisioned Washington's forces hauling their heavy artillery across the Hudson ice to overwhelm his depleted garrison. In expectation of a last-ditch defense of Manhattan, Knyphausen called on all inhabitants from sixteen to sixty to form a Loyalist Volunteer Corps, and so prompt was the response that General Tryon, the civil governor, granted 2600 commissions in five days. Arms were supplied from the Royal arsenal, the civilians purchased British regimentals at their own expense, and drills were held three times weekly on the snow-packed Commons.

Robert Townsend, in his assumed Tory character, did not dare refuse the call. Instead of the American blue-and-buff that he yearned to put on, he was forced to don the red coat and black-feathered buck hat of the British Provincials. He lowered his head as he marched in enemy uniform across the Commons, unwilling to meet the hostile eyes of his fellow countrymen behind the barred windows of Bridewell.

* * *

A change had come over Townsend in the past few months. His dispatches had been growing shorter and less frequent; and Abraham Woodhull, whose overwrought nerves made him irritable and sharp-spoken, was disturbed by Culper Junior's strange laxness. Early in April he complained to Tallmadge that Austin Roe had just returned from New York with "nothing but a short memorandum from C Jur and a scrap of paper which he said contained all worthy of notice . . . I think he is exceedingly to blame and guilty of neglect and have given him my Opinion in full upon the matter." By mid-month the messages ceased altogether, and Townsend informed General Washington that he

could not continue as an intelligence agent. Woodhull made a
hasty trip to the city when he learned the news, and on April
23rd he reported to Tallmadge from Setauket that he had
interviewed Culper Junior and "returned this day after making
every effort with his utter denial." He added cryptically: "As I
shall see you soon, I forbear stating his reasons."

There is no written record of their clandestine meeting at
Conscience Bay, and we can only guess at the "reasons" which
Woodhull disclosed to Tallmadge. It is hard to believe that
Culper Junior's abrupt resignation was due to fear for his own
safety; Townsend was not one to panic easily. His decision to go
back on his word must have been prompted by a deeper personal
motive, a matter of conscience which overrode even his stern
sense of obligation. The real cause, I suspect, was the lady known
as 355 . . .

Here again we come to a missing section of the pattern, a mystery even more inscrutable than the final movements of Nathan
Hale. Of all the secrets of the Culper Ring, the identity of
355 has been the most carefully preserved. Only a few random
facts have emerged from the past to guide us. We know from
Woodhull's early letter that she was "an acquaintance" who re-
sided in the city, and who could "outwit them all." This would
indicate that 355 was already involved in espionage work when
Robert Townsend met her. We know that sometime in 1780 —
perhaps at the same moment that Townsend resigned — she became his common-law wife, and their son was christened Robert
Townsend Junior. We know that shortly after Arnold defected
to the British she was arrested as a spy, on or about October
20th; Woodhull's letter of that date mentions the imprisonment
of "one that hath been ever serviceable to this correspondence."

And that is all we know. Her very name is lost to us. Robert
Townsend never revealed it during his lifetime. If his strait-
laced Quaker family knew of her existence, they kept it to

themselves; to this day the Townsend records at Raynham Hall list Robert as a bachelor. No fragmentary phrase in a letter or diary offers a clue to her background. Was she related to a prominent Tory family, perhaps the wealthy William T. Robinson, or Thomas Buchanan, or Benjamin Floyd of Brookhaven, or Henry Nicoll of New York, whose wife was the daughter of General Nathaniel Woodhull? Did her social position enable her to gain access to highly classified British intelligence, some of it known only to the Commander-in-Chief and his aide? Evidently Arnold suspected her of revealing the West Point plot; she was the only active member of the Culper Ring to be taken up when he fled to New York. General Clinton was too cautious and tight-lipped to betray any confidences; but Major André's vanity might have led him to babble military secrets to a charming companion.

Suppose, then, that 355 was one of the decorative females with whom the dilettante Major liked to surround himself. Her appeal was intellectual; she flattered him about his poetry, he talked to her unguardedly. Though she and Robert Townsend had fallen in love, she continued her flirtation with André, hoping to pry more information from him, and her meetings with Townsend took place at a hidden rendezvous, perhaps the Underhill house. I like to picture 355 as the opposite of the reserved and sober young Quaker: small, pert, vivacious, clever enough to outwit the enemy, but feminine enough to give Townsend a brief interlude of happiness that he would never know again. Her eyes would tease him out of his somber mood, her warm throaty laugh could bring an unaccustomed smile to his grave face. Their romance prospered over the winter, while Clinton was in Carolina with his aide. A legal marriage was impossible, since it was bound to be discovered when André returned, but in their own eyes they were already man and wife; and in April Townsend learned that she was carrying his child.

News from the South warned that the surrender of Charles-

ton was imminent, and we can suppose that Townsend, in light
of her condition, insisted that she quit the Culper Ring with
him. They would be married, they would leave the city together.
355 refused; her liaison with the British secret service was too
valuable a source of intelligence to abandon, she insisted, and
her duty was to remain here. It was their first quarrel. Racked by
his Quaker conscience, filled with guilt and self-blame, he notified Washington that he would serve no longer.

His resignation left the Manhattan unit without a head, and
Woodhull was unable to suggest a successor. "If any person
can be pointed out by 711 [Washington] at N.Y. who can be
safely relied on to supply C. Junr's place," he wrote Tallmadge,
"I will make myself known to him, and settle a plan for the
purpose," but he made it clear that he would not resume residence in the city under any circumstances. Tallmadge forwarded
the letter to Washington, and offered his personal opinion that
"even C. Senior grows timid & think the intercourse had better
be dropt for the present."

General Washington's reply was blunt, and betrayed the Commander-in-Chief's impatience with his temperamental agents:
"As C. Junior has totally declined and C. Senior seems to
wish to do it, I think the intercourse may be dropped, more especially as from our present position the intelligence is so long
getting to hand that it is of no use by the time it reaches me . . .
I am endeavoring to open a communication with New York
across Staten Island, but who are the agents in the City, I do
not know. I am &c., Go. Washington."

Although Culper Senior was cut to the quick by the General's
curt dismissal, he tried to conceal his feelings in a plaintive letter
of farewell. "I am happy to find that 711 is about to establish
a more advantageous channel of information than heretofore. I
perceive that the former he intimates hath been but of little
service. Sorry we have been at so much cost and trouble for so

little or no purpose. He also mentions my backwardness to serve. He certainly hath been misinformed. You are sensible that I have been indefaticable, and have done it from a principal of duty rather than from any mercenary end — and as hinted heretofore, if at any time theres need you may rely on my faithful endeavors."

The Sympathetic Stain was put away, no more signals fluttered from Anna Strong's clothesline, and grass grew over the buried box in Woodhull's pasture beside Conscience Bay. The Culper Ring was suspended.

* * *

Charleston fell to the British on May 12th. It was a personal triumph for General Clinton, and also for his versatile young aide. The story goes that a Tory resident named Edward Shrewsberry was ill at his home on East Bay during the siege, and his brother, a lieutenant serving with the American army, visited him frequently. On several occasions, he recalled, he met a young man, clad in homespuns, who was introduced to him as a Virginia patriot and a "back-country man who has brought down cattle for the garrison." After the capitulation of the city, Lieutenant Shrewsberry received permission to visit his Tory brother again, and encountered the same young man, now in British regimentals, who was revealed to be Major André. If the story is true, it gives a certain irony to the letter André wrote four months later, when he was arrested as a spy, protesting indignantly to Washington against "an implication of having assumed a mean character for treacherous purposes or self-interest."

With the surrender of General Lincoln and the capture of 5500 Continental troops and 391 guns, Clinton's southern campaign came to an end; and he left Cornwallis to subdue the remainder of Carolina and sailed back to New York with his victorious army. His return may have saved the Americans from total disaster. Old General Knyphausen, counting on reports of strong Tory sentiment in New Jersey and of mutinies and desertions in the rebel encampment at Morristown, had just sent an invasion force of nineteen regiments across Jersey in hopes of drawing Washington into battle. Whether the British would have overwhelmed Washington's threadbare and starving army will never be known. Sir Henry was of no mind to have his success in Carolina overshadowed by another and more impressive victory; and on his arrival he promptly countermanded Knyphausen's orders, recalled the marching regiments, and resumed his sullen command of New York City.

The Loyalists of Manhattan were cast down by the abortive end of the Jersey campaign, but their hopes revived later in June when the flower of Clinton's army, fully equipped and flushed with their southern victory, embarked on transports in New York Harbor. The war-weary residents, Judge Thomas Jones wrote, were "all agreed that a grand blow was to be struck in some quarter or another." As the mighty armada beat its course up the Hudson, the general supposition was that the river would be occupied from New York to Albany, cutting off all communication between the eastern and western colonies and strangling the rebels into submission. To the bewilderment of everyone, the fleet dropped anchor off Phillipseburgh in Westchester County, only fourteen miles from New York, ravaged the defenseless countryside and robbed the local farmers of their cattle and hogs and dunghill fowl, and then returned to the city. "A noble employment this," Judge Jones mocked, "for a British army of 16000 men, under the command of a British General sent to America to crush a rebellion."

General Clinton had his own private reasons for calling back his troops. A communication from his Philadelphia correspondent "Gustavus" assured him that Arnold would soon be given command of West Point; and it seemed only sensible to wait until the Hudson River fortress could be betrayed into his

hands without risking an assault. Another "Gustavus" letter
in cipher, sent direct from American headquarters in Morristown on June 12th and forwarded by secret courier to Clinton,
supplied the British commander with intelligence of more immediate value. "Six French ships of the line," Arnold informed
him, "several frigates, and a number of transports with 6000
troops are expected at Rhode Island in two or three weeks to act
under General Washington."

Sir Henry's eyes must have lighted as André decoded the message. Here was a golden opportunity to strike at the French
while they were disembarking at Newport. The troops would be
disorganized, they would have had no time to erect fortifications,
and an amphibious attack when the foe was in such a vulnerable
position could add new luster to the Clinton reputation. Admiral
Arbuthnot was ordered to have his transports prepared to sail
"at a moment's notice, as the movement of the army at this
time might be important." Supplies were loaded on board, the
British forces in New York were put in combat readiness, and
Clinton waited impatiently for word that the French fleet was
sighted.

The American Commander-in-Chief was no less concerned
about their arrival. Early in May, Major General Lafayette had
returned from Paris and proceeded at once to Morristown,
where Washington "folded him in his arms with profound emotion." The dashing young Marquis had come to deliver, in utmost secrecy, the welcome tidings that a fleet under Admiral
Tarnay was on the Atlantic, bringing six thousand troops commanded by Count de Rochambeau. Washington confided the
good news to Arnold when he visited the Morristown headquarters on June 12th; and the information was on its way to
the enemy by nightfall.

When the British abandoned their Hudson River campaign
and sailed back to New York, Washington's apprehensions increased. Somehow Clinton must have learned of the approaching

French landing, and he suspected that Sir Henry was preparing to pounce on them in a surprise attack. It was vital to know the British plans but, since the suspension of the Culper services, Washington had no means of obtaining reliable intelligence from the city. His need was so urgent that he overlooked his previous annoyance with his Setauket spies, and on July 11th he wrote Tallmadge from his new headquarters at Preakness in Bergen County, New Jersey: "As we may every moment expect the arrival of the French fleet, a revival of the correspondence with the Culpers will be of very great importance. If the younger cannot be engaged again, you will endeavor to prevail upon the older to give you information of the movements and position of the enemy . . . in short desire him to inform you of whatever comes under his notice."

It took three days for Washington's message to reach Major Tallmadge at Cortlandt's Manor. On June 14th, the same day that it was delivered, the Commander-in-Chief informed the President of Congress: "I have this moment received a letter from Major General Heath, dated Providence on the 11th, informing that on the afternoon of the 10th the French fleet arrived off Newport, that the signals of recognizance had been made, and the fleet was standing into the harbor when the express came away."

Rochambeau's army was already in process of disembarking, and there was no time to lose. Early the following morning Tallmadge rode at top speed across Connecticut to Fairfield, where he found Caleb Brewster in a local tavern, regaling the patrons with tales of his hairsbreadth escapes from the British. Brewster pulled Joshua Davis from the arms of his sweetheart, eighteen-year-old Abigail Redfield, rounded up the rest of his crew, and shortly after dark set out for Setauket, slipping undetected past a British frigate patrolling the Sound. They dragged their whaleboat over the sandspit and rowed with muffled oars across Conscience Bay to the hidden cove on

Strong's Neck, and Brewster hurried up the path to the Strong Mansion. There he learned from Anna Strong that Abraham Woodhull was confined to his bed with a fever. Aware of the pressing need for haste, Brewster exchanged his uniform for a set of seaman's clothes, and followed a back trail to the village.

British officers gathered in Roe's Tavern that night peered down their noses at a hulking figure in blue homespuns and stocking cap who shouldered through the door and ordered a tankard of beer. There was no sign of recognition in Austin Roe's face as he served Brewster, swept up the coins from the table, and sauntered out of the room. Brewster drained his glass in a long gulp, and followed Roe into the kitchen. He explained the emergency, and handed Roe Tallmadge's letter to deliver to Culper Junior; and at dawn on the 18th Roe saddled his fastest horse for the express ride to New York. Had he delayed another hour, he would have been overtaken by a Tory courier from East Hampton, galloping over the same route that morning with a message for General Clinton that the French fleet had arrived.

Robert Townsend resumed the role of Culper Junior as abruptly as he had quit it two months before. Again there is no explanation in the correspondence, and again we can only surmise. Perhaps his sense of duty overcame his scruples; perhaps he found it unbearable to be away from 355, and Washington's request furnished him with the excuse he needed. All that day and the next, while Roe remained in concealment at the Underhill house, the Manhattan spies gathered facts and figures about British military plans, some of them seemingly from Clinton's own headquarters. The method of smuggling this vital intelligence out of the city presented a new problem to Townsend. The British had posted guards at all the exits from Manhattan, and were searching everyone who might carry information of their anticipated move. Fortunately he still had enough Sympathetic Stain on hand to write his dispatch in invisible ink; but to follow the usual procedure of hiding it in a ream of blank paper, and adding other heavy parcels in order to avert suspicion, would encumber Roe and delay his return.

Townsend's solution was to write an ordinary business letter, addressed to Colonel Benjamin Floyd in Brookhaven: "New York, July 20th, 1780. Sir, I recd your favor by [here "Mr. Roe" is crossed out, but is still legible] and note the contents. The articles you want cannot be procured, as soon as they can will send them. I am, Your humble servant, Samuel Culper." Colonel Floyd's home had recently been plundered by raiders, and it would be natural for him to make purchases in the city. Not only would the letter seem plausible, but it would explain why Roe was returning empty-handed. No one could see the message on the reverse side, written in secret Stain.

The letter was read and passed by the British sentry at the Brooklyn ferry, and Roe rode back safely to Setauket. He stabled his horse, and strolled over to the Woodhull farm, ostensibly to inquire about his neighbor's health. Closing and bolting the door of Woodhull's chamber, he gave him Townsend's message and reported what he had learned. Woodhull propped himself up in bed, and in a shaky hand added a postscript to Tallmadge: "Your letter came to hand and found me very ill with a fever, and still continues . . . 724 [Austin Roe] returned this day in great haste with the enclosed dispatch from Culper Junior. Also assures of the arrival of Admiral Graves with six ships of the line and is joined by three more out of New York, also one of 50 and two of 40 guns and has sailed for Rhode Island and is supposed they will be there before this can possibly reach you. Also 8000 troops are this day embarking at Whitestone for the above mentioned port . . . You must excuse all imperfections at this time on the account of my before mentioned fever. Nevertheless you have perhaps all the needful — and pray for your success and exercions. And am yours sincerely, Saml. Culper."

Caleb Brewster had been waiting at the Strong Mansion for

Roe's return, and Woodhull sent him a personal note: "Sir, The enclosed requires your immediate departure this day by all means let not an hour pass: for this day must not be lost. You have news of the greatest consequence perhaps that ever happened to your country. John Bolton must order your returne when he thinks proper. S. C."

Brewster could not locate Tallmadge immediately on his arrival in Fairfield, and he persuaded another officer in the dragoons to carry the dispatch to Washington's Preakness, New Jersey, headquarters, where it arrived shortly before 4 P.M. on the 21st. In Washington's temporary absence, it was received by his aide-de-camp, Colonel Alexander Hamilton, who knew about the Sympathetic Stain and developed the secret intelligence on the back of the Floyd letter. Hamilton rushed the information to General Lafayette, who had left Preakness a few days before and was on his way to Newport. "The Gen'l is absent and may not return before midnight," Hamilton wrote Lafayette. "Though this may be only a demonstration, yet as it may be serious, I think it best to forward it without waiting for the Generals return."

Washington studied the stituation at his headquarters that evening. At this very moment, he realized, Clinton's troops might well be on their way to Newport. Only a swift counter-attack on New York could force them to turn back; and he knew his army was too weak to mount an assault. He picked up a quill pen, and twirled it absently in his fingers. Was it necessary to make a real attack, he pondered. Could Sir Henry be deluded into thinking that an offensive movement against Manhattan was threatened? Might his pen accomplish what his sword was unable to do?

The British transports were heading eastward on the Sound when a Tory farmer, held to be above suspicion, delivered to a British outpost a packet of letters which he said he had discovered on the highway. They were found to contain the details of General Washington's plans for a full-scale invasion of New York with an army of twelve thousand. Signal fires were lighted hastily along the Long Island coast, the fleet was halted at Huntington, and Clinton ordered his forces back to defend New York. Rochambeau completed his landing at Newport unmolested. Several days later, Clinton explained his failure to attack the French in a letter to Lord George Germain in London: "During this time Washington, by a rapid movement, had, with an army increased to 12000 men, passed the North-river, and was moving towards King's-bridge, when he must have learned that my armament had not proceeded to Rhode-Island. He, I apprehend in consequence of this, re-crossed the river, and is now near Orange Town [Tappan]."

The Commander-in-Chief, with his delight in subterfuge and intrigue, must have relished the success of his deception.

*   *   *

On the west bank of the Hudson, several miles below Fort Lee, a small blockhouse had been erected at the base of the Palisades, manned by a picket guard of seventy Tory refugees. Its purpose was to protect local woodcutters and cattlemen, whose large herds were fattening in the lush meadows around Bergen Neck in order to supply the British garrison at Paulus Hook. On July 21st, as part of the diversionary action against New York, Washington sent Major General Anthony Wayne with two thousand troops of horse and foot to drive the cattle within the American lines.

Mad Anthony, hero of Stony Point, was a briliant regimental commander, wary and cool and a natural leader of men. The job of rounding up the herds was assigned to his cavalry, under Major Henry Lee, the popular "Light Horse Harry" whose son Robert would command the Confederate armies in another war; and Wayne himself led three regiments, armed with four pieces of light artillery, against the blockhouse. The small cannon proved ineffectual, and after a brisk exchange of fire the Americans broke off the engagement and returned to their camp, the dragoons driving the plundered herds ahead of them.

The episode inspired Major André's most famous satiric poem, "Cow-Chase," a parody of the Old English ballade called "Chevy Chase." It ran serially in Rivington's *Gazette* during the summer, to the vast entertainment of the coffeehouses and taverns of the city. André was particularly intrigued by the coincidence that Wayne had at one time been employed as a tanner, and referred to the fact in his opening stanzas:

> *To drive the kine, one summer's morn,*
> *The tanner took his way:*
> *The calf shall rue that is unborn*
> *The jumbling of that day.*
>
> *And Wayne descending steers shall know,*
> *And tauntingly deride,*
> *And call to mind, in ev'ry low,*
> *The tanning of his hide.*

Wayne's explanation that his cannonballs could not pierce the solid walls of the blockhouse drew another barbed thrust:

> *Five refugees, 'tis true, were found*
> *Stiff on the block-house floor;*
> *But then, 'tis thought, the shot went round,*
> *And in at the back door.*

André was also amused by the fact that Wayne's horse had been shot from under him in the heat of the battle:

> *His horse that carried all his prog,*
> *His military speeches,*
> *His corn-stalk whisky for his grog —*
> *Blue stockings and brown breeches.*

The final stanza contained a note of prophecy that the author had not intended:

And now I've closed my epic strain,
I tremble as I show it,
Lest this same warrior-drover, Wayne,
Should ever catch the poet.

This ominous verse, written a couple of weeks previously, was published in the *Gazette* on September 23rd, the day that André was caught with the sketches of West Point in his boots. He was confined in Tappan to await trial, and the officer in whose custody he was placed was General Wayne.

V

"Similar Will Be Your Fate"

W EST POINT had not figured originally in Arnold's plans. In 1779, after months of secret negotiation, he had set £10,000 as his personal price for treason. Clinton had made no specific reply to his demand, but advised him that the surrender of "a corps of five or six thousand men would be rewarded with twice as many thousand guineas." It was Peggy Arnold who saw that command of the strategic Hudson River fort would give her husband added bargaining power, and vastly increase the value of his services to the British.

The former Peggy Shippen was as unscrupulous as she was beautiful. She had been pampered and petted all her life, by her Tory father and by the chorus of local swains who danced attendance on her, and male conquests were so easy that she looked on them with scorn. She was barely eighteen when the British occupied Philadelphia, a slim high-bosomed blonde with enticing eyes and a small spoiled mouth who "left every ballroom on a carpet of crushed hearts." Her sterile romance with John André, the idol of the army, was carefully contrived to enhance her own prestige; while she clung to his arm, she peered beneath lowered lids at the titled young British officers around her, and dreamed of marrying an earl and presiding at the Court of St. James's. The evacuation of Clinton's army left her momentarily desolate, but she was a materialist and settled for the next-best prospect, the crippled hero of Quebec and Saratoga who had just been appointed American military governor of Philadelphia.

Benedict Arnold was twice her age, a widower of thirty-seven with three sons almost as old as Peggy. He leaned on an ivory-tipped cane, and his enormous head and shoulders made him seem deformed; unable to dance, he sat alone in a corner with his twice-shattered leg extended on a camp stool, brooding and vindictive as a chained hawk. She sat beside him, caressed his leathery black hair, lifted her face coyly to his sensual lips. He was infatuated with this golden vision, and courted her with the same flamboyant love letter he had composed to his late wife and to a later sweetheart, Betsy Deblois. "Dear Peggy," he wrote, changing only Betsy's name, "suffer that heavenly bosom (which cannot know itself the cause of pain without a sympathetic pang) to expand with a sensation more soft, more tender than friendship." The sensation which swelled Peggy's bosom was not love but ambition. When she married Arnold in April of 1779, she was already scheming to obtain, through her famous husband, the wealth and social triumph on which she had set her heart.

Even on their honeymoon she began the slow process of poisoning his mind. Skillfully she nourished his vanity, fostered a growing jealousy of Washington, played on his grievances with Congress. Why should he be humiliated by these pettifogging civilians who withheld his salary, questioned his accounts, subjected him to public investigation? When he was tried by court-martial on the charge of using army equipment for private gain — a thoroughly justified accusation — she dwelt on the gross ingratitude of his countrymen. Although he was acquitted, the insult still rankled, and Peggy took full advantage of his injured pride. He was sacrificing himself for a worthless cause, she whispered in his ear. The rebellion was doomed; the French would annex America as another colony; only the great Arnold could end the war and restore the former bonds with

Great Britain. He would be rewarded with riches and a duke-
dom, and be remembered forever as the savior of his country.
What lingering doubts he might have had were washed away
in the flood of hysterical tears with which Peggy always had
her way.

From the beginning of the conspiracy, she was its master-
mind. Arnold was dull-witted, a man of reckless action, single-
minded as a charging bull; Peggy was clever and cunning and
infinitely patient. She made use of her previous immaculate affair with André to open negotiations with General Clinton; she
handled the secret correspondence when Arnold was absent from
Philadelphia; she was the author of the plot to deliver West
Point. And when the plot failed, everyone from Washington
down — including most American historians for two centuries —
considered her its innocent and pathetic victim.

Arnold's statement to Clinton that he had been promised
the West Point command was a trifle premature. Washington
was reluctant to give a comparatively minor assignment to a
general of Arnold's stature. In June, Arnold persuaded his
friend Robert R. Livingston, who had no suspicion of treachery,
to intercede for him, and Livingston wrote Washington asking
that the post "be confided to General Arnold, whose courage is
undoubted and who is the favourite of our militia." General
Philip Schuyler, another innocent intermediary, likewise recommended him; and Arnold himself appealed to the Commander-
in-Chief when he visited the Morristown headquarters on June
12th, the same day that he sent Clinton the confidential information about the French fleet. Washington recalled: "I told him
I did not think that [West Point] would suit him, as I should
have none in his garrison but invalids because it would be covered by the main army."

From Morristown, Arnold proceeded to West Point, which
he had never seen before, and was escorted around the fort by
its commandant, General Robert Howe. To encourage Clinton

222 CONSCIENCE BAY

by proving that it was vulnerable, he wrote Sir Henry a detailed account of the undermanned garrison and poorly defended redoubts. "There is only 1500 soldiers, which will not half man the works . . . The Point is on a low piece of ground comparatively to the chain of hills which lie back of it . . . On Rocky Hill there is a small redoubt to hold 200 men and two six-pounders pointed to the other works. The wall six foot thick and defenseless on the back; and I am told the English may land three miles below and have a good road to bring up heavy cannon to Rocky Hill. This redoubt is wretchedly executed, only seven or ten feet high, and might be taken by assault by a handful of men." General Howe remembered afterward that Arnold's particular interest in Rocky Hill "struck me oddly even then, though I had not the least suspicion of him."

On July 15th, Arnold stated his final terms to Clinton. Sir Henry would "secure to me my property, valued at ten thousand pounds sterling, to be paid to me or my heirs in case of loss . . . If I point out a plan of cooperation by which S. H. shall posess himself of West Point, the garrison, etc., etc., etc., twenty thousand pounds sterling would I think be a cheap purchase for an object of so much importance. At the same time, I request a thousand pounds to be paid my agent . . . a Personal interview with an officer that you can confide in is absolutely necessary to plan matters." On the 29th, Major André, signing himself "John Anderson," presented Clinton's counteroffer, which agreed to the sum of £20,000 for delivery of West Point, but refused "an absolute promise of indemnification to the amount of £10,000 whether services are performed or not," and also cut the advance payment of £1000 in half. Peggy decided that half a loaf was better than none, and Arnold accepted.

So positive was he that the plot would succeed that he hastened to convert his assets into cash. His house in New Haven was put up for sale at a sacrifice price of £1000 "as I have an

opportunity of making a purchase that is convenient to me."
Two days after presenting his ultimatum to Clinton, he wrote
Congress that "there is due to me upwards of four years' pay"
and requested "that honourable body to give orders that I may
receive four months' pay in specie, to enable me to purchase
horses, camp equipage, etc." This seemed to be a legitimate reason, and on the 25th Congress awarded him 25,000 Continental
scrip which, at the ratio of 50 to 1, was approximately the four
months' salary he had asked for. With the money in his pocket,
he set out for Washington's headquarters with high hopes.

He caught up with the Commander-in-Chief on the 31st at
Stony Point, while the army was crossing the Hudson by the
King's Ferry, and inquired about the General's decision. "I told
him that he was to have the command of the light troops, which
was a post of honour, and which his rank entitled him to,"
Washington stated later. "Upon this information his countenance changed and he appeared to be quite fallen; and instead
of thanking me, or expressing any pleasure at the appointment,
never opened his mouth."

If Washington was puzzled, Peggy Arnold was prostrated at
the general orders for August 1st, announcing that Arnold
would command the left wing. She was dining at the home of
Robert Morris in Philadelphia when a friend of the family arrived and congratulated Mrs. Arnold on the news that her husband had been appointed to a different but more honorable
command than West Point. "The information affected her so
much as to produce hysteric fits," Robert Morris recalled. "Efforts were made to convince her that the general had been selected for a preferable station. These explanations, however, to
the astonishment of all present produced no effect." Peggy flung
herself on the floor, sobbing that Arnold's injured leg would not
permit such a duty, that Washington was trying to kill him.
Only Aaron Burr, a fellow guest that night, was unmoved by

the demonstration. Burr possessed a mind as shrewd as Peggy's, and he observed her histrionics with one skeptical eyebrow raised.

Arnold was dumfounded at the General's decision, not only because his lucrative plan was shattered, but because he had urgent reasons for removing Peggy as soon as possible from the temptations of Philadelphia and bringing her to the isolated Hudson Highlands. His spinster sister Hannah, who had come down from New Haven to live with the family, entertained no love for her brother's young wife, and her letters to Arnold were full of malicious innuendoes about "a certain chancellor," evidently Robert R. Livingston, "who is a dangerous companion for a particular lady in the absence of her husband." Hannah added waspishly: "I could say more than prudence will permit. I could tell you of frequent private assignations and of numberless *billets doux*, if I had an inclination to make mischief. But as I am of a very peaceable temper I'll not mention a syllable of the matter."

Distracted by financial and marital worries, Arnold visited Washington again, limping tragically on his ivory-tipped cane, and pleaded that his leg would make it impossible for him to serve as an active cavalryman. To placate his old friend, Washington yielded. From his Fishkill headquarters on August 3rd, he issued new orders to Arnold to "proceed to West Point, and take command of that post and its dependencies, in which are included all from Fishkill to King's Ferry." Since the main American army was returning shortly to New Jersey, Arnold would be in charge of the river forts and the entire area north of New York through which Clinton's forces must march in order to attack the Point. Now his market value to Sir Henry was assured.

Virtually his first act, on assuming command, was to seek the names of the Manhattan spies who might penetrate Clinton's headquarters and discover his treasonable correspondence. On his way to his new assignment, he called on General Lafayette and asked for the names and addresses of Washington's New York agents, explaining that their dispatches could be transmitted more expeditiously by way of West Point. Lafayette replied courteously that the individuals had confided in the General, and their identity could not be divulged to anyone else. Rebuffed by Lafayette, he appealed to the former West Point commandant, General Howe, taking the precaution to send him a gift of "furniture & Liqueurs" to put him in the proper mood for Arnold's request. "As the safety of this Post & Garrison in a great measure depends on having good Intelligence of the movements & designs of the Enemy," he wrote from Robinson's house on August 5th, "and as you have been fortunate in the Agents you have employed for that purpose, I must request to be informed who they are, as I wish to employ them for the same purpose." He added: "I will engage upon honor to make no discovery of them to any Person Breathing."

Howe refused as politely but firmly as Lafayette, and Arnold turned next to Major Tallmadge, who he knew was in contact with Washington's spies. The Second Dragoons lacked sufficient horses, and Arnold notified Tallmadge that he had ordered remounts for the regiment, and then repeated the request he made to Howe. Tallmadge replied that "I feel myself, in behalf of the Regt. under peculiar Obligation to You for that Care & Attention shown to the Corps in procuring us so many Remounts," but explained that he had pledged his agents in the most solemn manner not to inform any person on earth of their names.

Arnold did not dare press the matter further, but he resolved to watch and wait for any clues. He was sure that Washington had received advance information of Clinton's proposed attack on Newport, which could only have come from someone who enjoyed the complete confidence of the British high command. In view of the fondness of both Sir Henry and André for the fair sex — though for basically different reasons — he wondered whether the mysterious informant might be a woman.

*   *   *

The war had lapsed into a state of dreamy lassitude during the dog days. Military activities were all but suspended, and New York lay inert in the August heat. All day long the sun baked the exposed streets, denuded of the last of their shade trees last winter, and the ripening stench of Canvas Town poisoned the air at night. Officers seized on any excuse to get out of town, escorting their sweethearts up the East River for a turtle feast, or crossing on the Brooklyn ferry to idle away an afternoon at the Hempstead track. An unnatural hush settled over the city, and even the moaning of prisoners was stilled.

Sir Henry had quit Manhattan for the clean breezes of Long Island, ostensibly to confer with the British Admiral at East Hampton but in reality to enjoy a few weeks of deer hunting in the rolling wooded hills at the island's tip. Accompanied by the ubiquitous Major André, and by Lieutenant Colonel Simcoe who joined the party at Oyster Bay, they journeyed east in stately procession. Woodhull sent a hurried dispatch from Setauket on August 16th: "General Clinton in person was escorted through this Town yesterday by the mounted Rangers, 17th Dragoons, and German Huzzars, in all about two hundred and forty horse." The entourage billeted themselves in Colonel Abraham Gardiner's luxurious mansion, overlooking the Royal fleet anchored in Gardiner's Bay. Guards were increased during the General's sojourn, and squadrons of dragoons roamed the coastline in search of rebel privateers who might attempt to kidnap the British commander. A small detachment of Tory refugees, under Captain Glover and Lieutenant Hoyt, was assigned to patrol the Setauket area.

Caleb Brewster had crossed the Devil's Belt by appointment on the 15th to pick up Culper's dispatch; but Woodhull was not back from a trip to New York, and Brewster decided to wait overnight for his return. Some enemy craft were lurking in Conscience Bay, and he secreted his whaleboat in a reedy cove near Drowned Meadow, at the lower end of Setauket Harbor. One of the crew was posted as sentry, and the rest of the men lay on their arms in the marsh grass to rest until morning.

Brewster remained awake, listening to the solemn grunt of frogs and gurgle of the rising tide. There was another sound in the darkness, a series of muffled splashes, and he reached for his musket and sat erect. The sentry had heard it also; his silhouette stood against the sky as he raised a flintlock to his shoulder. A musket exploded in front of him, with a flash of orange flame, and he flopped forward and thrashed in the mud.

Other muskets were splitting the night all around them, and Brewster and his crew raced toward the whaleboat, returning the fire as they retreated. There was the distant thud of a falling body, and at the same moment another member of the British patrol groaned and sank to his haunches, holding his stomach. Taking advantage of the momentary confusion, the crew clambered into the whaleboat, Brewster shoved off and leapt in after them, and they rowed out of range of the splashing lead. The guards on Misery Point at the harbor's mouth would be alerted by the firing, he knew; he steered the boat around the northern tip of Strong's Neck into Conscience Bay, and the crew hauled it over the sandspit to the open Sound. Dawn was already showing as they ran the gauntlet of enemy frigates back to Fairfield.

The midnight attack rankled, and Brewster's huge fists clenched at the thought of revenge. After brooding impatiently three days, he persuaded Joshua Davis to leave Abigail Redfield and accompany him on another expedition to Setauket. He informed Tallmadge on his return: "I took three boats last Saturday night and went over in search of Glover and Hoyght, but could hear nothing of them. They never stayed to bury their dead man. They carried another away with them mortally wounded. Setauket is full of troops. Austin came to me yesterday and told me I had best not come on till the middle of next week as the troops is so thick in Town and marching eastward . . . I shall want one man to make up my crew and should be exceeding glad of five more to man the other boat for the cussed refugees are so thick I cant go amiss of them."

Enemy patrols were not the only problem that Caleb Brewster faced. During the long inactive months, with nothing else to do, the idle whaleboat crews turned their thoughts to romance. Josh Davis had succumbed completely to the charms of Abigail, and Brewster could see the marital noose tightening around his partner's neck. His own summer flirtation with Anne Lewis, daughter of Jonathan Lewis of Fairfield, had been growing more serious lately; but Brewster was determined not to be trapped. He had evaded the British for four years; he was sure he could elude Annie. He was less confident about his weak-willed associate. To his concern, Davis balked at another trip to Setauket on the 22nd. "Abbie don't want me to be away, Cale. Not this week."

"Why not?"

An uncomfortable pause. "Well, fact is she's planning our wedding for Sunday."

"War's bad enough," Brewster growled, "without getting married too."

"I ain't the only one. She says Annie Lewis is talking about making it a double wedding."

Brewster shoved back the tavern table and sprang to his feet. "We're leaving for the other side right now. It's safer than here."

Culper Senior was ill when they slipped into Conscience Bay and, to Brewster's vast relief, the whaleboats had to wait over the weekend for his dispatch. During the delay, Brewster made good use of his time; and his letter to Tallmadge on August 27th gave a detailed account of British troop dispersement around Setauket. "This is a fine time to take some of the Officers," he wrote with characteristic braggadocio. "They are out with their hounds every day. I lay up back of Esqr. Strongs yesterday and there came a Lieutenant of 17th Regiment within gun shot of us, looking for Esqr. Strongs hounds afoot, but he begged so hard I thought it best not to take him as it was so near his house. They are riding continually from one staghorn to the other." He concluded: "The troops are all come from the Eastward, Sir Henry Clinton gone to New York and the British fleet has sailed from Gardiner's Bay."

Sir Henry's vacation had ended sooner than he expected. One rainy morning in late August a headquarters messenger delivered a code letter from Arnold, requesting an immediate conference with some trusted representative to complete arrangements for the surrender of West Point. Before noon, Clinton and André were on their way back to the city. The conspiracy, after sixteen dragging months, was coming to a head at last.

*   *   *

New York stirred to life in September. The streets were crowded again, and the brisk air held the hurrying promise of fall. The Theatre Royal had reopened, officers in gold braid and ladies in damask attended the weekly cotillions in the Long Room of the City Tavern, and Hessian guards clicked their heels before the Kennedy Mansion at Number One Broadway where Sir Henry and his staff had resumed official residence. A feeling of excitement pervaded British headquarters. Candles burned late at night behind the drawn shutters, and Clinton and André huddled together in long secret conferences. The Manhattan spies sensed that something important was in the wind, but André was unusually closemouthed, and there was no concrete

evidence to report to Tallmadge. "We Pray for your best endeavors," Culper warned in a cryptic letter. "The times require
you to be vigilent and active . . . I have made several discoveries of villany but have not time to write now."

Clinton's ambitious young aide had a personal stake in the
conspiracy. He knew that the success of the West Point coup
would redound to his own credit, and he persuaded the doting
General to let him lead a select corps in the assault on Rocky
Hill. Here was his chance to achieve advancement in the service,
to emerge as a colonel or even a brigadier, perhaps to be rewarded with a title. André was as impatient for the proposed
rendezvous as Arnold himself.

General Clinton had readied his transports at New York, in
preparation for a swift strike up the Hudson, but he concealed
his intentions by intimating that the fleet would sail for Maryland and Virginia. His ruse to hoodwink the Americans deceived
his own officers as well. Lieutenant Colonel Simcoe had been
promised by André that his Rangers would take an active
part in the West Point attack, and he was stunned at Clinton's
orders to embark instead on an expedition to the Chesapeake.
In great distress he dispatched a note from Raynham Hall to
his friend at headquarters. André's reply was discreet, and he
left it to Simcoe to read between the lines. "Rely upon it your
alarms are in vain," he assured him. "I should have been happy
to have seen you and hinted that apparent arrangements are not
always real ones, but I beg you to seek no explanation. I should
not say what I do but I cannot, without concern, see you in any
uneasiness I can relieve."

Arnold was just as busy preparing for the betrayal of his
post. He made every effort to render West Point defenseless,
scattering his troops and sending a party of two hundred crack
riflemen down the river to cut firewood for next winter. He
knew the weakness of the iron chain which was stretched across
the Hudson just below the fort to block enemy shipping — as

early as June he had informed Clinton that it could be broken by "a single ship, large and heavy-loaded, with a strong wind and tide" — and carefully discouraged any attempt to strengthen it. In his spare time, he compiled a detailed survey of the ordnance at all the batteries, the planned disposition of the garrison in case of attack, and his estimate of the number of men under his command. By adding the troops at Verplanck's and Stony Point, and inventing a few of his own, he made the total slightly higher than the figure of six thousand for which Clinton had offered to pay £20,000. The survey would be given to André when they met.

Their first attempt ended in disappointment. Arnold had suggested an interview at Dobb's Ferry on September 11th, and André rode north to Kingsbridge, boarded the British armed sloop *Vulture* at Spuyten Duyvil, and sailed up the Hudson to the appointed spot. As Arnold's barge approached Dobb's Ferry, on the morning of the 11th, it was fired on by several British gunboats whom André had neglected to warn, and the bargemen retreated hastily to an American post on the west shore. All that day the two conspirators waited, with only the width of the river between them, each hoping that the other would seek him out under a flag of truce. At nightfall Arnold was rowed back to West Point, and the frustrated André returned to the city to await further developments. Through excess caution, they had wasted their best opportunity for a safe contact.

On September 15th, addressing his letter to "John Anderson, merchant," and signing himself "Gustavus," Arnold submitted two alternate plans for their next attempt at a meeting. If André chose to come through the American lines, Arnold assured him that either Lieutenant Colonel John Jameson, who was in temporary command of the Second Dragoons at North Castle, or his deputy Major Tallmadge, would provide him with a military escort. "If you have any objections to this plan," he wrote "I will send a person in whom you may confide, by water, to meet you at Dobb's Ferry on Wednesday the 20th inst. between eleven and twelve o'clock at night, who will conduct you to a place of safety where I will meet you." The person was Joshua Hett Smith of Haverstraw, who claimed later he had been assured by Arnold that John Anderson was a secret agent for the Americans. "It will be necessary," Arnold added in his letter, "for you to be disguised."

Arnold did not hesitate to betray his personal friends as well as his country. The following day he received a confidential note from Washington, stating that the General would be at Peekskill on Sunday evening, on his way to Hartford to meet Admiral Ternay and General Rochambeau, and asking Arnold to send down a guard and instruct the quartermaster to have a night's forage for about forty horses. "You will keep this to yourself," Washington requested, "as I want to make my journey a secret." It was particularly important not to let the enemy know when and where the American Commander-in-Chief would cross the river and thus expose himself to a sudden raid by British gunboats; but Arnold did not hesitate to send a message in cipher to Clinton: "General Washington will be at King's Ferry Sunday evening next on his way to Hartford, where he is to meet the French Admiral and General, and will lodge at Peekskill." Clinton decided that an attempt to seize Washington might jeopardize the West Point plot, and did not avail himself of Arnold's information.

There was one final precaution to be taken. In case André should decide to come to West Point by land, Arnold sent a letter to Major Tallmadge at North Castle: "If Mr. John Anderson, a person I expect from New York, should come to your quarters, I have to request that you will give him an escort of two Horse to bring him on his way to this place, and send an express to me that I may meet him." Tallmadge attached no particular significance to Arnold's request until last-minute intelligence from Culper Junior gave it new and startling meaning.

*   *   *

Throughout his life Tallmadge refused to reveal the source of his advance warning, since he had pledged himself not to betray the confidence of the Culpers. In his *Memoir* he stated: "I might enlarge greatly in anecdotes relating to this momentous event in our revolutionary war. Some things relating to the detention of André, after he had been sent to General Arnold, are purposely omitted." Shortly before Tallmadge's death, he was again asked to tell the full story, and replied firmly: "There were only four officers of our army who knew all the circumstances relating to the capture and detention of Major André, with the other incidents above hinted at, and of this number I am the only survivor . . . I have deliberately concluded never to disclose [them], and my purpose cannot now be shaken."

Once again a page of history is blank, and we have no facts to guide us. There is an intriguing folk tale that André visited his friend Simcoe at the Townsend homestead in Oyster Bay, on the eve of his mission, and Townsend's young sister Sarah overheard the word "West Point" repeated several times. According to the legend, she saw a mysterious stranger leave a note in a corner cupboard addressed to John Anderson, and later André retrieved it while pretending to be searching for some of Sarah's doughnuts. The tale can be discounted for two reasons: André's own letter to Simcoe shows that he did not visit Raynham Hall for at least ten days before his departure on his mission; and Tallmadge admits in his Memoir that his first knowledge of the identity of John Anderson was when André himself revealed it after his capture. The Culpers may have made "discoveries of villany," but they do not seem to have associated them with the charming young major.

Equally implausible is the oft-told story that on the night before André's departure a Colonel Williams, whose headquarters were in the Kip homestead overlooking Kip's Bay, gave a dinner party for General Clinton and his staff. After toasts were drunk, the young adjutant general was called on for a song, and "with great sweetness and much pathos" he rendered the familiar camp ballade: "Why, soldiers, why, whose business 'tis to die." As he sat down, Sir Henry announced: "John André leaves the city tonight a major, but he returns a titled nobleman." There is no record of a Colonel Williams in the British army at that time; and it is difficult to believe that Clinton would confide so closely guarded a secret to a roomful of junior officers.

Still another frustrating tale about the conspiracy was supplied years later by a grandson of Colonel Abraham Gardiner. While Clinton and his entourage were vacationing at the Gardiner Mansion in East Hampton, he wrote, an eavesdropping servant heard Major André say that "if he must go he would, but he did not expect to return." He also recalled that a "mistress to Col. Simcoe said to Mrs. G. The Col's wife that one of your forts is to be delivered up to us soon by one of your Generals . . . Mrs. Gardiner thought of this soon after Major J. Davis [probably Joshua Davis of the whaleboat fleet] was in town at Huntington and she went to see him to inquire of her son who was a surgeon in the A. army." Unfortunately Mrs. G.'s discovery came to nothing. "She was on the point of mentioning to Major Davis what the woman told her," the tale concludes, "but by some means or other did not. She thought it was only the woman's foolish talk."

What, then, were the "circumstances" which Tallmadge declined to reveal? We can assume that the Manhattan spies were aware of the stir of excitement at British headquarters in September, and they could hardly have failed to wonder at André's absence from the city on his first attempt to meet Arnold. The unusual shipping activity in the harbor was observed not only by the Culpers but also by a secret correspondent sent into the city by General Greene, who informed Washington that "some secret expedition was on foot, but of its nature and direction, he could not obtain the smallest hint."

355 must have been particularly alert for any clue. Perhaps she caught a careless remark dropped by Clinton or André. Perhaps the young major, who loved the dramatic, indicated the importance of his mission when he bade her an eloquent farewell. It might have been no more than a suggestion of treachery in the north, a boast that an American general was about to defect to the British. She would have realized its significance, and reported it at once to Culper Junior.

Tallmadge had been trying to shorten the regular Culper channel from New York to Setauket and across the Sound to Fairfield. A week before, on September 13th, he informed Washington that "I have just engaged a man to bring letters from N.Y. via Kingsbridge if necessary." 355's warning, forwarded over this direct route, could have been in Tallmadge's hands when André started down the east shore of the Hudson on his ill-fated ride to the city.

*   *   *

André's plan to return to New York on the *Vulture*, as he had come, had been altered by several unforeseen events. At dawn on Friday, while he and Arnold were conferring in a grove of firs at the base of Long Clove Mountain near Haverstraw, an American four-pounder and howitzer at Teller's Point opened fire on the *Vulture* which was riding at anchor midstream. After six shots hulled the vessel, the captain decided prudently to drop a little down river. Joshua Hett Smith's boatmen refused to row the extra distance in daylight, past the active shore battery, and Arnold decided that André's only alternative was to return by land. Disregarding General Clinton's specific instructions against wearing a disguise behind the American lines, André exchanged his scarlet uniform blouse for a purple coat with gold-lace buttons which belonged to Smith, and donned a round civilian hat, uncocked. He felt that his nankeen waistcoat and white-topped riding boots would not identify him as an officer, but as a precaution he wore a long blue surtout buttoned around his neck, and, he stated at his trial, Arnold "himself made me put the papers I bore between my stockings and my feet."

Arnold wrote an order, as though from his Robinson House headquarters across the river from West Point: "Permit Mr. John Anderson to pass the guards to the White Plains, or below if he chooses, he being on public business by my direction. B. Arnold, M Genl." He instructed Joshua Hett Smith to escort André to the British lines, and hastened back to West Point, satisfied that his accomplice would experience no trouble. Smith waited until the evening of September 22nd — four years to the day after Nathan Hale was hanged — and he and André and a Negro servant took the King's Ferry across the Hudson to Verplanck's Point. They rode south as far as Crompond, eight miles below Verplanck's, where they were warned of raiding parties in the area. Smith was apprehensive, and insisted on spending the night. "We slept in the same bed," Smith stated in his testimony, "and I was often disturbed with the restless motions, and uneasiness of mind exhibited by my bed-fellow, who on observing the first approach of day, summoned my servant to prepare the horses for our departure. He appeared as if he had not slept an hour during the night."

André grew more relaxed as they rode south toward Pine's Bridge over the Croton River, the southern boundary of the American lines. There had been no untoward incidents, and a few more miles would bring them safely within British territory. The acclaim and title he coveted were almost within his grasp. Smith observed that "the nearer we approached the bridge, the more his countenance brightened into a cheerful serenity . . . He descanted on the richness of the scenery around us, and particularly admired, from every eminence, the grandeur of the Highland mountains, bathing their summits in the clouds from their seeming water base at the north extremity of Haverstraw Bay. The pleasantry of converse, and mildness of the weather, so insensibly beguiled the time that we at length found ourselves at the bridge before I thought we had got half way."

They stopped for breakfast at the farmhouse of an old Dutch woman on Cat Hill. To Smith's alarm, she informed them that the Cow Boys or the Skinners had raided her the night before, and taken all the supplies of her cupboard save for some Indian meal, which she mixed with water and boiled to make soupaan. Smith was of no mind to venture into the dangerous Neutral Ground below the Croton, and announced to André that he would proceed no further. "He was affected at parting," Smith stated, "and offered me a valuable gold watch in remembrance of him, as a keep sake, which I refused." After giving him some money and directions about the road to follow, Smith and his servant turned back and left André to ride the remaining fifteen miles to the White Plains alone.

The Neutral Ground was the local name for that section of Westchester County which lay between the two opposing lines. It was a no-man's land, without military guards or patrols, and was infested with rival gangs of highwaymen and freebooters who looted the countryside at will. Some bandits called themselves Skinners and leaned to the patriot cause; they operated under a New York ordinance which permitted them to claim as prize any valuables they might find on a captured enemy. Others were more or less Tory in sympathy and, because of their fondness for stealing cattle, were known as Cow Boys; they were under the vague command of the Loyalist Colonel James de Lancey, the celebrated "Cow Boy of the Bronx." Sometimes they fought one another, sometimes they worked in collusion. Like jackals they ranged in small packs, too cowardly to attack by day, conducting their nefarious business under cover of darkness.

A group of three illiterate Skinners, Paulding and Williams and Van Wert, had finished a night of plundering, and on Saturday morning were resting and playing cards beside a wooden bridge, a half mile below Tarrytown. They heard hoofbeats approaching, and concealed themselves in some bushes. The lone rider wore a tight-buttoned blue cloak, but beneath its skirt they caught the gleam of polished leather. Good boots were valuable; they stepped out with raised firelocks and forced him to dismount. Noting that one of the highwaymen wore a plundered Hessian uniform coat, André assumed they were Loyalists and identified himself as a British officer on pressing business. When he realized the blunder, he hastily produced his pass from General Arnold, but it was too late. They searched him, stole his gold watch and the pocketful of coins that Smith had given him, and pulled off his boots. One of them noticed some papers concealed inside his stockings, but they could not read, and might have let him go had he not chattered about giving them a hundred guineas if he were freed. The size of the sum convinced them that they had captured an important prize, and they took him to the nearest American outpost at North Castle in hopes of a reward.

Major Tallmadge and a detachment of dragoons had been reconnoitering the country between the White Plains and East Chester, and he did not return to North Castle until late Saturday evening. There he learned from Lieutenant Colonel Jameson, the acting commandant, that a prisoner had been brought in during the day by some Skinners, and the Colonel had examined certain papers he was carrying and discovered them to be notes and sketches of the West Point defenses. Assuming that the pass signed by Arnold was a forgery, he had dutifully sent the prisoner north under guard to the General at the Robinson House, preceded by a fast courier with a personal letter to Arnold describing the capture. At the same time, he forwarded the seized papers to Washington, who had concluded his meeting with Rochambeau and was somewhere on the road between Hartford and West Point. The name on Arnold's pass, Jameson added, was John Anderson.

Tallmadge remembered seeing the same name on his previous dispatch from General Arnold. The Culper warning of treachery was fresh in his mind — though he had not connected it with Arnold until this moment — and he came to an instant decision. "I suggested to Jameson a plan which I wished to pursue," Tallmadge wrote in his *Memoir*, "offering to take the entire responsibility on myself, and which, as he deemed it too perilous, I will not disclose further." Despite his reticence, it is obvious that Tallmadge proposed the drastic step of seizing General Arnold and holding him prisoner until Washington could examine the incriminating papers. Such an act of insubordination was beyond the limited imagination of his superior officer, who believed in strict adherence to the rules. After a heated argument, Tallmadge persuaded him to order André and the guards back to North Castle; but Jameson stubbornly refused to recall the courier who was speeding to West Point with the letter which would warn Arnold that the plot had been exposed.

As André rode north that Saturday night, his hopes began to rise again. The conspiracy had failed through his own ineptness; but if he could reach Arnold before Washington discovered the facts, he might still save his neck. The party was almost at Peekskill, only ten miles from West Point, when Jameson's orders caught up with them, and the unhappy André was brought back to North Castle. It was Tallmadge's first glimpse of the stranger who still called himself John Anderson, and he sensed at once that this was no ordinary secret agent. "As soon as I saw Anderson," he wrote in his *Memoir*, "and especially

after I saw him walk (as he did almost constantly) across the
floor, I became impressed with the belief that he had been bred
to arms. I communicated my suspicion to Lieut.-Col. Jameson
and requested him to notice his gait, especially when he turned
on his heel to retrace his course across the room."

It was deemed best to transfer the prisoner to Second Regiment headquarters at Lower Salem, and Tallmadge was assigned to guard him in his new place of detention. He noticed
that Mr. Anderson's agitation and anxiety were increasing every
hour. Sometime on Sunday André learned that the telltale
papers found on him had been sent to Washington instead of
Arnold, and that the Commander-in-Chief would have charge
of the affair. His assumed name could protect him no longer.
About three o'clock that afternoon, he asked Tallmadge to be
favored with a pen and paper, and in his presence addressed a
letter to General Washington stating that "the person in your
possession is Major John André, adjutant general of the British
army." He did not mention Arnold, but admitted that he had
come through the lines to obtain intelligence, and had been "betrayed . . . into the vile condition of an enemy in disguise
within your posts." He requested that he be "branded with nothing dishonourable, as no motive could be mine but the service of
my king, and as I was involuntarily an imposter." John André,
as consummate a performer as Peggy Shippen Arnold, had begun to play the role of injured innocence which would sway
everyone but Washington himself.

Washington was late for breakfast at the Robinson House
that Sunday morning. He requested his aide, Colonel Alexander
Hamilton, to convey his apologies to General and Mrs. Arnold;
and the rest of the party, including Knox and Lafayette, rode
on ahead to Arnold's quarters on the bluff opposite West Point.
They were in the middle of their meal when Jameson's advance
courier arrived with the warning letter. Arnold read it without
a change of expression, excused himself to his guests, and hur-

ried upstairs to his private chambers where Peggy lay in bed with their month-old baby son. A couple of minutes later, as Washington was approachng, Arnold bolted through a rear exit, mounted his horse, and shouted to an aide to inform His Excellency that he had gone across the river to the fort. He galloped down a shortcut to his barge, and ordered the unsuspecting crew to row him downstream to the *Vulture*. The eight bargemen followed him aboard the British warship, whereupon Arnold informed them that they were under arrest, and ordered them taken below as prisoners.

Peggy Arnold remained in her room until Washington had breakfasted and departed for West Point, expecting to meet Arnold there. Conceivably she spent her time destroying all correspondence and papers concerning the conspiracy; no letters from Arnold to Peggy were ever found. Having removed the evidence, Peggy embarked on her finest dramatic performance. Arnold's aide, Lieutenant Colonel Varick, heard a shriek, ran upstairs, and met Mrs. Arnold "with her hair dissheveled and flowing about her neck," he wrote his sister. "Her morning-gown with few other clothes remained on her — too few to be seen even by gentlemen of the family, much less by any strangers." Peggy was not above using her physical appeal to arouse sympathy. "She seized me by the hand," Varick continued, "with this — to me — distressing address and a wild look: 'Colonel Varick, have you ordered my child to be killed?' Judge you of my feelings at such a question from this most amiable and distressed of her sex, whom I most valued."

Varick helped her to her bed, and tried to console her, assuring her that General Arnold would soon be home from West Point with General Washington. "She burst again into pitiable tears and . . . exclaimed: 'No, General Arnold will never return; he is gone, he is gone forever; there, there, there, the spirits have carried [him] up there, they have put hot irons on his head' — pointing that he was gone up to the ceiling." When she learned that Washington had come back from the Point without Arnold, she insisted to Varick that "there was a hot iron on her head and no one but General Washington could take it off, and wanted to see the general."

On his return to the Robinson House, Hamilton gave Washington the captured papers brought by Jameson's second messenger, who had ridden all the way to Hartford and back to West Point; but for the moment the Commander-in-Chief kept the news of Arnold's defection from the others. Varick informed him of Mrs. Arnold's request, and the General went to her room. Peggy promptly resumed her act. "I attended him to her bedside," Varick recalled, "and told her there was General Washington. She said no, it was not. The General assured her he was, but she exclaimed: 'No, that is not General Washington; that is the man who was a-going to assist Colonel Varick in killing my child.' She repeated the same sad story about General Arnold. Poor, unhappy, frantic, and miserable lady."

Hamilton was also moved by her distress. Washington had sent him galloping down the east shore of the Hudson to Verplanck's, in a vain effort to halt Arnold's barge, and later that afternoon Hamilton informed Peggy Arnold regretfully that her husband had escaped. "It was the most affecting scene I was ever witness to," he reported to his fiancée, General Schuyler's daughter Betsy. "One moment she raved, another she melted into tears . . . All the sweetness of her beauty, all the loveliness of innocence, all the tenderness of a wife, and all the fondness of a mother showed themselves in her appearance and conduct. We have every reason to believe that she was entirely unacquainted with the plan, and that the first knowledge of it was when Arnold went to tell her that he must banish himself from his country and from her forever."

Even Washington was persuaded that she had no part in the plot. Not only were Peggy's tears convincing, but a letter from Arnold, sent ashore from the *Vulture* under a flag, urged that the "mistaken vengeance of my country . . . ought to fall only on me; she is as good and innocent as an angel, and is incapable of doing wrong." Washington arranged with great solicitude to send the overwrought lady to her father in Philadelphia, and ordered Major Franks, another of Arnold's aides, to escort her on the journey. The General and his staff bade her farewell with deep emotion, and Hamilton wrote Betsy: "Her sufferings were so eloquent that I wished myself her brother, to have a right to become her defender."

At Paramus, New Jersey, the party stopped for the night at the home of Peggy's old friend Mrs. Theodosia Prevost, later to become the wife of Aaron Burr. The cool and analytical Burr had always been skeptical of Peggy's hysterics, and in a private diary he set down Theodosia's account of what happened that evening: "As soon as they were left alone, Mrs. Arnold became tranquillized and assured Mrs. Prevost that she was heartily tired of the theatricals she was exhibiting . . . that she had corresponded with the British commander, and that she was disgusted with the American cause and those who had the management of public affairs, and that through great persuasion and unceasing perseverance she had ultimately brought the general into an arrangement to surrender West Point." Burr, who had known Peggy from childhood, kept the story secret until both the Arnolds were dead, and it could no longer do any harm.

*   *   *

Washington never set eyes on John André. On Sunday evening he sent orders to Lieutenant Colonel Jameson to deliver his prisoner at once to the Robinson House, warning him to supply a strong enough escort to prevent his escape or recapture by the enemy. "He had better be conducted to this place by some upper road rather than by the route through Crompond . . . and is to be most closely and narrowly watched." The orders were received at midnight, and Tallmadge and a party of a hundred dragoons conducted André north through a heavy rain and arrived at dawn. From Robinson's House, André was taken across the Hudson to West Point, and thence down river in a barge. As André sailed past the stone abutments of the fort, he must have recalled with wry humor the promise by Clinton that he would be allowed to lead a select corps to assault those gray walls and achieve immortal fame. Now his name would be lost to posterity.

The party disembarked at Stony Point, and Tallmadge and the escort of dragoons led the prisoner south to Mabie's Tavern at Tappan, where André was to be imprisoned during his trial. The journey was long, and André and Tallmadge spent the hours talking together. A quarter of a century later, Tallmadge recorded their conversation in his *Memoir*:

"As we progressed on our way to Tappan, before we reached the Clove, where we dined, Major André was very inquisitive to know my Opinion as to the result of his Capture . . . I endeavored to evade the question, unwilling to give him a true answer. When I could no longer evade this Importunity, I said to him that I had a much loved Classmate in Yale College by the name of Nathan Hale, who entered the army with me. After the British Troops had entered N. York, Genl. Washington wanted Information respecting the strength, position & probable movements of the enemy. Capt. Hale tendered his services, went into N. York, & was taken just as he was passing the out posts of the Enemy; said I with Emphasis, do you remember the sequel of this Story; Yes, said André; he was hanged as a Spy; but you surely do not consider his Case & mine alike. I replied, precisely similar, and similar will be your fate. He endeavored to answer my remarks, but it was manifest he was more troubled than I had seen him before . . ."

Major Tallmadge had reasons of his own to be troubled. He recalled Arnold's elaborate efforts to learn the names of his secret correspondents in New York, and feared that the traitor

might have discovered their identity elsewhere. Evidently he
had already given Clinton some clues. In a warning letter to
Washington, Sir Henry demanded the release of André and
intimated that there were certain American spies in his power
"whom he had foreborne to execute from a desire to spare the
horrors of war." The death of André would bring certain and
swift retribution against the Culper Ring in Manhattan.

BOOK THREE

Honor Bound

Before these accounts are finally closed, justice and propriety call upon me to signify that there are Persons
within the British Lines — if they are not dead or removed — who have a claim upon the Public under the
strongest assurances of compensation from me for their
services in conveying me private intelligence; and which
when exhibited I shall think myself in honor bound
to pay.

— GEORGE WASHINGTON

I

"Rebels! Turn Out Your Dead"

M AJOR ANDRÉ was hanged at high noon on Monday,
the 2nd of October. He had requested Washington to
"adapt the mode of my death to the feelings of a man of honour" and permit him to be shot as a soldier rather than swing on
a gibbet; but the General refused to alter the sentence of the
court-martial. André had been condemned as a spy, he held,
and he should die as a spy. To spare the prisoner's feelings, he
was not told of Washington's decision; and he learned the
truth for the first time when he mounted the small hill above
Tappan Village and saw the crossbar between two apple trees
and the dangling loop of rope.

He was dressed in full British regimentals and white-topped
boots brought from New York by his body servant Peter, his
curls powdered, his stock adjusted with meticulous care. General Greene led the procession of general and field officers between a double line of soldiers which stretched half a mile from
Mabie's Tavern to the place of execution. Only Washington
remained at headquarters. André followed in slow step, the
lugubrious strains of the dead march making a strange contrast
to the gay autumn foliage and brilliant sunshine. Beneath the
gallows was a baggage wagon with a plain pine coffin, and a
grave had been dug nearby. He climbed onto the wagon and, dis-

daining the blackened hangman, adjusted the rope around his neck and drew the knot tight on the right side of his throat.

His final statement was in character. Nathan Hale's last thoughts had been of his country; André's were of himself. He bowed courteously to General Greene and said: "You will bear me witness that I die like a brave man." Delicately he tied his own scented handkerchief over his eyes, the drums beat the long roll, and the wagon was driven from beneath him. He died on the first outward swing of the rope.

André's fate, though admittedly just, was universally lamented. General Greene was too overcome to speak. General Anthony Wayne, forgetting the satiric thrusts in the "Cow-Chase," wept openly. Major Tallmadge walked beside the prisoner to the hilltop and parted with him under the gallows, "entirely overwhelmed with grief that so gallant an officer and so accomplished a gentleman should come to such an ignominious end . . . I was obliged to leave the parade in a flood of tears." Robert Townsend, who might have been hanged himself if André's mission had succeeded, wrote Tallmadge from New York: "I have never felt more sensibly for the death of a person . . . He was a most amiable character. The army in general and inhabitants think that General Washington must have been destitute of feeling or he would have saved him." Alexander Hamilton, as gullible about André as he had been about Peggy Arnold, pleaded passionately with Washington to spare the charming young Britisher from the gibbet; and the General's refusal marked the beginning of a coldness between them which terminated a few months later in Hamilton's angry resignation as Washington's aide.

Sir Henry Clinton had been torn between sorrow and guilt at the capture of his court favorite. During the trial at Tappan, he dispatched an outraged letter to Washington, insisting that André had come through the American lines under a flag and acted under Arnold's orders, and therefore could not be con-

sidered a spy. The fifteen-man board of general officers, headed
by Greene, had heard André's own confession that there was no
flag and that he had come ashore "in a private and secret manner," and they ignored the protest. When Clinton received no
reply, he sent General Robertson as his personal emissary to
Corbet's Point, near Tappan, with another letter of protest.
In an anonymous reply to Clinton, probably unauthorized by
Washington, Hamilton suggested that André might be exchanged for General Arnold; but Sir Henry felt it would be
dishonorable to betray the traitor. Arnold himself tried to
intervene with a last-minute notice to Washington that, should
André hang, "I call upon heaven and earth to witness that
your Excellency will be justly answerable for the torrents of
blood that may be spilled in consequence." His threat arrived
at Tappan on Monday noon, just as André stepped to the gallows.

*   *   *

Arnold's flight to New York had scattered the Culper Ring
like a covey of quail at the shadow of a circling hawk. Townsend paid hasty visits to all of his Manhattan agents and warned
them to go underground, turned over the Oakman & Townsend store to his business partner, and left for the country, pre-
sumably with 355. Since he could not bring her to his family
home at Oyster Bay, he hid out with Abraham Woodhull in
Setauket while the vindictive general was combing the city for
suspects. "The conduct of Arnold, since his arrival at N.Y.,"
Tallmadge wrote Washington on October 11th, "has been such
that, though he knows not a single link in the chain of my correspondence, still those who have assisted us in this way are
at present too apprehensive of Danger to give their immediate
usual intelligence. I hope as the tumult subsides matters will
go on in their old channels . . . I have wrote Culper Junr.
assuring him that his name or character are not known by any

officer but myself in the army." Washington reported to Congress: "Unluckily the person in whom I have the greatest confidence is afraid to take any measures for communicating with me just at this time, as he is apprehensive that Arnold may possibly have some knowledge of the connection and have him watched."

As the weeks passed and no Culper associates were apprehended, Tallmadge began to breathe more easily. Robert Townsend returned to the city and wrote in relief on October 20th: "I am happy to think that Arnold does not know my name . . . no person has been taken up on his information. I was not much surprised at his conduct, for it was no more than I expected of him. Genl. Clinton has introduced him to the General officers on parade as General Arnold in the British service. This will tend to gloss his character with the venal part of the enemy, but the independent party must hold him in contempt; and his name will stink to eternity with the generous of all parties."

Culper Junior's relief was short-lived. The blow fell without warning on the very day that he dispatched his optimistic letter. "I was at New York about the 20th," Woodhull informed Tallmadge sadly. "Several of our dear friends were imprisoned, in particular one that hath been ever serviceable to this correspondence. This step so dejected the spirits of C. Junr. that he resolved to leave New York . . . Depend my endeavors shall continue, as I hope never to lose sight of our cause, truly sensible our all is at stake. I conclude your affectionate Friend and Humble Servt., Samuel Culper."

355 and Hercules Mulligan were seized simultaneously, evidently on Arnold's accusation. Mulligan was thrown into the Provost, on the charge of collaborating with the rebels; but Arnold had brought no proof with him when he fled from West Point, and the glib Irishman managed to talk his way out of a conviction. 355 was not so fortunate. The evidence against her was too strong, and, like Nathan Hale, she was condemned

without a trial. Townsend learned of her arrest that night when he joined a group of British officers at a Coffee Shop table. "Picked up a woman spy today," a major from headquarters remarked. "Supposed to have informed the rebels about West Point. The wench refused to name any of her associates, I hear."

Townsend tried to sound casual. "Did they hang her like poor André?"

"Worse than that, old chap. They put her aboard the *Jersey*."

The *Jersey* was the oldest of the five prison ships in Wallabout Bay, a waterlogged hulk which had once been a 64-gun war vessel, fourth rate. She was stripped of her masts and rigging and all her guns, and slime covered her sloping sides and hung in green beards from the rusting anchor chain. Over a thousand prisoners were penned below deck in this floating charnel-house. Officers were crammed into the former gun room, American sailors and soldiers occupied the two lower decks, and French and Spanish captives were kept in the narrow airless space above the keel.

The ship bore the nickname "Hell," and the British Marine guards, carrying out the analogy, subjected their victims to every kind of fiendish indignity and cruelty. "If you were to rake the infernal regions, I doubt whether you would find such another set of demons as the officers and men who had charge of the old *Jersey*," Captain Alexander Coffin of the American navy recalled after the war. "On my arrival I found eleven hundred prisoners; many of them had been there from three to six months, but few lived over that time. They were generally in the most deplorable situation, mere walking skeletons, with scarcely clothes to cover their nakedness, and overrun with lice from head to foot. The food was all condemned provisions from ships of war, which no doubt were supplied with new in their stead and the new charged by the commissaries to the *Jersey*. There were never provisions served out to the prisoners that would have been eatable by men that were not literally in a starving situation . . . There were hogs kept in pens by the ship's officers. I have seen the prisoners watch an opportunity and with a tin pot steal the bran from the hogs' trough and when they had an opportunity boil it on the fire and eat it."

The prisoners' quarters were never cleansed, and were ankle-deep in refuse and human excrement. Portholes were nailed shut and hatches battened down at night, and the emaciated men lay on rags and gasped for breath in the nauseous and stifling hold. Once a day gondolas manned by four prisoners under guard were sent ashore for fresh water, which was dumped into a common butt and left to stagnate. Cooking was done in a copper vessel, poisonously corroded by the salt water which was hauled up out of the East River. Swarms of rats spread the plague, and yellow fever and smallpox raged unchecked. Lacking medical attention, the men tried to inoculate themselves by scratching their fingernails on the sores of infected fellow prisoners. "We bury six to eleven men a day," an inmate on the *Jersey* wrote in a smuggled letter. "We have 200 more sick and falling sick . . . Our morning's salutation is 'Rebels! Turn out your dead!' "

Occasionally a recruiting officer would visit the *Jersey*, and offer the captives their freedom if they would join the Royal Navy; but most of them preferred a slow death by disease or starvation to turning against their country. So bitter were the rebels at this British offer, one survivor recalled, that they filled a snuffbox with vermin, and dumped the ugly contents down the back of the recruiting officer's neck the next time he came to harangue them.

Only the strongest survived, and many of those went insane. Prisoners would be awakened in the night by the warning cry: "Madman with a knife!" and would cower in total darkness as their demented cellmate stumbled back and forth over the prostrate bodies, his blade slashing. Often a man would discover the comrade beside him stiffened in death in the morning. A letter published in 1783, signed "An American," stated that 11,644 perished on the *Jersey* and other prison ships, and "had taken up their abode under the surface of the hill" on the banks of Wallabout Bay. Other bodies were tossed overboard without ceremony, or were left exposed on the mud flats until a high tide washed them back into the East River.

Perhaps Robert Townsend knew that night that he would never see 355 again. He left the Coffee Shop and walked slowly down Wall Street to Murray's Wharf, and out to the end of the lonely pier. The dark river thrust against the creaking pilings, and in midstream the swinging lamps of a man-of-war bobbed with the tidal current. A year ago in June he had stood here with Abraham Woodhull, and agreed to serve as a secret agent. And what had it gained him? Across the river, lost in the curving shadow of Wallabout Bay, was the old *Jersey*, and the woman he loved, and his child that she was carrying. He could not visit her, he could not even admit that he knew her for fear of jeopardizing the Culper Ring. He had no heart to remain here in New York, so close to her and yet so helpless. He walked back to the Underhill boardinghouse to pack his possessions, resolved to quit the city forever.

*   *   *

Arnold showed no sign of penitence at André's death. "He wants feeling!" Washington declared. "He seems to have been hackneyed in villainy, and so lost to all sense of honour and shame that while his faculties will enable him to continue his sordid pursuits there will be no time for remorse." A few days after the hanging, when General Clinton was still prostrated with grief, Arnold wrote him a callous letter asking if he might have the £10,000 he had originally requested rather than the £6,000 which André had offered. Clinton kept his bargain and made Arnold a brigadier, but the cash reward for his treason remained at the original figure.

Clinton's private dislike of Arnold was shared by all his staff, who made no secret of their wish that Arnold had been hanged instead of André. "General Arnold is a very unpopular character in the army," a British officer commented, "nor can all the patronage he meets with procure him respectability. The subaltern officers have conceived such an aversion to him that they unanimously refused to serve under his command, and the detachment he is to lead was, on this account, officered from the Loyal American corps." Even the Tories detested him, and commented scathingly that he was trying to "raise a regiment of as great scoundrels as himself, if he can find them."

Arnold limped through the streets of New York in British uniform, facing the cold stares of passers-by, embittered and alone. His colossal egoism could not conceive that he had done wrong; he saw himself rather as a martyr who had sacrificed everything to save America from ruin. In his supreme self-confidence, he issued a "Proclamation to the Officers and Soldiers of the Continental Army," published in Rivington's *Gazette*, urging his fellow countrymen to turn against their leaders and enlist in his new regiment called the "American Legion." He had the effrontery even to write Major Tallmadge and invite him to "join me with as many men as you can bring over with you. If you think proper to embrace my offer, you shall have the same rank you now hold, in the cavalry I am about to raise." Tallmadge forwarded the letter to Washington, unable to fathom "the motives which induced the Traitor to address himself particularly to me. I have determined to treat the Author with the contempt his conduct merits."

The politic James Rivington was taking no chances. Fearful that Arnold might suspect him of peddling intelligence to the enemy — a business in which the American general was an acknowledged expert — he went to great lengths to make his *Gazette* even more rabidly Tory in tone. Though he never published an account of André's execution, he reported the trial in highly partisan terms and described Washington as a "murderer." In November he descended to still lower depths of scurrility and slander. Purporting to be quoting an "Excerpt of a Letter from a German wine merchant to his friend in the Empire," Rivington embarked on a savage attack on Washington's personal character, skillfully worded to resemble a foreigner's broken English.

"It is known," the counterfeit letter stated, "that the General keeps at head quarters an extraordinary and beautiful soldiers girl. I have seen her, but to describe her is my pen not able . . . A long while ago this charming creature was big with child, and the impregnation by express order of the General kept very secret, but who can keep any thing secret from womens? Lady Washington discovered soon the whole affair, and in lieu of being enraged, she did prepare with her own hands the swadling cloaths, shirts, and other little furnitures for the young hero, which the soldiers girl in December last brought into the world, and by order of the General got the name Habaccuc. One says Lady Washington has congratulated her husband, as she saw him again the first time, and expressed to him joy together over it, that he could bring forth that, which, she in vain had expected from him. Dear Friend, where are more such like Lady's?"

A few days later Rivington printed a further report that the girl was Betsy Sidman, the daughter of a "tap-house keeper," and that she had renamed the boy George Washington and presented him to the General, only to find herself "drummed from the camp . . . pursuant to orders, which Lord Sterling saw punctually executed." Rivington's alleged informer added: "The General's present *convenience* is the wife of a corporal, taken into his service as a housekeeper . . . the cuckold corporal, by his wife's interest, has lately been made a serjeant."

Jemmy Rivington polished his slender hands in satisfaction. Surely no one reading these items would question his loyalty to the Crown.

*   *   *

So long as Arnold remained in New York, brooding and vengeful, it was useless to find someone who might replace Culper Junior. The correspondence from Manhattan was temporarily abandoned; and in November Tallmadge, as eager for action as Caleb Brewster, submitted a bold plan to Washington. Woodhull had advised him that Fort St. George, located at Mastic on the southern shore of Long Island, was poorly defended, and its Tory garrison could be captured with ease. In addition, Woodhull wrote, a large quantity of hay and winter feed had been collected by the enemy at Coram, eight miles from Setauket. Tallmadge proposed a double mission to reduce the fort and destroy the magazine of forage.

Washington gave his consent, and Brewster crossed the Devil's Belt to Conscience Bay, hid his whaleboat, and reconnoitered the enemy situation on the south shore. He reported to Tallmadge on the 13th: "Forrage is at Corum yet in stacks where tavern is kept. Their remains about forty Ruffiigeus at Mastick on Mr. Smith's place. They have no cannon, nothing but muskets." He continued with pardonable pride: "I took a prize a coming across today. A fine large boat from New Haven, which had been to carry passengers over. We run up long side of them and made them believe we came from Loyd's Neck. They enformed me who secreted the persons in New Haven for four weeks and their connections, and I wrote it all down. We up sail and came off together and they engaged to pilot us to New Haven harbour . . . We got about two thirds across the Sound before they found out their mistake and I got them safe under guard. I am Dear Sir, your most obedient humbil servant, C. Brewster."

Fort St. George had been erected by a group of Loyalists from Rhode Island to protect their foraging parties who were cutting firewood for the British. They had taken over the two-story manor house of General John Smith, fronting on South Bay, installed a pair of swivel guns to cover the harbor, and surrounded the house with a deep ditch and abatis of sharpened pickets tilted at a 45-degree angle. The fortified residence was at the northwest point of a triangular stockade which enclosed a parade ground of several acres. Its twelve-foot walls, made of pointed posts joined together by a transverse rail, presented a formidable barricade. To insure the success of his attack, Major Tallmadge made a trip to Mastic to survey the works in person, and drew a detailed map of the defenses.

His raiding force was hand-picked: two companies of dis-mounted dragoons totaling forty men, and twenty whaleboat-men under Brewster and Davis and George Smith of Smithtown. They embarked from Fairfield at four o'clock on the afternoon of November 21st, and at nine that evening landed unobserved at Old Man's Point. Tallmadge put his troops in motion to cross the island, but a driving sou'easter forced them to return to their whaleboats, and they huddled beneath them for shelter through the night and all the next day. At dusk on the 22nd the rain abated, and the expedition marched stealthily to the south side of the island, halting at dawn within two miles of Fort St. George. Tallmadge arranged his plan of attack, placing two small detachments at strategic positions around the fort, with orders to remain concealed until the enemy opened fire on the main column, headed by Captain Edgar and himself.

Daylight was just showing as they advanced on the sleeping garrison. The pioneers, who preceded them with axes, were within forty yards of the fort before they were discovered. A sentry, pacing in front of the stockade, challenged the approach-ing column and fired his musket. Before the smoke had cleared, Tallmadge's sergeant ran him through with his bayonet. The

first enemy shot was the signal for the other detachments to
charge. The pioneers chopped an opening in the stockade, and
a rear platoon remained beside the hole to prevent any prisoners
from escaping. "I led the column directly through the Grand
Parade against the main fort," Tallmadge recounted in his
Memoir, "which we carried with the bayonet, in less than ten
minutes, not a musket being loaded. At the same instant that
I entered on one side of the fort, the officers commanding the
two smaller detachments mounted the ramparts on the other
side, and the watch-word, 'Washington and glory,' was repeated from three points of the fort at the same time."

The Tory garrison lowered its flag in surrender, but this
proved to be a ruse. "While we were standing, elated with victory, in the center of the fort," Tallmadge wrote, "a volley
of musketry was discharged from the windows, which induced
me to order my whole detachment to load and return the fire. I
soon found it necessary to lead the column directly to the house,
which, being strongly barricaded, required the aid of the pioneers
with their axes. As soon as the troops could enter, the confusion
and conflict were great. A considerable portion of those who had
fired after the fort was taken, and the colors had been struck,
were thrown headlong from the windows of the second story
to the ground. Having forfeited their lives by the usages of
war, all would have been killed had I not ordered the slaughter
to cease."

While the prisoners were being secured, lookouts noted that
several ships in the harbor were getting under way. The swivel
guns in the fort were brought to bear on them, and they were
soon secured. Methodically the raiders demolished the enemy's
works, destroyed a large quantity of stores, and burned the
supply vessels. Some valuable items of plunder were made up
in bundles and placed on the shoulders of the prisoners, pinioned
two and two together; and the expedition started back triumphantly to Old Man's Point with the Tory commandant, a

couple of other officers, and fifty rank and file from the garrison.

Tallmadge turned over command of the detachment to Captain Edgar, selected a dozen men and mounted them on horses taken at the fort, and set out to destroy the British storage depot at Coram. Although a regiment of British regulars were encamped east of Huntington, only a few miles away, Tallmadge's party reached Coram without being challenged. They overpowered the guard around the storage magazine and set the hay afire, and an hour later rejoined the main line of march. That afternoon they reboarded their whaleboats at Old Man's, and by midnight were back at Fairfield without the loss of a man.

Washington was so gratified that he wrote a personal letter to Tallmadge, congratulating him on his successful enterprise and expressing his thanks "for your judicious planning and spirited execution of this business . . . You have my free consent to reward your gallant party with the little booty they were able to bring from the Enemy's works." Caleb Brewster was too wary of Annie Lewis's possessive eye to linger in Fairfield for the General's felicitations. The day after the expedition returned, he set out again across the Sound to pick up another dispatch from Culper Senior.

The message included a marked copy of the *Gazette* for November 18th. "On Tuesday last," the paper noted briefly, "arrived in town the lady and son of Brigadier General Arnold."

*   *   *

Peggy Arnold, on her return to Philadelphia in September, had met with an icy reception. The local papers were still full of Arnold's crime, and the *Pennsylvania Packet* openly implied that his wife had shared in the plot: "We should have despised and banished from social intercourse every character, whether male or female, which could be so lost to virtue, decency, and humanity as to revel with the murderers and plunderers of their countrymen." Peggy remained in her room at Judge Shippen's home, ostracized by society and threatened with stoning if she ventured out on the street. On October 27th, the Supreme Executive Council of Pennsylvania, suspecting that Peggy might be corresponding with the traitor in New York, resolved "that the said Margaret Arnold departs this state within fourteen days from the date hereof, and that she do not return again during the continuance of the present war." Peggy and her infant son were escorted across New Jersey to Paulus Hook, still a British post, and ferried to New York, where she rejoined her husband in the former John Watts Mansion at Number Three Broadway, next door to Clinton's headquarters.

Washington could show deep loyalty and devotion to his friends, but he was capable of steely anger when one of them betrayed him. His bitterness toward Arnold was so intense that he was willing to go to any lengths to capture the traitor and bring him to justice. Late in September, while André was still alive, the Commander-in-Chief summoned Colonel "Light Horse Harry" Lee, whose dragoons were considered the elite of the Continental Army, and requested him to send a trusted emissary into New York to kidnap Arnold. His timely delivery to Tappan, the General said, "will possibly put it into my power to restore the amiable and unfortunate André to his friends." Washington expressly stipulated that Arnold was not to be killed "as his public punishment is the sole object in view."

Light Horse Harry had just the man in mind: a young sergeant major from Virginia named John Champe who was "rather above the common size, full of bone and muscle, with a saturnine countenance, of tried courage and inflexible perseverance." Sergeant Champe needed all these qualities for his perilous mission. Lee's plan called for Champe to desert his regiment, escape to New York, enlist in Arnold's American Legion, and, with the aid of a couple of secret agents in Manhattan, seize the traitor some dark night and bring him back by boat to the Jersey shore at Newark, where Lee would be waiting.

The first step was to make the desertion seem so genuine that it would deceive not only the enemy, but also Champe's own corps of dragoons. As Lee recalled it later, he gave Champe some money and the regiment's orderly book — since it would seem more convincing if an absconding sergeant major brought along official papers — and the emissary mounted his horse, requesting his commander to delay pursuit as long as possible because he would have to "zigzag in order to avoid the patrols" on the road to Paulus Hook. The plan was nearly ruined by Lee's overeager staff, who were kept unaware of the mission. Shortly after Champe's departure, an excited officer of the day informed the Colonel that he had encountered a fleeing American dragoon "who, being challenged, put spur to his horse and escaped." Lee tried to stall the pursuit as long as possible, but, since he could not call it off without arousing suspicion, reluctantly issued orders to a cornet to set out in chase. Champe had less than an hour's head start, and at dawn, as he mounted a hill north of Bergen, he saw his pursuers half a mile behind him. Abandoning his attempt to reach Paulus Hook, the fugitive galloped through Bergen and straight down to the Hudson, where two armed British galleys lay at anchor. The cordon was less than three hundred yards away when Champe dismounted, plunged into the river, and swam out to the enemy craft under a barrage of lead from his own dragoons.

His spectacular escape was proof to the British of his allegiance to the Royal cause, and he was transported to New York and taken to the acting adjutant general, Major Oliver de Lancey, Jr., who had taken André's place. Champe told a harrowing story of increased disaffection among the Americans, since Arnold had set the heroic example. De Lancey was so enchanted that, twenty-four hours after his arrival, Champe was repeating his tale to Sir Henry Clinton, who rewarded him with two guineas and wrote a letter of recommendation to General Arnold. The sergeant managed to convince even the skepti-

cal Arnold of his integrity, and was given his same rank in the
American Legion. In a dispatch to Lee in November, smuggled
out of the city by "one of the two incogniti" whose names
Champe had been given, he wrote that he now "had every op-
portunity he could wish to attend to the habits of the general."
Lee reported his preliminary success to Washington, and the
General, although it was too late to save André, ordered
Champe to "prosecute with unrelaxed vigor the remaining ob-
jects of his instructions."

Champe made his preparations with great care. He contacted
the second confidential agent, who may have been Hercules
Mulligan, and arranged for "a proper associate" in the kidnaping. Champe had observed that Arnold was accustomed "to
return home about twelve every night, and that previous to
going to bed he always visited the garden," not to commune with
his soul but simply to relieve himself before retiring. Champe's
plan was to "seize him and, being prepared with a gag, to apply
the same instantly." Trussed and gagged, Champe and his associate "intended to have placed themselves each under Arnold's
shoulder, and to have thus borne him through the most unfrequented alleys and streets" to a waiting boat at a Hudson River
wharf, "representing Arnold, in case of being questioned, as a
drunken soldier whom they were conveying to the guard-house."
To ensure a quick exit from the garden, Champe carefully
knocked out several palings from the fence at the rear of the
Watts Mansion, and "replaced them, so that with care and without noise he could readily open his way to the adjoining alley."
Once aboard the boat, Champe was sure that the Royal Navy
patrol craft in the Hudson could be avoided in the darkness.

The great design missed by a day. On the date set for the
midnight kidnaping, Sergeant Champe and the rest of Arnold's
Legion were ordered aboard a transport, and sailed to Virginia
as part of an expedition to aid Cornwallis. Once more Champe
was obliged to escape from his regiment and work his way to the

camp of General Greene in North Carolina; and Greene supplied him with a horse and sent him back to his own outfit. His fellow dragoons were understandably puzzled at the warm greeting that Colonel Lee gave the supposed deserter.

When Arnold sailed for Virginia on December 20th, he had high hopes of reward. He had been given a separate command, as he desired, and his orders were to conquer rebel territory and damage rebel property. He saw a triple opportunity: to distinguish himself in the King's service, and to succeed Cornwallis as supreme commander in the South; to exercise his personal vengeance on his countrymen; and, most important of all, to make a fortune in prize money. Sir Henry Clinton saw the possibility also, and sought to curb Arnold's avarice by ordering Lieutenant Colonels John Simcoe and Dundas to accompany him, and desiring Arnold to "consult those gentlemen previous to your undertaking any operation of consequence." Despite this precaution, Arnold waged a ruthless campaign in Virginia, slaughtering civilians and plundering public and private stores and leaving the town of Richmond in smoldering ruins. The governor of Virginia, Thomas Jefferson, offered 5000 guineas for his capture; and Lafayette, sent by Washington to oppose him, was ordered to put the traitor to death if he were taken. Instead of being cowed, the inhabitants, even those with Tory leanings were roused to fury by his indiscriminate violence, and Cornwallis found the whole countryside united against him.

Arnold's departure removed the immediate threat to the Culper Ring, but a new and more serious menace was taking shape late in 1780. Slowly but surely, Clinton's counterintelligence was compiling a dossier of information on the Manhattan spies. One Nehemiah Marks, Tory son of a leading merchant in Derby, Connecticut, was acting as "despatch agent" for the British and running secret messages across the Sound from Long Island to Stamford, the same route used by Brewster's whaleboats. Several times Marks had reported that a certain "Bruster" was carrying rebel dispatches; and on November 26th a British "State of Intelligence" paper corroborated his findings: "There is one Brewster who has the direction of three Whale boats that constantly come over from the Connecticut shore once a week for the purpose of obtaining Intelligence. They land at Draun Meadow Bay" — meaning Drowned Meadow, just east of Setauket. By December, Marks had worked his way so deeply into American secrets that he wrote ungrammatically but jubilantly: "I have found ought wair Bruster holds a Correspondence of intiligince & who Surplies him." Marks named specifically Nathaniel and Philip Roe, relatives of Austin Roe, and also mentioned "a place Called old mans."

Even more specific was information supplied to the British by William Heron of Redding, Connecticut, a clever Tory agent known as "Hiram the Spy," who assured Clinton's headquarters in New York: "Private dispatches are frequently sent from your city to the Chieftain here by some traitors. They come by way of Setalket, where a certain Brewster receives them, at or near a certain woman's."

The enemy spyglass was gradually coming into focus on Conscience Bay.

HONOR BOUND

🙟🙠

II

The Two-Faced Mr. Rivington

A RNOLD's treachery dealt a heavy blow to his country-men's already sagging morale. A mood of despondency had settled over the Continental Army, after Major General Horatio Gates's debacle the previous August. Ignoring Washington's recommendation to put General Greene in charge of the south-ern campaign, Congress had given the arrogant little political general over-all command in South Carolina. Gates had always assumed full credit for the defeat of Burgoyne at Saratoga, and was confident that he could bring Cornwallis to his knees; and in his eagerness he drove his half-starved and weary forces in an all-night march to engage the British at Camden. Since he lacked rum for the troops, he issued a gill of raw molasses to each man, which proved to be so violent a cathartic that his army was literally caught with its breeches down when the enemy attacked. The militia threw away their arms and stam-peded in headlong flight, the gallant Baron de Kalb was killed trying to rally his men, and General Gates, outdistancing all the rest, galloped sixty miles to Charlotte before he paused for breath. James Rivington seized on the occasion to ingratiate himself further with the British by publishing a mock advertise-ment in his *Royal Gazette:*

Reward! STRAYED, DESERTED, OR STOLEN, on the 16th of August last, near Camden in the state of South

Carolina, a whole ARMY, consisting of horse, foot and dragoons, to the amount of near TEN THOUSAND with all their baggage, artillery, wagons, and camp equipage. The subscriber has very strong suspicions, from information received from his aid de camp, that a certain CHARLES, EARL CORNWALLIS, was principally concerned with carrying off the said ARMY. Any person who will give information . . . shall be entitled to demand from the Treasurer of the United States the sum of

THREE MILLION of PAPER DOLLARS

as soon as they can be spared from the public funds.

HORATIO GATES, M.G.
and late Commander in Chief of the
Southern Army.

That winter of 1780–1781 saw patriot hopes at their lowest ebb in the war. Nerves were raw; everyone suspected everyone else of plotting treason; animosity built up toward Rochambeau and his French forces, still idling at Newport. The Continental troops had cause to be discontented. They had not been paid for over a year, and Washington pleaded with Congress in vain for funds. Regulars were being detained beyond their three-year term, whereas short-service militiamen could re-enlist every few months and draw a generous bonus. Rations were so scarce that General Glover appealed to the Massachusetts Assembly on December 11th: "It is now four days since your line of the army has eaten one mouthful of bread. We have no money, nor will anybody trust us." Washington reported grimly that "the soldiers eat every kind of horse food but hay." They lacked sufficient bedding, and in bitter weather three or four men shivered under a single blanket. Many were without shoes or adequate clothing; soldiers patched their tattered uniforms until they would no longer hold together, and at Fishkill a building had to be set aside as a retreat for naked men. "No European army would suffer the tenth part of what the American troops suffer," Lafayette declared. "It takes citizens to support hunger, nakedness, toil, and the total want of pay."

On New Year's Day of 1781, the resentment of the troops broke out in open mutiny. Twenty-four hundred noncommissioned officers and men of the Pennsylvania line, in winter quarters at Morristown under command of Major General Anthony Wayne, decided to take matters in their own hands and lay their grievances before Congress. Shortly before midnight, while Wayne was enjoying a bowl of New Year's punch with his staff, the rebellious troops gathered in the parade ground, cheering and firing muskets in the air, led six dray horses from their stalls and hitched them to gun caissons, and started their march to Philadelphia. Wayne and his officers dashed from their quarters and tried to block their way with swords and espontoons, firing pistols into the ranks and killing one man and wounding others. The sullen column filed past them and headed south through New Jersey to the resolute beat of drums. They had passed Princeton and were almost at Trenton when Wayne caught up with them and, in an impassioned appeal to their loyalty, persuaded them to halt until the Congress could hear their complaints.

General Clinton's alert spies had brought him word of the mutiny at Morristown the day after it occurred. His staff officers urged him to dispatch troops at once to attack the disorganized patriot army; but Sir Henry, arguing that an overt move might drive the mutineers back to the American side, chose a more discreet course. Secret messengers infiltrated the lines with a proclamation from the British commander, offering to take the rebels under protection of the Royal government, pardon them for past offenses against the Crown, and pay them all arrears in good British gold instead of worthless Continental dollars. The Pennsylvanians were outraged at Clinton's imputation of treason; they sought justice, but they had no thought of "turning Arnolds." Two of the spies bringing the commander's olive branch were arrested by the mutineers and turned over to American authorities, who hanged them on January 10th at a crossroads near Trenton. Joseph Reed of Congress arrived in a few days with promises of adjustment, and the mollified troops returned to duty. Once again the cautious Sir Henry had wasted a priceless moment to strike.

Washington's confidential agents in New York were no less alert. Hercules Mulligan had been released from the Provost, when Arnold's charges against him were dismissed for lack of evidence, and resumed his clothier business, keeping his ears open for any significant intelligence. Late in February his brother Hugh, owner of the Kortwright importing firm, received a hurried order to place a quantity of provisions aboard a transport which was to carry three hundred cavalry up the Sound. Casual conversation with the British commissary officer revealed that the expedition would be landed at New London, Connecticut, to ambush the American Commander-in-Chief as he traveled through Lebanon on March 5th on his way to confer with Rochambeau at Newport.

Hugh Mulligan passed the information to his brother, and Hercules forwarded it by the whaleboat route to Washington's headquarters at New Windsor, New York. Lafayette promptly advised the Duc de Lauzun, whose French light horse were stationed at Lebanon, to "be prepared with his cavalry to repel the invaders," and Washington journeyed safely by an alternate route. At Newport he was escorted to Count de Rochambeau's quarters in the Vernon House by a huge procession, led by thirty boys bearing lighted candles fixed on staffs. An awestruck French officer entered in his diary: "His face is handsome, noble and mild . . . I mark as a fortunate day, that in which I have been able to behold a man so truly great."

Aware that there had been a leak somewhere, British counterintelligence redoubled its efforts to learn the identity of "S.C." and "C ——— J ———," and end their covert correspondence with

Washington. The illiterate Nehemiah Marks managed to make contact with a turncoat American officer, and reported to Clinton that "one that has a Commission in the Rebels Servis" had promised to "due every thing to assist Mee to find ought thee peticler men that Send the intelegance from New York." Hiram the Spy had already pinpointed Caleb Brewster's landing place near the home of Anna Strong in Setauket; but Brewster had a variety of alternate coves and estuaries, and continued to elude the enemy. Early in February of 1781 he slipped into Conscience Bay, by appointment with Culper Senior, but found the British troops so thick in Setauket that he prudently returned to Fairfield for a couple of additional whaleboats, "both for my own safety," he explained to General Washington, "and to annoy them if they fell in my way.

"On the 12th, at night," his letter continued, "I crossed again with three boats and affected my purpose, and on the morning following just as we were embarking to return I discovered a boat rowing from the eastward." Brewster was never one to turn down a chance for action. "I lay concealed until she came opposite to me when I detached one of my boats in pursuit; she discovering our strength immediately came on shore and proved to be a crusing refugee boat carrying eight men, a list of their names and characters I have the honor to enclose to your Excellency." The prisoners, including three Loyalists who had escaped from the Simsbury mines, were delivered to the Provost Guard at Fishkill; and Washington gratefully instructed Brewster to "dispose of the Boat and what you took in her for the benefit of the captors."

More valuable to Caleb Brewster than the booty was the opportunity to escape from Anne Lewis, however briefly. As the Culper correspondence lagged, following Townsend's decision to quit New York, he found himself spending more and more idle time in Fairfield; and the depressing prospect of matrimony was beginning to weigh on his mind. Not only was his partner

Josh Davis tied to Abigail Redfield's apron strings, and on the
verge of becoming a benedict, but every day his own Annie
was growing more demanding. He was like a whaleboat without
oars, he reflected, caught in the current and borne helplessly to
the brink of disaster. His relief was unbounded when he learned,
early in the spring of 1781, that Culper Junior was back in Manhattan and ready to resume his espionage activities.

The reappearance of Robert Townsend was as abrupt as his
earlier departure. On March 18th, Woodhull wrote Tallmadge:
"C. Junr. is again in New York, and entering into busineses as
heretofore, and you may soon I hope receive his dispatches."
The reason for his sudden return to the city was never given;
but it seems more than probable that Townsend had learned of
the death of 355 aboard the *Jersey*, perhaps in childbirth.
A Mrs. Deborah Franklin of Brooklyn, according to the recollections of her own son, visited the prison ship several times to
see "this woman," and evidently she carried the infant ashore.
The child was named Robert Townsend Junior and was reared
in secrecy, either by Mrs. Franklin or by a lady in New York
whose identity remains unknown. Townsend paid for his upbringing, but he did not dare visit his son during the war.

*   *   *

Patriot hopes revived during the spring with encouraging
news from South Carolina. Horatio Gates had resigned his commission in disgrace, and General Nathanael Greene, Washington's original choice for the command, had succeeded him in
December. The chubby-faced and affable little Rhode Islander
proved to be a master strategist, as aggressive and adroit as
Cornwallis was slow-moving and muddling. Greene knew that
his forces were outnumbered three to two, and concentrated on
a guerilla campaign. He placed half his troops under old General Daniel Morgan, rugged veteran of Quebec and Saratoga,
with instructions to harass the British outposts in the western

part of the state, but avoid a direct engagement if possible. Greene himself moved to northeastern Carolina to support the local patriots in their fight against the Loyalists.

Dan Morgan retreated skillfully before Banastre Tarleton's pursuing infantry until his patience wore out at being chased by "a damned Britisher." On January 16th, learning that Tarleton was only a day's march away, Morgan decided to make his stand in a cattle pasture called the Cowpens. His crack Virginia riflemen in their fringed white hunting shirts were stationed on the rise of a hill, and General Dan, like a crusty old bear, growled a single order: "Look for the epaulets." He lured Tarleton into a headlong attack by pulling back his militia, and then surrounded the British legion and cut them to pieces with rifles and bayonets and sabers. Tarleton lost 900 killed and wounded to Morgan's total loss of 72, and Cornwallis confessed to Lord Rawdon: "The affair almost broke my heart."

The portly Earl was in for further heartbreak. Having sacrificed his light troops at the Cowpens, he adopted the desperate expedient of stripping his army for action by destroying all the tents, wagons, rum casks, and provisions save what the men could carry on their backs. Greene, still outnumbered, fought a rear-guard action which Alexander Hamilton called "a masterpiece of military skill and exertion," falling back in orderly ranks to the swollen and yellow Dan River and taking all the boats with him to the far side. For a month he postponed the engagement which Cornwallis sought, while the Whig countrymen rallied behind him and the panic-stricken Tory volunteers deserted Cornwallis in droves.

At last his forces exceeded those of the British, and on March 14th he faced Cornwallis at Guilford Courthouse. Adopting Morgan's tactics, Greene placed his raw Carolina militia in the center of the line, and put his picked troops behind them with orders to "shoot down the first man that runs." Light Horse Harry Lee's green-coated dragoons shattered the enemy with deadly marksmanship, and Cornwallis's horse was shot out from under him, tumbling the indignant nobleman into a briar thicket. After Cornwallis had lost over a fourth of his army, including his finest officers, Greene sensed the proper moment to withdraw and maneuvered a brilliant retreat. Cornwallis sent a boastful dispatch to London, claiming a victory for having driven the Americans from the field, and Charles James Fox commented caustically in Parliament: "Another such victory would destroy the British army."

Cornwallis had come privately to the reluctant conclusion that in some mysterious manner he was being outgeneraled, and in April he quit the soil of the Carolinas forever, and headed for the coast of Virginia. "I cannot help expressing my wishes that the Chesapeak may become the seat of war," he wrote Sir Henry Clinton, "even (if necessary) at the expense of abandoning New-York; untill Virginia is in a manner subdued, our hold of the Carolinas must be difficult, if not precarious."

Instead of following Cornwallis, Greene made the bold command decision to regain South Carolina and Georgia and bring them once more under patriot control. One by one the southern forts fell to Lee's dragoons, and Cornwallis fumed in frustration as he saw all his work of the past year undone. At the same time young Francis Marion, the dreaded "Swamp Fox," embarked on a systematic campaign of terror, plundering the Loyalist inhabitants and, like a Carolina Robin Hood, giving the spoils to the poor. His band of no more than a hundred men, mounted on swift horses stolen from the countryside, would strike without warning and then melt away silently into the cypress swamps, leaving a Tory settlement in ashes or the bodies of a scouting party heaped beside the road, stripped of clothes and weapons.

It was civil war, brutal and merciless. The British charged the patriot partisans with slaughtering troops who had surrendered, and claimed that "the houses of desolate widows have been laid waste, and innocent and neutral persons murdered."

The patriots in turn accused their Tory neighbors of hanging paroled militiamen and perpetrating inhuman atrocities against the aged and harmless. The fact is that both sides were guilty. Fourteen-year-old Andrew Jackson, who fought in the patriot ranks and was captured at Sands House, admitted frankly: "In the long run, I am afraid the Whigs did not lose many points in the game of hanging, shooting and flogging. They had great provocation, but upon calm reflection I feel bound to say that they took full advantage of it." The future President of the United States had a personal taste of the savage treatment shown to prisoners. All his life he bore the scars of saber wounds inflicted by a British lieutenant when young Jackson refused to clean his jack boots.

As the tide turned against Cornwallis, Rivington tried to bolster the spirits of his Tory readers by filling his *Gazette* with mythical accounts of British victories and American reverses. In addition to his slanted news items, he published forged letters, scandalous attacks on patriot leaders, and such outright lies as the report that Colonel Ethan Allen and his troops had deserted the army and claimed Vermont for George III. When he ran out of falsehoods to cheer his audience, he resorted to satiric verse mocking the rebels:

> *The Devil loves liberty, and so do the Congress,*
> *The Devil is a Deceiver, and so are the Congress,*
> *The Devil loves Rebellion, and so do the Congress,*
> *As the Devil is in Hell; where will be the Congress?*

Even Rivington's forced optimism could not keep the New York Loyalists from realizing that Britain's campaign in the South had run into serious trouble; and they turned their accusing eyes on Sir Henry Clinton. Why was he sitting idle on Manhattan Island with a disciplined army half again as large as that of Washington? Why did he not attack the rebel forces, if only to relieve some of the pressure on Cornwallis? Why did he refuse to send support to his beleaguered colleague in Virginia, and prevent another catastrophe such as had overtaken Burgoyne? Was he overcautious, or incompetent, or perhaps, as some of his critics hinted, anxious to "prolong the war" for personal profit?

General Clinton sought to justify his inactivity on the grounds that he lacked sufficient troops. "To possess territory demands garrisons," he explained to Germain in London. "If it has required 6000 to hold Carolina, where nature has traced out a defensible boundary . . . surely my Lord, I cannot hope with a field army of 6000 men first to subdue and then to cover and protect the neighboring populous tracts . . . I become every day more sensible of the utter impossibility of prosecuting the war in this country without reenforcements." He had another reason for remaining in New York, though he did not mention it to Germain. For a long time, he had suspected Cornwallis of conniving to supersede him as supreme commander. If he withdrew his garrison to aid his archrival, Washington might seize the opportunity to capture the city, and Sir Henry's career would end in disgrace.

Washington was as anxious as the Loyalists to know whether Clinton would sail south to assist Cornwallis's hard-pressed army, and he wrote Tallmadge to request "the C——s, of whose fidelity and ability I entertain a high opinion," to supply information. The Commander-in-Chief stated his needs explicitly. "At present I am anxious to know (for the reports have been very numerous vague and uncertain) whether another embarkation is preparing, and if so to what amount, and where destined. What the present force of the Enemy is; particularly on Long Island, in New York and at King's Bridge . . . indeed what the situation, prospect, and designs of the enemy are, so far as they can be penetrated into."

The British intelligence net had been drawing tighter around the Manhattan spies, and the Culpers were unwilling to expose themselves. Robert Townsend flatly refused to put any further information on paper, lest the letter be intercepted and his handwriting recognized, and Woodhull warned Tallmadge that "the enemy have lately been made to believe that a line of intelligence is supported here [New York]. They are jealous of every person that they may see from this part." His next trip to the city bore out his fears. "The enemy have got some wind of me," Culper Senior wrote in terror, "for when passing Brooklyn Ferry was strictly examined and told some vilian supported a correspondence from this place. I do assure you am greatly alarmed, and shall not think it safe for me to go to New York very soon."

Tallmadge met the emergency by recruiting a new agent who could visit New York without arousing suspicion. On May 2nd, he sent Washington a full report of British activities on Manhattan with a covering note to the General: "The Author of the letter signed S. G. is a Gentleman of my acquaintance & capable from his own knowledge & opportunities with which he is particularly favored, of giving information to be depended on. I had an interview with him when last on L. I. I proposed to him to assist us in the way of intelligence. I have hopes of his undertaking . . . I have also enclosed a Rough Draught of the Enemies Works at Brooklyn Ferry, taken by S. G. on the Spot."

S. G. were the reversed initials of George Smith, a lineal descendant of the original patentee of Smithtown, Long Island. Smith had served as a second lieutenant in Captain Daniel Roe's Suffolk County company, along with Brewster and Joshua Davis, and participated in several whaleboat raids from Connecticut, including Tallmadge's attack on Fort St. George. In the summer of 1780 his father died, and he received permission as a "Reffugee Resident of Stratford" to return to Smithtown to settle the estate. Since his permit allowed him to move freely around the Island and in and out of New York, he became an invaluable addition to the Culper Ring. His correspondence was

interrupted only once, late in 1781, when Tallmadge reported
to the General that S. G. had journeyed to Manhattan "to make
discoveries on the banks of the North River near Fort Washington . . . As he was returning from N.Y. unfortunately for us
he was taken up on suspicion of being a spy, and tho' no papers
were found on him which could lead to a discovery, he is still detained. Another person who was very friendly was confined at
the same time."

George Smith did not remain a prisoner for long. Less than
a week after he was apprehended, he wrote Tallmadge from
New York: "I have not time to give you the particulars of the
trial . . . let it suffice to say that we were acquited by the court
with honour, while our accusers have the mortification of lying
in provost." His harrowing experience failed to deter him from
adding a detailed account of Clinton's troops who had "come to
Long Island and are cantooned from Brookline to Increase
Carpenter's house, two miles to the eastward of Jamaica."

*   *   *

On the Fourth of July, Washington's army appeared suddenly at Dobb's Ferry, only twelve miles from Manhattan Island. The following morning a rebel scouting party was spotted
on the heights above King's Bridge. Two days later Rochambeau and six thousand French troops, very dashing in their
white uniform coats with pink or green or blue lapels and yellow
leggins, completed their march from Newport to join forces
with the Americans in a line that extended from the Hudson
to the Bronx River.

New York was in a ferment of apprehension. British spies
had brought news that another French fleet under Admiral de
Grasse was about to weigh anchor in the West Indies, bound for
the Colonies, and General Clinton expected momentarily to
see his harbor blockaded and his waterfront raked with cannon
fire. Deceived by an intercepted letter from Washington, which

the American commander cunningly contrived to have captured, Clinton was convinced that the combined armies and fleet were planning an immediate assault on Manhattan; and in his panic he ordered Lord Cornwallis to send back part of his forces from Virginia to aid in the defense of the threatened city. "I think we have already effected one part of the plan of the campaign," Washington confided to Lafayette, whose troops were chivvying Cornwallis like an elusive gadfly, "that is, giving a substantial relief to the southern States, by obliging the enemy to recall a considerable part of their force from thence."

For seven nerve-wracking weeks, a series of American feints kept Clinton paralyzed with fear. General Lincoln was sent forward to feel out the British garrison at King's Bridge, and retired after a brisk skirmish. On July 22nd, five thousand Continental and French troops assembled on Harlem Heights, their bayonets glinting in the morning sun, while Washington and Rochambeau and a corps of engineers calmly reconnoitered the enemy works on the northern rim of the island. Later that day the two commanding generals visited Throg's Neck, ignoring a few harmless salvos from British vessels anchored offshore, and that night they enjoyed a leisurely dinner at the Van Cortlandt Mansion, a mile above King's Bridge. "Nothing could have been more alarming as well as mortifying than my situation at the present crisis," Clinton complained to Lord George Germain. "The enemy's parading army on the heights in my front for two days and no possibility of any stirring against it, as I had not an armed vessel to cover either of my flanks."

Sir Henry was even more alarmed and mortified early in August when Washington and a group of French generals crossed the Hudson and traveled down the New Jersey side of the river, clearly visible to the enemy on the opposite shore, and inspected the whole length of Manhattan. The General was mounted on a fine blooded hunter, presented to him by the State of Virginia, which he had personally trained to jump barriers in

a fox chase, and the ease with which he cantered over the rough
terrain of the Palisades was admired by the French noblemen
in his party. The Marquis de Chastellux recalled that he "rode
very fast, without rising in his stirrup, bearing on the bridle, or
suffering his horse to run as if wild." Abbé de Robine, Rochambeau's army chaplain, described him with Gallic grandiloquence
as "that most singular man — the soul and support of one of the
greatest revolutions that has ever happened, or can happen . . .
In these extensive states they consider him in the light of a
beneficent God, dispensing peace and happiness around him.
Old men, women and children, press about him when he accidentally passes along, and think themselves happy, once in their
lives, to have seen him . . . The Americans, that cool and se-
date people, are roused, animated, and inflamed at the very
mention of his name."

It was the first time that Washington had seen New York
since the disastrous Battle of Manhattan, and he gazed with
silent emotion at the half-ruined city, devastated by five years
of war. "The island is totally stripped of trees," he recorded in
his journal, "but low bushes, apparently as high as a man's
waist, appear in places which were covered with wood in the
year 1776." He swept his spyglass slowly over the enemy fortifications along the river, the flat wasteland of Canvas Town, the
black skeleton that had been Trinity Church, the British colors
flying over the Battery; and he wondered when he would
set foot again on Manhattan, at the head of a liberating army,
and raise the American flag in place of the Union Jack.

On August 14th a message from the West Indies was delivered to Washington, forwarded by Admiral de Barras who
commanded the French warships lying at Newport. "Received
dispatches from the Count de Barras," he entered in his journal,
"announcing the intended departure of the Count de Grasse with
between 25 & 29 Sail of the line & 3200 land Troops on the
3rd Instant for Chesapeake Bay . . . Matters now having come

to a crisis, I was obliged to give up all idea of attacking New York; & instead thereof to remove the French troops & a detachment from the American army to the Head of Elk, to be transported to Virginia for the purpose of Cooperating with the force from the West Indies."

Washington was quick to grasp this means of bringing the southern campaign to a triumphant climax. Exhausted by chasing Lafayette's smaller army for two hundred miles around Virginia, the puffing Lord Cornwallis had dug in at Yorktown to catch his breath. With De Grasse's fleet blockading the peninsula by sea, and Washington and Rochambeau joining forces with Lafayette and the new French troops brought by the Admiral to invest Yorktown and cut off any retreat by land, His Lordship's doom would be sealed.

The transfer of the Continental Army from the Hudson to Virginia had to be kept secret as long as possible, Washington realized, to avoid alerting Clinton who might dispatch reinforcements to Cornwallis or send his British fleet scurrying south to waylay De Grasse before he reached the Chesapeake. Such a massive troop movement to the southward was bound to be observed by Tory spies; but for a little precious time it could be made to appear that the allied armies were marching through New Jersey in order to attack New York by way of Staten Island.

General Washington, who had already shown himself a master at intrigue, embarked on the greatest deception of his career. In an elaborate effort to hoodwink Sir Henry, the armies halted in New Jersey and began laying out an apparently permanent camp, including huts and artillery parks and a field bakery with four ovens at Chatham. To add to the illusion, French troops moved along the Palisades, their white uniforms clearly visible to British observers in New York, and a flotilla of small boats assembled in the rocky recesses along the Jersey shore to suggest an amphibious assault.

The Virginia fox-hunter had learned other tricks from the fox. An express with specifications for the new camp passed so close to the British lines that he was captured, and the plans were brought promptly to Clinton. As an added insurance, the wily American commander arranged to have a talk with "an old inhabitant of New York" who was known to be spying for the British, and asked the Tory agent a number of naïve questions about the landing beaches on Staten Island and the terrain around Sandy Hook, explaining innocently that he was "fond of knowing the Situation of different parts of the Country." He warned the spy "by no means to lisp a Word of what had passed between them" and, to make his fabrication still more convincing, started an American regiment down the road to Sandy Hook under his very eyes. The British agent, bursting with false information, was at Clinton's headquarters that same night.

Even the marching armies were kept in the dark about their objective, and fictitious communications were circulated to deceive not only Clinton's informers but the Continental troops as well. "Our situation reminds me of some theatrical exhibition," wrote Washington's surgeon, Colonel James Thacher, "where the interest and expectations of the spectators are continually increasing, and where curiosity is wrought to the highest pitch." British spies duly reported that French and American forces were progressing through New Jersey, keeping far enough west to escape direct observation by enemy patrols, but their destination remained a mystery. A perceptive Hessian colonel notified Clinton that depots of food and forage had been established in the southern part of the state, and that a French officer had sent his American mistress to Trenton; but Sir Henry was still positive that his sly opponent would double back on his tracks to Sandy Hook. Not until the armies had crossed the Delaware did Clinton realize how completely he had been duped.

Washington confessed his deception in a letter written from

Mount Vernon five years after the war was over: "It was determined by me, nearly twelve months before hand, at all hazards, to give out, and cause it to be believed by the highest military as well as civil officers, that New York was the destined place of attack, for the important purpose . . . of rendering the enemy less well prepared elsewhere. It never was in contemplation to attack New York, unless the Garrison should first have been so far degarnished to carry on the southern operations as to render our success in the siege of that place as infallible as any future military event can ever be made . . . That much trouble was taken and finesse used to misguide and bewilder Sir Henry Clinton, in regard to the real object, by fictitious communications, as well as by making a deceptive provision of ovens, forage, and boats in the neighborhood is certain: Nor were less pains taken to deceive our own army; for I had always conceived, where the imposition does not completely take place at home, it would never sufficiently succeed abroad." He added enigmatically: "The knowledge of innumerable things, of a more delicate and secret nature, is confined to the perishable remembrance of some few of the present generation."

Clinton's lack of initiative and perception was bitterly resented by the New York Loyalists. Judge Thomas Jones, never one to mince words, denounced "the stupidity, the ignorance, the irresolution, and the indecision of the Commander-in-Chief, Sir Henry Clinton." His superior forces had failed to attack when the French and Americans were lined up like sitting ducks at King's Bridge. He had allowed the Continental Army to march south through New Jersey without making the slightest effort to impede its progress. Benjamin Franklin's Tory son William observed tartly: "We have only to lament that we have not penetration enough to fathom the policy of his deep laid schemes. For deep laid they must be because unintelligible."

General Benedict Arnold was among the most scathing in his

criticism of the British commander. He was still galled by the fact that Clinton had sent two officers with him to Virginia, with secret orders to put him under arrest "if they suspected him of any sinister intent," and then had recalled him peremptorily in June, leaving the command with Cornwallis. Arnold had returned to New York with less prize money than he had expected, frustrated and vindictive. To pacify the American traitor, Sir Henry acceded to his request to lead an expedition against New London on what proved to be the most wanton and needless raid of the war.

Arnold's announced purpose was to punish rebel privateers who were bringing their booty to New London for sale; but his real object was to vent his spleen on his countrymen by plundering and destroying the Connecticut seaport town, only fourteen miles from his birthplace. With a considerable fleet and some two thousand marine and land troops, Arnold sailed from New York on September 5th and entered New London harbor the following morning. Fort Griswold, on the west side of the bay, and Fort Trumbull, a short distance up the Thames River, were stormed and quickly taken. Colonel William Ledyard, after defending Fort Griswold for forty minutes, surrendered his sword to a British major, who thrust it through his body. Seventy-three men of the small garrison were likewise slain in cold blood after the colors were struck, and thirty more were left critically wounded. Arnold pillaged both New London and Groton and set them afire, and as the twin columns of smoke mingled over the ruins he sailed back to New York with his spoils.

It was Arnold's final appearance on the American stage, and unwittingly he had aided the patriot cause which he hated. His futile expedition had tied up a number of ships-of-war and spare troops which Clinton might have sent south to harass Washington. At the very moment that New London was in flames, the Continental Army reached the Head of Elk in

Maryland, on the last leg of their unopposed march to Yorktown.

*   *   *

The New York Loyalists were beginning to see the handwriting on the wall, and even Jemmy Rivington's false reports in
the *Gazette* could not cheer them. Rivington himself admitted
that the period was "the most critical era of the war." The city
was in an economic depression, and his once profitable book-
publishing business had dwindled to eight titles in a year. He
was using inferior paper because the mill on Long Island could
no longer supply him with proper stock. A printer's strike had
forced him to increase the wages of his help. Early in 1781 he
had to abandon his subscription policy and hawk his newspaper
on street corners, since he could not afford to pay for deliveries.
As his former sources of income faded, he turned more and more
to espionage as a means of meeting his debts.

There is no way of determining the exact moment that Rivington started to peddle British secrets to the Americans; but it
could have been as early as 1779 when he opened his Coffee
Shop with Robert Townsend as a silent partner. His position as
King's Printer and an arch-Tory provided him with perfect
cover. The British never realized his duplicity, though some of
his contemporaries considered him quite capable of double-
dealing. The Reverend Ashbel Green, later President of Princeton, called him "the greatest sycophant imaginable; very little
under the influence of any principle but self-interest, yet of
the most courteous manners to all with whom he had intercourse." Isaiah Thomas claimed in his *History of Printing* that
when the New York publisher saw the patriot cause brightening
"he deemed it prudent to conciliate the minds of the leading
American characters . . . and sent out of the city such communications as he knew would be interesting to the commanders
of the American army." Charles Thomson, Secretary of the Con-

tinental Congress, told his biographer years later that Rivington secretly gathered information for American military leaders,
and that "it was he who gave an intimation of an intention to
poison General Washington, whilst he was quartered on the
North River." Whatever his contribution, it is certain that
Jemmy Rivington's only motive was personal gain. He was the
complete opportunist, untroubled by loyalty or honor, two-
faced to the last.

In September of 1781, while Cornwallis was besieged at
Yorktown, he conducted his most lucrative transaction with
the Americans. Major Allan McLane, one of Washington's
trusted secret agents, had been sent early in July on a confidential mission to confer with Count De Grasse in the West
Indies and discuss the destination of the French fleet. Mc-
Lane had accompanied De Grasse to the Chesapeake, landing
in Virginia on August 26th, and was promptly dispatched by the
Board of War to do espionage work on Long Island. His instructions were to obtain information on the movements of the British
fleet, and, according to McLane's papers, to "correspond with
R of New York" in order to secure the Royal Navy's signal code.
An entry in McLane's journal, written in his own hand, states:
"After I returned in the fall was imployed by the board of war
to repair to Long Island to watch the motion of the Brittish fleet
and if possible obtain their Signals which I did threw the assistance of the noted Rivington. Joined the fleet Under the
Count D Grass with the Signals."

How the secret code was conveyed to McLane has never
been discovered; but Rivington, an expert bookbinder, had
several methods of smuggling information out of the city. He
could write his message on thin paper and slip it between the
boards of a bookcover, which were then glued together and
covered with leather. Even less elaborate, he could fasten the
message face down as the endpaper of a book, using a flour
paste which could be moistened and the paper peeled off with-

out damaging the handwriting. It would have been a simple matter for one of the Culper agents in Manhattan, such as George Smith, to carry this innocent-looking volume past the unsuspecting Hessian guards and deliver it to McLane at an appointed rendezvous.

British officers gathered in Rivington's Coffee Shop late in September were stunned at the news brought by a fast frigate from Yorktown. The Royal armada of nineteen ships of the line, which had sailed south on August 31st under Admirals Graves and Hood, had engaged De Grasse's fleet off Cape Henry, and in the exchange of broadsides ten British ships had been seriously damaged. The French seemed to possess an uncanny ability to outmaneuver Admiral Graves, the courier reported, almost as though they could decipher his coded signals. During the battle, Count de Barras had slipped unobserved into the Chesapeake with eight more ships-of-war brought down from Newport. Outnumbered and badly crippled, Admiral Graves's armada was limping back to New York with shattered spars and rigging, leaving Cornwallis to his fate.

Jemmy Rivington paused in the doorway of the Coffee Shop, clasping his lean delicate hands in simulated distress at the news. His blue eyes were veiled, and his face bore only the trace of a tight triangular smile.

*   *   *

General Cornwallis had blundered into a trap of his own choosing. He could have remained at Portsmouth, where the broad Elizabeth River gave him access to the sea, and the Dismal Swamp protected him against an assault by land. But Clinton had ordered him to establish a base on the Chesapeake "to give protection to battle ships," and Cornwallis had selected the worst possible situation, a narrow strip of land between two rivers called York Peninsula. When De Grasse's fleet blocked the mouths of both the James and York, and Lafayette's meager

force at his rear was augmented by 3200 fresh troops from the
West Indies, the jaws of the trap began to close.

Still Cornwallis might have crossed to the mainland and
escaped, had it not been for a spy named Private Charles Morgan who performed a feat as remarkable as that of Sergeant
Champe. Posing as a deserter from Lafayette's army, Morgan
successfully infiltrated the enemy camp, made his way to Cornwallis, and convinced the worried Earl that Lafayette had
enough boats to follow him across the James if the British attempted a retreat. Cornwallis remained behind his Yorktown
breastworks, still hoping that Clinton would send another
fleet to drive off De Grasse and evacuate him by sea, until the
armies of Washington and Rochambeau had sealed off the
neck of the peninsula from river to river. General Weedon of
Virginia exulted to Greene that "we have got him handsomely
in a pudding bag."

On September 14th Washington rode into Williamsburg
where, seven years before, he had proclaimed to the House of
Burgesses that "the crisis is arrived when we must assert our
rights." A salute of twenty-one cannon signaled his arrival, and
he was greeted effusively by General Lafayette. St. George
Tucker, who was only a few feet away, wrote that the Marquis
"absolutely kissed him from ear to ear more than twice, as well
as I can recollect, with as much ardour as ever an absent lover
kissed his mistress on his return." Washington established his
headquarters in the stately brick Wythe House, fronting on
the Palace Green, and waited for De Grasse's frigates to transport the remainder of the French army from Baltimore to the
port of debarkation above College Creek.

The siege of Yorktown was begun on Friday the 28th. "Having debarked all the Troops and their Baggage," Washington
recorded in his journal, "we commenced our march for the
Investiture of the Enemy at York . . . About noon the head
of each column arrived at its ground. The Line being formed

all the Troops — officers & men — lay upon their arms during the night." The Commander-in-Chief and his staff bivouacked on the ground in the open air, and an officer noted that Washington "slept under a mulberry-tree, the root serving for a pillow."

With less than half the manpower and only a third the guns of the combined French and American armies, Cornwallis realized that his situation was critical. His troops abandoned all their exterior works outside the town, which were promptly possessed by the allied armies. The besiegers formed a semi-circle around Yorktown, and set to work in great secrecy digging forward trenches only six hundred yards from the British redoubts. On the stormy night of October 5th the trenches were occupied, and a parallel nearly two miles long was completed three days later, under a constant bombardment of shot and shells from the aroused enemy. Batteries were erected, and on October 9th "his Excellency General Washington put the match to the first gun," Thacher wrote, "a furious discharge of cannon and mortars immediately followed, and Earl Cornwallis received his first Salutation."

Day after day the British commander scanned the ocean for the white sails of the relief expedition which Clinton had promised; but Admiral Graves's battered fleet was still under repair in New York, being fitted with new spars and masts. Sir Henry had assured Cornwallis that the armada would sail on October 5th, bringing five thousand troops to his rescue; but repairs went slowly, and Clinton wrote again to advise the harried Earl that he could not get under way before the 8th. Cornwallis warned that his situation had become desperate, and Clinton sent another dispatch stating that he really hoped to stand out to sea by the 12th. Cornwallis, resigned to the inevitable, replied quietly that his situation by now was "so precarious that I cannot recommend that the fleet and army should run great risque in endeavouring to save us."

For a week the bombardment continued unabated. Bursting shells sent showers of debris into the air, barricade walls toppled, the flames of burning Yorktown reddened the sky. Thomas Nelson, Governor of Virginia, directed the cannon fire at his own fine brick mansion, which he suspected was Cornwallis's headquarters, and it was leveled in an hour. Cornwallis withdrew his weary forces to the innermost fortification, defended by two strong redoubts on the British left. At eleven on the night of October 14th, the allied armies mounted an assault on the redoubts, with Lafayette's French chasseurs storming the work on the right, and Colonel Alexander Hamilton commanding the American battalion assigned to the left. A flare and six shells gave the signal to attack. Lafayette's chasseurs rushed through the abatis of felled trees and put up ladders against the sides of the first redoubt. Hamilton, placing one foot on the shoulder of a kneeling soldier, vaulted over the shell-torn parapet of the second, followed by his men. There were a few minutes of savage hand-to-hand fighting, with rifle butts swinging and bayonets slashing, and the enemy troops held up their hands in surrender. Both redoubts were taken, and the American loss was only nine men killed and twenty-five wounded.

Penned in the inner fort, his rations gone and his shells nearly expended, Cornwallis made a last desperate effort to escape. On the night of Tuesday the 16th, he tried to ferry his army across the York River; but a violent storm drove the boats downstream, some of them partly loaded with troops. Washington's cannonading resumed again at dawn, and Cornwallis knew that his crumbling works would be flattened in a few more hours. "We at that time could not fire a single gun," he reported later. At ten o'clock on Wednesday morning, the 17th — just four years after the surrender of Burgoyne at Saratoga — a redcoated drummer boy mounted the ruins of the British parapet and beat a parley.

On that same morning, after being delayed in New York

two more days by weather, Clinton finally dispatched Admiral Graves's armada to relieve Cornwallis. Five days later, near Cape Charles, a small British vessel intercepted the fleet, and its skipper informed them that he had escaped from Yorktown on the 16th and had not heard any firing since then. A little further down the coast, two more refugees in a canoe were overtaken and brought aboard. They gave the news of Cornwallis's surrender.

Early on Friday, the 19th of October, Washington sent the final articles of capitulation to Lord Cornwallis to be signed. His terms were just and generous: the British army was to surrender to the Americans, the navy to the French; officers were to retain their side arms and private property; soldiers would be kept in Virginia or Maryland or Pennsylvania, but Cornwallis would be permitted to return home on parole. The ceremony would take place that same afternoon. "The garrison of York will march out to a place to be appointed in front of the posts, at two o'clock precisely, with shouldered arms, colours cased, and drums beating a British or German march. They are then to ground their arms, and return to their encampments."

At noon of the 19th the allied armies were drawn up in a double line, extending more than a mile along the Hampton Road. The Commander-in-Chief sat on his fine courser at the front of the American column; General Rochambeau headed the French troops. Promptly at two o'clock the vanguard of the conquered army was seen approaching, their standards cased. "Every eye was prepared to gaze on Lord Cornwallis, the object of peculiar interest and solicitude," Colonel Thacher noted, "but he disappointed our anxious expectations; pretending indisposition, he made General O'Harra his substitute as the leader of his army . . . When it is considered that Lord Cornwallis has frequently appeared in splendid triumph at the head of his army, we conceive it incumbent on him cheerfully to participate in their misfortunes and degradations, however humiliating; but it is said that he gives himself up entirely to vexation and despair."

General O'Harra advanced between the two lines toward the American commander, followed by his troops in slow and solemn step. The British wore immaculate new uniforms furnished for the occasion, the Scots sported bright regimental tartans and kilts, the Hessians were in blue coats with crossed shoulder straps of yellow canvas. As they marched, the British band struck up the ironic strains of "The World Turned Upside Down," which Colonel Leslie's troops had sung in their retreat from Salem Bridge in 1775:

> *Goody Bull and her daughter together fell out.*
> *Both squabbled, and wrangled, and made a damned rout.*
> *But the cause of the quarrel remains to be told.*
> *Then lend me your ears, and a tale I'll unfold . . .*

Halting before General Washington, O'Harra removed his hat, apologized for Lord Cornwallis's inability to appear, and reached for the gold hilt of his sword. With intuitive courtesy, Washington pointed to Major General Lincoln, who had been obliged to surrender his own sword at Charleston a year ago. O'Harra offered the sword instead to Lincoln, who promptly handed it back. Amid a profound silence, the enemy troops marched to the Surrender Field, the command "Present arms! Lay down arms! Put off swords and cartridge belts!" was given, and one by one the men stacked their rifles and muskets on the mounting pile. The proud British army of over seven thousand elite wheeled and returned to their tents, now prisoners of war. As the Americans marched back to their own camp, their exuberant voices filled the autumn air with a popular new ballade, inspired by the Yorktown siege:

> *Cornwallis led a country dance,*
> *The like was never seen, sir.*

Much retrograde and much advance,
And all with General Greene, sir.

Now hand in hand they circle round
This ever-dancing pair, sir:
Their gentle movements soon confound
The earl as they draw near, sir.

His music soon forgets to play —
His feet can move no more, sir,
And all his bands now curse the day
They jig-ged to our shore, sir.

Official intelligence of the surrender of the British army at Yorktown reached London on a rainy Sunday in November, and was delivered to Lord George Germain at his home in Pall Mall. Jumping into a hackney coach, Germain and the Under Secretary of State drove at top speed to the residence of Lord North in Downing Street. The Prime Minister received the disastrous news, Germain said, "as he would have taken a ball in his breast." On the outcome of Cornwallis's expedition, Lord North knew, had hung the fate of the American contest, as well as his own stay in office and probably the duration of the Ministry. He brandished his arms and paced up and down the room "in the deepest consternation and distress."

"O God! it is all over," he exclaimed wildly, "it is all over!"

III

A Silent Adieu

LORD CORNWALLIS sailed for England aboard the *Robuste* on December 15, 1781, accompanied by Lieutenant Colonel Simcoe, now an invalid, and Brigadier General Benedict Arnold of the British army. Clinton had warned Arnold that he should not trust himself to anything but a King's ship, for rebel animosity toward him ran so high that they might attempt to overhaul him on the high seas. Animosity toward Sir Henry himself was no less high among the Tories, he admitted to Arnold with bitterness. Everyone blamed him for the Yorktown disaster, whereas in fact it was all the fault of the bumbling British Ministry which had failed to send him reinforcements and thwarted him at every turn. Arnold, traitor to the end, made notes of the General's incautious remarks, to be quoted later when he intrigued against Clinton in London.

Peggy Shippen Arnold did not sail on the same vessel with her notorious husband. Philadelphia gossip reported that she went "in a private ship, as more agreeable for her than a man-of-war . . . They gave for the cabin 300 guineas, and then took in what company they chose, chiefly military I believe. I do not hear of any females but her maid."

Other familiar figures made their exits from the stage as the Revolutionary drama entered its last act. Lord George Germain was ousted from the British cabinet immediately after Cornwallis's defeat. Lord North resigned a few months later, and the Marquis of Rockingham, a stalwart Whig, accepted the post on condition that there should be "no veto to the independence of America." Lafayette sailed home just before Christmas, and General Washington sent his "ardent vows" of an undying attachment and begged him to return in the spring. But France was beginning to stir with a revolution of her own, and Washington never saw his beloved Marquis again.

In May of 1782 Sir Henry Clinton was recalled to testify before Parliament, partly through Arnold's machinations, and Sir Guy Carleton succeeded him as Commander-in-Chief of His Majesty's forces in America and Commissioner for Peace. The departure of the dour Clinton was greeted with universal acclaim, and Governor Livingston of New Jersey observed that "as fertile as England is in the production of blockheads, I think they cannot easily send us a greater blunderbuss, unless, peradventure, it should please his Majesty himself to do us the honor of a visit."

In contrast to his predecessor, General Carleton was a humane and capable public servant, whose courteous manners and strong sculptured features were reminiscent of Washington himself. During the Seven Years' War, Carleton had fought beside many officers of the present Continental Army; and his able defense of Quebec against Montgomery and Arnold, and his subsequent adroit management of Canada, had won for him the respect not only of his superiors in London but also of his opponents in America. The Rockingham administration directed him to avoid further hostilities; to withdraw the British garrisons and their dependents from Savannah and Charleston and New York; and to employ "every circumstance which can tend to revive old affections or extinguish late jealousies." His first act was to arrange the release from a New York prison of Sir James Jay, brother of John Jay and inventor of the Sympathetic Stain used by the Culper Ring.

As the old faces faded, new ones arrived to take their place. Almost every prominent British naval commander including twenty-four-year-old Viscount Nelson, whose name was to become immortal at Trafalgar, found some excuse to drop anchor in New York Harbor and join in the glittering round of balls and assemblies and cotillions. The city was enjoying one last wild fling before the inevitable end of British occupation, and garrison officers and Loyalist civilians, like passengers on a sinking ship, kept up their courage with forced gaiety and hollow laughter. Local society was set all of a tizzy in the fall of 1781 when King George III, "in compliment to his American subjects," permitted his son, the future William IV, to sail to New York as a midshipman with Admiral Digby's fleet. It was the first visit of a Prince of Wales to America, and he was greeted rapturously by the swooning younger set. During the winter he tobogganed down the slope of Bayard's Mount and learned to skate on Collect Pond, with an admiral on each arm, and was barely rescued from drowning when the ice tactlessly gave way beneath his Royal presence.

He had a narrower escape the following spring. In March of 1782 a group of patriots under Colonel Matthias Ogden concocted a bold scheme, fully approved by General Washington, to kidnap both the sailor prince and the Admiral. "The spirit of enterprise, so conspicuous in your plan for surprising in their quarters and bringing off the Prince William Henry and Admiral Digby, merits applause," Washington wrote Ogden, "and you have my authority to make the attempt, in any manner, and at such time as your judgment shall direct." Loyalist spies became aware of the plot, and it was reluctantly abandoned.

Like everything else that Britain attempted in the war, Carleton's mission of reconciliation came too late. Events had moved beyond any possibility of compromise between Britain and the Colonies, and Sir Guy tried in vain to correspond with Washington on the subject of peace, or forward under a flag a proposal by the House of Commons for a joint commission to draw up a treaty. Washington, scrupulous about entangling himself in civil affairs, refused to discuss anything but military matters, and viewed Carleton's expressions of friendship with skepticism. These "delusive offers of Peace," he warned, might be merely a "fresh opiate" to drug his countrymen into stupor. On August 2, 1782, Carleton informed Washington that Thomas Grenville had been sent by His Majesty from London to Paris to discuss peace negotiations, with orders that "the independence of the thirteen Provinces should be proposed by him in the first instance, instead of making it a condition of a general treaty." Washington, always on his guard, was suspicious that these overtures might mask some new enemy design; and on August 10th he wrote Major Tallmadge from Newburgh: "I wish you without delay to open again, or at least to renew effectually, the channel of intelligence through the C.s. I know your correspondents have heretofore been well informed and that the only great difficulty has been in the circuitous route of communications."

Tallmadge made contact at once with George Smith. "Immediately repaired to Fairfield," he replied to the General on August 18th, "and effected an interview with S. G. to whom I communicated the purport of your Excellency's letter. At the same time I forwarded, by him, similar instructions to S. C. Senior and Junr. The absence of Captain Brewster on a short cruise to the eastward, may perhaps occasion some delay, but I cannot but believe that my correspondents will exert themselves on this occasion, as I have wrote pressingly on the subject." Tallmadge added that he had found still another agent to work with the Culper Ring. "From some intimations I have reason to believe that a certain Character, in great repute among the Refugees and very particularly intimate with Coll. Upham [former aide-de-camp to General Clinton] would be happy in an opportunity to render important services to the State and army. His character is by no means notorious, but very sagatious. I have ventured to write him on the subject of intelligence, and have great hopes from his services."

The name signed by this "sagatious" character, though it may not have been his own, was John Corke, and his correspondence was sent from "Near Croton, N.Y." Tallmadge described him in a later dispatch as "an officer in one of the Refugee corps, who is exceedingly intimate at hq." As a Tory officer, residing at Croton in the Neutral Ground, he could travel back and forth to the city without being challenged; and it is just possible that John Corke was the mysterious messenger who carried the Culper warning of Arnold's treachery by way of King's Bridge two years previously. A letter from him, dated September 19th, was delivered in person to Major Tallmadge in Westchester County, and bore good news for the weary American army:

> When I last saw my friend Col. Upham at N.Y. . . . he jumped from his chair in a great passion & swore by God that there was now no Alternative, but that the Independence of America would be unconditionally acknowledged, & that no Conditions would be insisted on for the Refugees.
>
> It is said at N.Y. that an Expedition is forming & by many Conjectured to be against the French Fleet at Boston or those at Portsmouth, a number of British Troops I saw embarking when I left the City, but the above mentioned Aide assured me that they were bound to the W. Indies or Halifax. For my own part, & from the above assurance, I have no expectations that any offensive operations will be undertaken by the British this Campaign. The above Gentleman, with whom I am most intimately connected, informed me that it is now under Consideration to send off all the B. troops to the W. Indies & to garrison the City till the Spring with the Jager & foreign Troops as well as Loyalists . . . It is a fact that a fleet is going to Charlestown to bring off that Garrison . . . Sir Guy says he thinks it not improbable that the next Packet may bring orders to leave the City.

A Fleet is getting ready to sail for the Bay of Fundy about the 1st of Oct. next, to transport a number of Refugees to that Quarter. The Aide above referred to informs me that he thinks it probable he shall go there himself with his Family. Indeed I never saw such general Distress & Dissatisfaction as is painted on the Countenance of every Tory at N.Y.

J.C.

John Corke's letter is almost the last legible document in the Culper correspondence. The secret agents were taking extra precautions, since General Carleton had issued firm orders that "any Persons being discovered to have written Information would be treated as Spies." Henceforth their intelligence was either oral, or written in Stain which has faded so badly that it can no longer be deciphered.

Caleb Brewster viewed the approaching end of hostilities with dark misgiving. Not only would life be dull without the excitement of battle but, if he could no longer take his whaleboat across the Sound to Conscience Bay, his bachelor days were numbered. Anne Lewis had been growing more and more insistent of late, settling her plump form on his lap and resting her head on his shoulder. "Cale, aren't we ever going to get married?"

"Now, Annie, 'course we are," Brewster would assure her, searching frantically for a means of escape. "Right after the war, dear."

"But the war's over now."

A low growl. "This war ain't over till I stop fighting."

It was with considerable relief that he was able to report to Tallmadge in November, after a reconnaissance trip to Long Island, that a detachment of six hundred British light horse and infantry had arrived at Huntington to establish a winter encampment. They felt themselves secure from rebel attack, due to the lateness of the season, and Brewster, eager for any excuse, urged Major Tallmadge to organize an expedition and beat up their quarters. In a personal interview with Washington at Newburgh, Tallmadge received permission to undertake the mission, but the General ordered him not to execute the raid until he named the precise time. "The fact was," Tallmadge explained in his *Memoir*, "Gen. Washington had planned an expedition down the North River. His intention was to have thrown a large detachment of his army below Fort Washington, while he moved with the main body to Fort Independence and Kingsbridge. The enemy thus placed between two fires, would have been forced to yield, while, with my detachment on Long Island, they would have found themselves attacked on all sides."

Tallmadge received his orders at last, naming the night of December 5th. "My detachment consisted of four companies of light infantry — chosen troops — and a body of dismounted dragoons, to mount the captured horses of the enemy," he wrote. "I had also a body of Connecticut levies attached to my command, amounting in all to about 700 men. On the evening of the 5th of December, 1782, the different detachments met (for the first time) in the vicinity of Stamford, from whence they moved to Shipan Point, where I had ordered the boats to assemble. Here, finding such preparations, the officers began to suspect that something pretty serious was going on.

"When the sun had set, the weather being severe, I ordered the whole detachment to parade on the shore, where our little fleet had assembled. As soon as the platoons were assigned to each boat, they began to embark, but before one-half of the troops had entered the boats, I discovered a squall of wind rising from the West, accompanied by rain, which, from its violence, made it necessary to disembark the troops. The violence of the wind and rain, mixed with snow, continued through the night, so that we were obliged to draw up our boats and turn them over to protect the troops from the pelting storm. The next morning the rain had ceased, but the face of the Sound was a perfect foam, so that no boat could have kept above water for five minutes."

The blow continued all that second day and night, and on the following morning Tallmadge was informed that three boats from Long Island had taken refuge on one of the Norwalk islands, a few miles to the eastward, stormbound like themselves. "The wind and sea abating somewhat of their violence, and the enemy's boats appearing on the Sound returning to Long Island," his *Memoir* relates, "I ordered six of my best boats (with sails) to be manned, and Capt Brewster, an experienced sailor, was directed to look up the enemy, and if possible to capture them. The boats put off from the shore, and although their course was before the wind, three of them were obliged to turn back. The enemy seeing our boats bearing down upon them, pressed all sail as well as oars, and steered for Long Island.

"Capt. Brewster steered his course so judiciously, that before they had reached the middle of the Sound (being here about 12 miles wide) he fell in with two of their heaviest boats, when they engaged with great fury. On the first fire, every man in one of the enemy's boats fell, being either killed or wounded. Capt. Brewster received a ball in his breast, which passed through his body. He, however, captured the two boats, and one escaped."

Brewster managed to keep his injury secret from the rest of the crew until the enemy surrendered, and then collapsed from loss of blood and was carried unconscious back to Fairfield. When he opened his eyes, he was lying in bed in the Lewis home, and Annie was hovering over him like a ministering angel. He closed his eyes again, resigned to the inevitable.

The third enemy boat had reached Huntington Bay in safety, and Tallmadge knew that its crew would alert the British garrison. He called off the expedition, "more severely mortified and chagrined than I had ever been in my life." His spirits rose a little when he learned that Washington's surprise attack on New York had likewise been abandoned, some British ships having anchored above Fort Washington the previous evening. As it turned out, Tallmadge noted, their joint failure was all for the best. "When these two attempts were to have been made, in which doubtless many lives would have been lost, the preliminary articles of peace had been actually signed," on November 30, 1782.

*   *   *

Just as hostilities had begun a year before war was actually declared, so the war continued a year after the provisional agreement for peace was accepted. During the spring and summer of 1783 the negotiations in Paris dragged on with agonizing slowness. Benjamin Franklin and John Adams, joined in April by John Jay who arrived from Madrid, haggled endlessly with the British envoys, and insisted that America be recognized as a separate and equal nation. "Since we have assumed a place in the political system of the world," Jay argued, "let us move like a primary and not a secondary planet." Washington wrote General Greene: "Dr. Franklin's laconic description of the temper of the British nation seems most apt. 'They are,' says he, 'unable to carry on the war, and too proud to make peace.' "

Early in April the British packet *Prince William Henry* from Falmouth brought to New York a Royal proclamation declaring an end of hostilities. It was read aloud by Mayor David Mathews from the balcony of City Hall, and Carleton promptly notified Washington, who informed the Congress. On the 19th of April in 1775 the embattled farmers on Lexington Common had fired the first shot of the war. On the 19th of April in 1783, by another of the weird coincidences of the Revolution, Congress proclaimed an armistice with the ringing of the Liberty Bell in the belfry of the State House in Philadelphia.

The soldiers of the Continental Army, poorly fed and still unpaid, found it hard to distinguish between an armistice and a definite treaty of peace; and Washington foresaw the real danger of another mutiny if they were held in the ranks. He met the crisis by obtaining from Congress the discretionary power to grant furloughs, with the understanding that the term of service would not expire until the treaty was actually signed. All that summer men straggled back in small units to their farms and firesides, seeking to resume their former means of livelihood after eight long years.

Even more forlorn was the situation of the prisoners-of-war who were released under the armistice. British and Hessian troops, interned in Philadelphia and the South, were permitted and even urged to settle among their late enemies, and great numbers of them made their permanent homes in the land they had failed to conquer. But no provision was made for the American prisoners set free from the crowded cells of Bridewell and the Provost and the hulks in Wallabout Bay. Half dead from disease and privation, without funds or the ability to work, they wandered through the streets of Manhattan like emaciated ghosts, begging on the street corners of the busy impersonal city at which they had gazed with such longing from the decks of their floating jails. One Elijah Fisher, discharged on April 9th from the "old Jarsey prison-ship," set down his sentiments after a lonely walk in New York:

"I com down by the markett and sits Down all alone, al- most Descouraged, and begun to think over how that I had ben in the army, what ill success I had met with there and allso how I was ronged by them I worked for at home, and lost all last winter, and now that I could not get into any besness and no home, which you may well think how I felt; but then Come into my mind that there were thousands in worse circumstances than I was, and that I had done nothing to reflect on myself, and I resolved to do my endever and leave the avent to Prove- dance, and after that I felt as contented as need be."

Caleb Brewster was having no part of an armistice. His wound had begun to heal under Annie's tender care, his strength was gradually coming back, and by some miracle, during the long recuperation, he had managed to stay single. His partner Joshua Davis had married Abigail Redfield in January of 1783; but Brewster was resolved not to take the fatal plunge as long as there was an enemy left to fight. Hostile privateers still plied the waters of the Sound, plundering merchant shipping and carrying on what was known as the "London Trade," and the sloop-of-war *Fox*, commanded by Captain Johnson, had attacked several unarmed vessels in full sight of Fairfield. One spring morning Annie found her patient seated on the edge of his bed, struggling feebly to pull on his seaboots. "Where on earth do you think you're going?"

Brewster rose with an effort. "They just sighted the *Fox* off Stratford Point," he said, clinging to the bedpost to steady himself. "I'm taking after her."

"Now, Cale, you know you're too weak."

"There's a war on, Annie," Brewster said sternly, and stumbled out the door.

Some members of his old whaleboat crew were waiting for him on the waterfront, and they boarded a small sloop and hoisted sail in pursuit. As they drew near, the enemy craft opened fire with her swivel guns, ripping jagged holes in their rigging and sending a shot through the mast. Brewster held on to the helm and brought his crippled sloop alongside, and leapt onto the deck of the *Fox*, followed by his crew with fixed bayonets. Captain Johnson and two sailors were killed and several others wounded, and in less than two minutes the *Fox* surrendered. Not a man of Brewster's detachment was hurt, and they brought the prize into Fairfield harbor in triumph. It was virtually the last engagement of the Revolution.

The exertion was too much for Caleb Brewster. A couple of his crewmen helped him back to the Lewis house, white-faced and gasping for breath, and Anne pulled off his seaboots and rolled him into bed. Brewster's lips moved, and she bent her head to hear.

"War's over," he murmured. "I'm all done fighting." A long silence. "Guess you and me might's well get spliced, Annie."

*   *   *

The April proclamation announcing the end of hostilities, read from the City Hall balcony, fell like a stone on the Loyalists assembled in Wall Street below. "Despair was written on every countenance," the *Pennsylvania Packet* reported, "nothing but groans and hisses prevailed, attended by bitter reproaches and curses upon their king for having deserted them." They had risked their lives and fortunes for the British cause, relying on repeated assurances by His Majesty that he would never abandon them, and this was their reward. However sincere their reasons for opposing independence, they would be the object of blind and unremitting patriot vengeance. Their property would be confiscated, their businesses ruined, their very lives threatened by their own countrymen. "We have made them our enemies," Beverly Robinson protested to Clinton in London, "by adhering to and endeavoring to support the government of England, for which we are slighted and cast off as beggars."

Already the Loyalists were having a taste of patriot temper. As the British forces were withdrawn from the interior after the armistice, a mob in Woodbridge, New Jersey, surrounded a Tory named Cavalier Jouett, and with sticks and whips gave him a "Continental jacket." In Goshen, New York, another King's man was seized by his Whig neighbors who shaved off his hair and eyebrows with a pocketknife, tarred and feathered him, placed a sheepskin foolscap on his head, and paraded him through town for four hours with a cowbell around his neck and a sign on his forehead reading: "Look ye Tory crew and see what George your king can do." Nor did the proposed peace terms hold out any hope of restitution. The American commissioners in Paris declared unanimously that indemnification of the hated Loyalists was immoral and impossible, and Benjamin Franklin, who had disowned his Tory son William, flatly refused to "receive again into our bosom those who have been our bitterest enemies, and restore their properties who have destroyed ours; and this while the wounds they have given us are still bleeding."

There was no choice but self-exile. Loyalists with sufficient means transported their families to London or Bristol or Glasgow. Others less fortunate sought refuge in the barren and frozen hills around the Bay of Fundy where, a quarter of a century before, the banished Acadians had taken asylum. Thousands of émigrés settled in the unappropriated lands of eastern Canada, or sailed to the Bahamas and the West Indies, or traveled by land to Montreal and west along the St. Lawrence to the Canadian lake country where they founded a settlement called Toronto.

New York Harbor bristled with masts over the summer as the Tory exodus swelled to a stampede. Fleets of vessels, British and American alike, arrived from every Atlantic port as well as the West Indies and England to aid in the mass evacuation. British and Hessian troops who were being sent home further strained the transportation facilities, and private shipowners made fortunes overnight by charging exorbitant prices. Rivington's *Gazette* reported that some nine thousand refugees left New York in the week after the armistice was announced. On a single day in June, three thousand more embarked on fourteen transports. On August 16th, 5339 names were listed as outbound passengers, and a month later a record fleet sailed through the Narrows one morning with over eight thousand aboard. Hardly a day passed without the departure of another loaded brig or schooner or sloop, its afterdeck crammed with native-born Americans taking a last look at their homeland. An estimated twenty-nine thousand expatriates had landed in Nova Scotia by fall; and the refugee city of Port Roseway mushroomed in a few months to a population of nine thousand, exclusive of adjoining Black Town with "about 1200 free blacks" who refused to return to slavery under their American owners and instead looked to England for liberty.

The city was one vast auction ground. Every thoroughfare was heaped with personal possessions put up for forced sale by the refugees, or surplus stores of cattle and wagons and firewood which the army commissaries had to dispose of before their regiments were evacuated. Mountainous piles of furniture, bedding, mirrors, kitchen utensils, pictures, books, and clothing blocked the sidewalks, and the *Gazette* was filled with daily notices of "bargains for hard money." Adding to the general confusion, thousands of patriots swarmed into New York from the surrounding countryside, eager to recoup the losses they had suffered when they fled the city seven years before. Tory families were evicted from their homes by the former owners, and forced to sleep on the wharves while awaiting departure. Rebel resentment was so violent that the Loyalists armed themselves with spear canes when they walked the streets, and British sentries were posted "almost every hundred yards" to arrest anyone who broke the yet undeclared peace.

The humane Sir Guy Carleton did his best to bring order out of chaos. Working with American authorities, he appointed a joint commission to supervise all embarkations and make sure that no stolen goods were taken aboard, and also issued a stern proclamation to his army that every officer and man must meet his obligations before leaving the city. On May 6th, as an added gesture of cooperation, General Carleton traveled up the Hudson to Dobb's Ferry for an unprecedented wartime conference with the American Commander-in-Chief. Washington met the British party on the west shore of the river, and rode personally with Carleton in a chariot to the De Wint house in Tappan, less than a mile from the hill where André was hanged. The two chiefs of staff discussed arrangements for the final evacuation of New York when the Definitive Treaty was signed, and Carleton confessed that he was "no longer able to discern the object we contend for." After an amiable conference, Washington "pulled out his watch and observing that it was near dinner time, offered wine and bitters."

They sat down to an elegant repast catered by Sam Fraunces, proprietor of Fraunces' Tavern on Pearl Street, at a modest cost of £500. Two days later, Carleton returned the courtesy with a second conference and equally sumptuous collation aboard his frigate *Perseverance*. As the American general departed, the frigate fired seventeen guns "in honor of Washington's exalted rank. This was the first complimentary salute fired by Great Britain in honor of an officer of the United States, and virtually the first salute to the nation."

Convinced at last that the British were sincere, Washington relaxed his secret surveillance of the enemy, and intelligence reports from the Culper agents dwindled during the spring and by midsummer ceased altogether. The final message from Samuel Culper Senior, dated July 5th, was an apologetic statement of expenses. "I am unable to particularize dates," Abraham Woodhull explained, "for I kept only the most simple account that I possibly could, for fear it should betray me, but I trust it is a just one — and do assure you I have been as frugal as possibly could. I desire you would explain to the Genl. the circumstances that attended this lengthy correspondence that he may be satisfied we have not been extravagant. And in the Interum wishing you health and prosperity I remain your ever mindful and Humble Servant, Saml. Culper."

*   *   *

The Definitive Treaty of Peace between Great Britain and the United States was signed in Paris on September 3, 1783. An

unfinished study in oils by Benjamin West, successor to Sir
Joshua Reynolds as president of the British Academy, shows
the American commissioners at the historic moment: the benign
Benjamin Franklin, seventy-seven years of age, eyes twinkling
behind octagonal spectacles; John Adams, the poised aristocrat;
Henry Laurens, wan and sickly after his long imprisonment
in the Tower of London; and John Jay, forty years younger
than Franklin, whose diplomacy and iron will were credited by
his associates with securing the terms that America desired. Dr.
Franklin hailed the termination of the bloody struggle with a
fervid hope that "mankind will at length, as they call themselves reasonable creatures, have reason and sense enough to
settle their differences without cutting throats; for, in my opinion, there never was a good war or a bad peace."

A vast change had taken place in New York during the false
dawn between the armistice and the actual end of the Revolution. The cultured and wealthy bluebloods, the patrician first
families of the old Loyalist city, had been replaced by a cos-
mopolitan population of Irish and Germans and Scotch, plain
and hard-working and democratic. Signs of enemy occupation
were fast disappearing. Churches which had been commandeered
for hospitals or prisons, and residences taken over for army
barracks, were being cleaned and restored to their former uses.
Merchants reaped a rich harvest selling goods they had bought
from the fleeing Tories at sacrifice prices. Trade was reopened
with the rest of America, and vessels flying the Stars and Stripes
tied up alongside British transports at Whitehall and Murray's
Wharf. Already the war seemed long ago and unreal when General Carleton notified Washington that he would withdraw the
last of his forces on November 25th.

"His Majesty's troops will depart from Kingsbridge and
McGown's Pass on this Island on the 21st instant," he wrote,
"and I shall resign the possession of Herrick's and Hempstead,
with all the eastward on Long Island, the same day. Paulus

Hook will be relinquished on the day following . . . and I
shall retire from this city and from Brooklyn on Tuesday next
at noon, or as soon after as wind and weather permit."

With the evacuation of the British army only a few days
away, Major Tallmadge suggested to Washington that it would
be wise "to take some steps to assure the safety of several persons within the enemy's lines, who have served us faithfully
with intelligence during the war"; and he obtained permission
to go to New York, under cover of a flag, to protect his spies
from mistaken Whig vengeance. He was received with great
courtesy by Sir Guy Carleton, and dined at his table with the
highest-ranking officers of the army and navy, exchanging toasts
to General Washington and to the King. It was a strange sensation, he wrote, to walk the streets of Manhattan in American
uniform, "surrounded by British troops, Tories, cowboys and
traitors," and he was amused to note how the refugees "would
now come around to me, and beg my protection against the
dreaded rage of their countrymen."

He was allowed to move about the city freely, and one by
one he visited the secret agents with whom he had corresponded
so long. Some of them, like George Smith and John Corke and
Hercules Mulligan, he had known during the war or had met
while stationed in New York in 1776; but the head of the
Culper Ring was only a name to him. Woodhull had given him
the address of the Underhill boardinghouse, and Woodhull's
sister Mary led him upstairs to Robert Townsend's chamber. He
knocked and entered.

He had visualized Culper Junior as a staid businessman in
his late forties; and he was not prepared for this lean and grave
young man, no older than himself, though his chestnut hair was
already streaked with silver. His face bore the marks of personal
tragedy, his eyes were hollow and haunted. He was packing his
belongings in a small hair trunk, and Tallmadge asked in sur-

prise: "You'll be here when General Washington arrives to-morrow?"

Townsend shook his head. "I'm leaving the city in the morning."

"But His Excellency wants to meet you and express his thanks. He is ready to recommend you for government office, if that is your aim, and he feels honor bound to give your service the public acclaim that it deserves."

"Acclaim?" Townsend bent over to close the lid of the trunk. "For betraying everything I believed in? For losing what I valued most?" He fastened the trunk strap and looked up at Tallmadge. "I've lived four years of my life in fear, and I'll live the rest of it in shame," he said slowly. "All I ask is to be for-gotten."

*   *   *

New York was astir early on Tuesday morning, in readiness for the great event. A week earlier "a large and respectable num-ber of inhabitants, lately returned from a seven years exile," had met at Cape's Tavern on Broadway, and decided to "form a badge of distinction"; and this morning every patriot sported a union cockade of black and white ribbon on the left breast, and a sprig of laurel in his hat. American flags, brought out of hiding places in chests and closets, appeared miraculously on all the houses. The sight of the rebel colors was too much for William Cunningham, who had recently been discharged as Provost Marshal. At dawn on Tuesday, having imbibed heavily all night, he set about tearing down the flags with "some scores of double-headed damns." He met his match at Day's Tavern on Murray Street. As he started to rip the Stars and Stripes from the door, the fiery little Mrs. Day flew at him and pummeled him with her fists until "the powder flew from his wig" and he beat an ignominious retreat amid the jeers of the onlookers.

General Carleton had suggested to Washington that they co-

ordinate the departure of the British with the arrival of the
Americans in order to avoid any disorder, "as I doubt not that
your Excellency is, with me, desirous to prevent every species of
enormity on this interesting occasion." Accordingly General
Washington traveled to Tarrytown a week before the event, and
was joined on the 19th by New York Governor George Clinton
and his suite. The following night they lodged at the Van Cortlandt Mansion below Yonkers, and on Friday the 21st they
rode south as far as Harlem, where they remained until Carleton completed his arrangements to withdraw.

At eight o'clock on Tuesday morning the American army,
with the light infantry as its main guard, reached the upper
barrier at McGown's Pass. They halted so close to the British
rear guard that General Knox, in command of the troops,
chatted cordially with the Royal officers. Salutes were exchanged,
the British wheeled smartly and started their march toward
New York, and the Americans followed close behind them,
down the Post Road and the Bowery Lane to another barrier
near the Bull's Head Tavern. The troops broke ranks and
sprawled on the grass, enjoying wine and fruit served to them
by the welcoming committee. At one o'clock the redcoats left
the second barrier and resumed their march south, the Americans dogging the footsteps of their former enemies down the
cobblestone avenues of the city to Wall Street. The British
swung east to Murray's Wharf for embarkation, while the Continental troops headed west toward Broadway, drums beating
and fifes squealing "God Save Great Washington," the Yankee
version of "God Save the King." They drew up in front of
Cape's Tavern, and a small artillery detail continued down
Broadway to the Battery to fire a salute as the American colors
were raised over Fort George.

Here they encountered an unexpected obstacle. After dismantling the fort and hauling down the Union Jack from the

tall flagpole on the parade grounds, some British soldiers had carefully removed the blocks and halyards, knocked off the cleats by which the pole could be climbed, and coated the staff from top to bottom with tallow. The artillery detail lowered their guns irritably, and a young sailor volunteered to shinny up the greased pole. After several fruitless attempts, someone ran to Golet's ironmongery in Hanover Square, and brought back an axe and hammer and nails. A board was split into cleats, the sailor tied the halyards around his waist, and started a slow ascent, nailing the cleats one by one above him as he mounted. The halyards were reeved, the Stars and Stripes run up, and the artillery discharged their muskets in a delayed salute. British soldiers, who had been watching the scene from their longboats in the harbor, rowed in satisfaction to their transports.

General Knox and a body of mounted civilian dignitaries galloped up the Bowery Lane to the Stuyvesant Mansion, just north of the barrier, where Washington and Clinton and their staffs were waiting. After a formal exchange of compliments between the General and the civic leaders, the procession started toward the city, the Commander-in-Chief and the Governor in the lead, escorted by a body of Westchester Light Horse, and followed by the Lieutenant Governor and members of the Council riding eight abreast. At the Tea Water Pump on Chatham Street, they were joined by another group of prominent citizens who fell in behind them on foot, also marching eight abreast.

Washington's eyes moved from side to side as he entered New York for the first time since that disastrous September Sunday in 1776. It was hard to believe this was the same town; the shade trees were gone, the orchards leveled, the neat picket fences removed for fuel. Weeds sprouted around the once handsome estates, and the mansions were dilapidated and empty. Some side streets were still blocked by earthworks, and the abandoned trenches had filled with stagnant water. The parade swung down Queen and across Wall to Broadway, and ahead of him Washington saw the stark ruins of Trinity Church, monument to a vanished city that would never be again.

New Yorkers wearing black and white cockades jammed the sidewalks along the line of march, cheering and weeping with joy, waving hats decked with laurel sprigs, holding up their children for a glimpse of the great leader whose force of character alone had held a divided and quarreling country together until victory was won. Robert Townsend stood at the curb, looking up at the Commander-in-Chief as he passed. His eyes were fixed on the granite face, full of wisdom and compassion and sadness. This was the man under whom he had served, not as a soldier but secretly and without acclaim. There was no need for medals. The gratitude of Washington was enough.

He stepped back unnoticed and disappeared in the crowd.

                    *   *   *

At eight the following morning Washington left his quarters at Fraunces' Tavern and walked alone down Queen Street to Number 23, the home of Hercules Mulligan. It was his first breakfast in New York, and he took it with his confidential correspondent whose timely warnings had twice thwarted British attempts on his life. As a further gesture of appreciation, he ordered a complete civilian wardrobe from Mulligan's tailor shop. The genial Irishman did not hesitate to take advantage of such distinguished patronage, and his shop prospered under its new title: *Clothier to Genl. Washington.*

The Commander-in-Chief had another personal debt to discharge. Accompanied by two members of his staff, he called next at the print shop of James Rivington at Queen and Wall Streets. The officers were astounded that Washington would visit the Tory publisher who had printed such slanderous calumnies about him, and one of them reported the incident later to Light Horse Harry Lee. They were politely received and ushered into a parlor, he said, and Rivington begged the

officers to be seated, and then asked Washington: "Will Your
Excellency do me the honor to step into the adjoining room
for a moment that I may show you a list of agricultural works
I am about to order from London?" They retired to Rivington's
private office, but the door came ajar, and the staff officer swore
to Lee that he "distinctly heard the clinking of two heavy
purses of gold as they were successively placed on the table."

Patriots were baffled by Washington's indulgence of the hated
Rivington, and the *Salem Gazette* sneered that he was "allowed
to reside in the Country for reasons best known to the great men
at helm. Where is Arnold?" Jemmy Rivington smiled enigmatically and offered no explanation. The Royal arms woodcut was
dropped from the masthead of his paper, and he changed its
name to the *New-York Gazette and Universal Advertiser*. On
December 6th he published a glowing account of the farewell
ceremony at Fraunces' Tavern "last Thursday noon" in honor
of the "illustrious, gracious and much loved Commander, General Washington. The passions of human nature were never
more tenderly agitated than in this interesting and distressful
scene." He concluded with a fawning statement that "his Excellency will set out for his seat, named Mount Vernon, in Virginia, emulating the example of his model, the virtuous Roman
general, who, victorious, left the tented field, covered with
honors, and withdrew from public life, *otium cum dignitate.*"

Washington had long dreamed of retirement, and in October
he had written the Marquis de Chastellux of his "anxious desire
to quit the walks of public life, and under the shadow of my
own vine and my own fig tree to seek those enjoyments and
that relaxation, which a mind that has been constantly upon
the stretch for more than eight years stands so much in need of."
He had grown gray in the service of his country, and infinitely
weary, and he longed to hear the rippling current of the Potomac
and smell the fragrance of jasmine and red clover and watch his
new colts frisking in the pasture. "I can truly say that the first

wish of my Soul is to return speedily into the bosom of that
country which gave me birth, and, in the sweet enjoyment of
domestic happiness and the company of a few friends, to end
my days in quiet, when I shall be called from this stage."

On December 4th the last of the British forces withdrew from
Staten Island, and Washington was free to go home. That noon
his officers repaired to Fraunces' Tavern where the retiring
Commander-in-Chief had appointed to meet them and take his
final leave. Some forty-four of the highest military leaders were
present, a shining roster of the Revolution: Greene and Putnam
and Knox; Steuben and Schuyler and Lincoln; Wayne, Morgan,
Marion; Moultrie, Stark, Hamilton, gathered for the last time
to bid their chief farewell.

Benjamin Tallmadge, now a lieutenant colonel by brevet,
paused in the entranceway of the tavern on his way to the ceremony, gazing for a moment into the public taproom on the lower
floor. The round table in the corner was deserted, and his mind
peopled it again with the group who were seated around it that
July night in 1776 when a courier from Philadelphia brought
the news that Congress had declared independence. Alexander
Hamilton, a pink-cheeked young captain then. Hercules Mulligan, later to become an important link in the intelligence chain.
Nathan Hale, the devoted zealot, who was to die two months
later in the performance of a peculiar service for his country.
Out of Hale's effort had come the first espionage organization;
he could be called the father of American intelligence. His
shadow walked beside Tallmadge as he mounted the stairs to
the Long Room.

"We had been assembled for but a few minutes," Tallmadge
wrote in his *Memoir*, "when his Excellency entered the room.
His emotion, too strong to be concealed, seemed to be recipro-
cated by every officer present. After partaking of a slight re-
freshment, in almost breathless silence, the General filled his
glass with wine, and turning to the officers he said: 'With a

heart full of love and gratitude, I now take my leave of you. I most devoutly wish that your latter days may be as prosperous and happy as your former ones have been glorious and honourable.'

"After the officers had taken a glass of wine, General Washington said: 'I cannot come to each of you, but shall feel obliged if each of you will come and take me by the hand.' General Knox, being nearest to him, turned to the Commander-in-Chief, who, suffused in tears, was incapable of utterance, but grasped his hand; when they embraced each other in silence.

"In the same affectionate manner, every officer in the room marched up to, kissed, and parted with his General-in-Chief. Such a scene of sorrow and weeping I had never before witnessed, and I hope may never be called on to witness again. It was indeed too affecting to be of long continuance — for tears of deep sensibility filled every eye — and the heart seemed so full that it was ready to burst from its wonted abode. Not a word was uttered to break the solemn silence that prevailed, or to interrupt the tenderness of the interesting scene. The simple thought that we were then about to part from the man who had conducted us through a long and bloody war . . . and that we should see his face no more in this world, seemed to me utterly insupportable.

"But the time of separation had come, and waving his hand to his grieving children around him, he left the room and passing through a corps of light infantry, who were paraded to receive him, he walked silently on to Whitehall, where a barge was in waiting. We all followed in mournful silence to the wharf, where a prodigious crowd had assembled to witness the departure of the man who, under God, had been the great agent in establishing the glory and independence of these United States.

"As soon as he was seated, the barge put off into the river, and when out in the stream, our great and beloved General waved his hat, and bid us a silent adieu."

The Day After Yesterday

GENERAL WASHINGTON never learned Culper Junior's real name. Robert Townsend pledged both Tallmadge and Woodhull to silence, sold his New York business, and retired to Raynham Hall to live out his days in obscurity. Once, many years later, some young nieces and nephews happened to open a small hair trunk in the attic, and discovered a British uniform, neatly folded; it was the uniform Townsend had been forced to wear as a member of the Loyalist Volunteer Corps. He seemed very embarrassed by their discovery, but offered no explanation. He never married, nor did his sister Sarah; legend says that she always kept the valentine which Lieutenant Colonel Simcoe wrote her, reading and rereading it so many times that the paper came apart at the folds. After Samuel Townsend's death, they stayed on in the old house, a pair of lonely ghosts living in the forgotten past.

Robert Townsend died on March 7, 1838, at the age of eighty-four. In his last will and testament, he left the major part of his estate to his natural son. In the case of all the other beneficiaries, the name of the mother was given; but the final bequest was to "Robert Townsend Junior, now a member of the Legislature of this state for the City of New York" and did not mention 355. Among his papers were found a bill for a quarter's schooling for Robert Junior, and a bill for carpenter's tools when his son began his trade. The boy must have known that his mother's bones were interred in a common grave with the prison-ship victims, for he worked diligently to raise funds for a proper memorial to the martyrs. In 1808, as an influential member of the Tammany Society of New York, he co-signed a circular announcing a plan "for the interment of that portion of the Remains of our Countrymen now lying on the shores of Long-Island. The Committee have procured from John Jackson, Esq., on whose farm they were deposited, and where they now lie, a Deed of a piece of ground, conspicuously and advantageously situated, being the head of the Navy Yard."

The entombment took place in May, in a lot on Jackson Street, now Hudson Avenue, just outside the Brooklyn Navy Yard wall; but for three-quarters of a century the bones lay in an underground vault without a monument to mark their location. "Behold their place of interment," a shocked observer wrote in 1864, "in a locality, used as a receptical for filth and refuse, and where even the coarse, disgusting noise of swine is heard." When Jackson Street was regraded, the vault was partly uncovered, and become more and more dilapidated until "the remains were in an exposed state." In 1873, some "twenty hogsheads of bones" were moved to a more appropriate lot in Washington Park, now called Fort Greene, and deposited in a brick vault, twenty-five by eleven feet. So little interest did the event arouse that the newspapers of that day made no mention of their transfer. Later another hundred skeletons were dug up in the course of excavations for an extension of the Navy Yard, and were added to the rest. Not until 1908 was a suitable monument erected, a granite shaft designed by Stanford White, and dedicated by President-elect William Howard Taft.

Here 355 lies today in her final resting place, and it would appear that the secret of her identity is buried with her. Every avenue of research I have explored has come to a complete dead end. Robert Townsend Junior was buried near his mother's first place of entombment; but the door of his vault — possibly at his father's request — does not give 355's name. There is no mention of her arrest or death in the General Clinton papers in the Clements Library in Michigan; in the files of Rivington's *Gazette* in the New-York Historical Society or the American Antiquarian Society in Worcester, Massachusetts; or in George Washington's voluminous papers in the Library of Congress. I have searched in vain in the New York and Long Island and Nassau County Historical Societies, the New York Genealogical and Biographical Society, and the New York Public Library. The Townsend Society of America has no record of her. The probate court of Queens County, Jamaica, where Townsend's will was filed in 1838, and the East Hampton Free Library, which has the will today, provided no clue, nor did the Oyster Bay Library or the Queensborough Public Library in Jamaica. The New York State Library reported that their Townsend family genealogy contains no information on Robert Junior. Werner's *Constitutional History* mentions him as a member of the state legislature from January 3 to May 16, 1837, but in those early days the parents of the legislators were not recorded. In London, neither the British Admiralty nor the War Office could find any reference to her in their lists of American prisoners-of-war; and the logbooks of the *Jersey*, which might have noted the unusual circumstances of her childbirth, are missing from 1780 onward, probably lost at sea. 355 remains as anonymous in death as she was in life, an American heroine without a name.

The secret of Culper Junior's own identity was solved by accident only a few years ago. In 1939 Morton Pennypacker, a Long Island historian, noticed a striking similarity in handwriting between the letters of Robert Townsend of Oyster Bay and the secret correspondence signed with the alias "Samuel Culper Junior." Calligraphic experts confirmed Pennypacker's findings, and Townsend, who had always feared that his handwriting might betray him, was revealed by it at last. In the same manner, the name of "S. G." was discovered in 1959 by Mrs. Virginia Eckels Malone, historian and columnist for the *Smithtown News*, who established that the hitherto unknown member of the Culper Ring was George Smith of Nissequogue, lineal descendant of the founder of Smithtown.

It is doubtful that Washington ever met Samuel Culper Senior, though he knew Abraham Woodhull's name. Like Townsend, Woodhull had no desire for public acclaim, and preferred the seclusion of his Conscience Bay farm after five harrowing years of secret service. A year after the war ended, he married Mary Smith, daughter of Obediah Smith, and in 1799 he was appointed first judge of Suffolk County, and served for ten years. He died in 1826, and was laid to rest in the cemetery of the Setauket Presbyterian Church.

Caleb Brewster and Benjamin Tallmadge also became benedicts in 1784. With no more whaleboat raids to offer him a means of escape, Brewster yielded to the determined Annie Lewis of Fairfield; and Tallmadge was wed in March to his childhood sweetheart Mary Floyd, daughter of William Floyd who signed the Declaration of Independence. That same year Tallmadge and Brewster and the supposed Loyalist Benjamin Floyd, whom Tallmadge had described as being "of more service to the Whig interest in Setauket than every other man in it," formed a business partnership and purchased the property of Benjamin's genuinely Tory brother Richard. Later Tallmadge settled in Litchfield, Connecticut, and served eight distinguished terms in the United States House of Representatives, where he was chairman of the Committee on Military Affairs.

Austin Roe likewise failed to meet George Washington. In 1790, after his election as President, Washington visited Setauket, and spent the night of April 22nd at the Roe Tavern, which he described in his diary as "tolerably decent with obliging people in it." Austin Roe was not among the people. While hurrying to Setauket to greet the President, the intrepid Paul Revere of the Culper Ring, who had ridden the express route to New York so many times without mishap, fell from his horse and broke his leg.

Hercules Mulligan prospered after the war, trading on the patronage of President Washington to earn a handsome income as New York's leading clothier. He raised three sons and five daughters, retired from business in 1820, and purchased a fine home at 280 Bowery Lane. He died in his eighty-fifth year, and was buried in Trinity churchyard, only a few paces from the grave of his friend Alexander Hamilton. The family vault was shared with his brother-in-law, Thomas Whaly, and the marble slab bears the simple and misspelled inscription: *Whalie and Mulligan's Vault.*

The devious James Rivington did not fare so well, despite Washington's efforts to protect him with an armed guard upon the American occupation of the city. His contribution to the Culper Ring was kept secret, as were all the confidential activities of the spies; and, though his collaboration was suspected by historians, the proof was not established until 1959. Dr. Catherine Snell Crary, of the History Department at Finch College, published an article in the *William and Mary Quarterly*, disclosing for the first time a handwritten statement by Major Allan McLane that "the noted Rivington" had furnished him with the British naval code. Perhaps Rivington's own reluctance to acknowledge his dealings with the patriots was because the canny publisher, always an opportunist, had arranged with Sir Guy Carleton for his sons to receive commissions in the British army and half pay for life, despite the fact that they had never seen active service.

In 1783, as soon as the British evacuated New York, Rivington's sworn enemy Isaac Sears returned from New Haven to the city. He had accumulated a small fortune by profiteering

during the war, and he purchased the Kennedy Mansion at
Number One Broadway and later became president of the New
York Chamber of Commerce. In December "King" Sears, accompanied by General John Lamb and Colonel Marinus Willett, visited Rivington's print shop and ordered him to cease
publication of the *Gazette* if he valued his life. The newspaper
was suspended; but the animosity of the patriots was still bitter,
and exploded into violence a couple of weeks later. Nicholas
Cruger, who claimed he had been imprisoned by the British
because of Rivington's testimony against him, encountered "the
scoundrel who had used him so basely," a friend signing himself
"Vindicator" wrote. "When this modern Lucifer had the in-
solence and audacity to come up to Mr. Nicholas Cruger in the
street, what man of the smallest spirit, so circumstanced, could
avoid knocking him down, and kicking him afterwards?"

Still "King" Sears persisted in his persecution. While Rivington was recuperating from his beating, Sears visited his home,
broke some windows, and warned again that if he continued in
business his house would be destroyed and his throat cut. His
source of income was ended, his unpaid bills mounted, and in
1797, at the age of seventy-two, he was confined in the debtors'
jail and "reduced to real Penury." A visitor to the jail reported
that Jemmy Rivington was "still a cheerful old man," although badly treated and penned with six others in one cell. His
health suffered from his confinement, and he died in 1802 and
was buried in the cemetery of the New Dutch Church.

Captain John Montresor, the British engineering officer who
befriended Nathan Hale during his final hours, made out as well
as Isaac Sears in the war. General Sir Henry Clinton, on Montresor's advice, decided in 1779 to demolish all the batteries and
redoubts which the rebels had built on Long Island and Staten
Island, and to fill up and level the lines and entrenchments. The
performance of this business, the outraged Judge Thomas Jones

recorded, was committed to the care and direction of Captain Montresor, "Clinton's confidential friend," and "to pull down what the rebels had erected at no expense," Judge Jones fumed, "cost John Bull more than £150,000 sterling, £100,000 of which the 'confidential friend' put into his own pocket, returned to England, purchased one of the genteelest houses in Portland Place, a noble county in Surrey, set up his carriages, had a house full of servants in rich livery, and lived in all the splendour of an eastern prince." War was a business, Montresor believed, and he had made the business pay.

Provost Marshal William Cunningham, who hanged Hale, met a similar fate himself. In 1791 Cunningham was arrested in London for forgery and sentenced to die on the gallows. In his last statement, made before he mounted the scaffold, he confessed: "I shudder at the murders I have been accessory to, both with and without orders from government, especially while in New York, during which time there were more than 2000 prisoners starved in the different churches, by stopping their rations, which I sold."

* * *

They are all gone now, and mostly forgotten, and the New York they knew belongs to yesterday. The cedar-crested hills are flattened, the sparkling lakes and streams have vanished, the little town lies buried like Pompeii under a laval flow of concrete. Cherry Hill, once the city's finest residential district and home of George Washington after his inauguration, is crushed beneath the abutment of Brooklyn Bridge, a flower under a heavy heel. The apple orchard where Nathan Hale was executed is now a modern apartment building called Manhattan House; there is no commemorative tablet or marker. The old Brooklyn Ferry, later known as the Fulton Street Ferry, has ceased to exist. Wallabout Bay has been largely filled in, and is the site of the present Brooklyn Navy Yard; the rotting timbers of the old *Jersey*, scuttled in 1783, rest somewhere beneath the complex of dry docks and machine shops.

At the upper end of Manhattan Island is the northernmost outpost of Fort Washington, ironically a part of Fort Tryon Park, named after the hated Royal governor who ravaged and burned much of Westchester and Connecticut. The site of the main fort is a children's playground, located on Fort Washington Avenue between 183rd and 185th Streets, called James Gordon Bennett Park. An exposed shelf of rock, protruding above the hard-packed dirt, is all that remains of the bloody parade ground where a couple of thousand patriots were killed or taken prisoner in the worst single disaster of the war. It is marked by a plain wooden flagpole, and on a sliver of marble, laid flush with the cement pavement and walked on by heedless passers-by, is inscribed: *Fort Washington Built and Defended by the American Army 1776.* The flagpole and sidewalk are defaced with chalk scribblings, *Ira Loves Judy* and *Jean Loves James*, and the only raised monument is an efficient Geodetic Survey plaque, explaining that this is the *Highest Natural Point on Manhattan, 265.05 Feet Above Sea Level. U.S.C. & G.S. Datum.* Across the river, Fort Lee still commemorates the name of the petty traitor who tried to overthrow Washington.

Long Island has not done much better by the past. The reedy cove called Drowned Meadow, where Brewster's whaleboat was attacked, is now the sprawling city of Port Jefferson, and Setauket Bay is known as Port Jefferson Harbor. The name of Old Man's Bay, for no apparent reason, has been changed to Mt. Sinai Harbor. Setauket is still the same charming town, with gracious lawns and shade trees, and some buildings of the Revolutionary period remain. Caroline Episcopal Church is pretty much as it was in 1777 when its Tory minister, the peppery Reverend Lyon, spotted some Hessian soldiers raiding his garden during the service, and interrupted his sermon to announce to the British officers in the congregation: "Here I am preaching the blessed Gospel, and there are your damned redcoats stealing my potatoes." The salt-box birthplace of Caleb Brewster has been preserved; but the Woodhull home beside Conscience Bay and the Selah Strong Mansion on Strong's Neck have been destroyed by fire, and there are no signs to indicate their exact location. In 1930, Austin Roe's Tavern was moved from its historic site on the Old Post Road, and is now a private residence on Briar Hill, beautifully maintained with its original beams and paneling intact.

Raynham Hall, the Townsend family home in Oyster Bay, is operated as a museum, and the rooms are carefully roped off from the public. The State Education Department has put up a couple of blue and yellow historical markers in the street, distinguished by two errors in spelling and one in fact: "Queens Rangers" should read "Queen's Rangers," "lead" should be "led," and "Col. Simcoe" was actually a lieutenant colonel. Nowhere was there any mention of the location of the Townsend burial plot when I visited the homestead; even the museum caretaker could not tell me where it was. I found the site at last, on the property of a Mr. Fensterer at 51 Simcoe Avenue, named for the bullying British officer who abused Abraham Woodhull's aged father. The graveyard could be reached only with Mr. Fensterer's permission, and the visitor had to pass through two garden gates to a small rear lot between the Fensterer garage and a neighbor's barn, overgrown with weeds and littered with tin cans and refuse. At the time I saw it, the headstone of Samuel Townsend, Robert's father, had almost weathered away, and flakes of sandstone lay in the rank grass. Beside it was the grave of Culper Junior, the stone tilted at an angle, the lettering all but illegible. In front of the stone, a consummate touch of irony, was a faded American flag and a D.A.R. metal plaque reading: *A Revolutionary Soldier.*

A year ago, under the determined leadership of Mrs. Miner Hill, president of the Oyster Bay Historical Society, the town decided to pay a belated tribute to its noted son. The long-neglected burial plot was cleaned up and planted with flowering shrubs, the sagging tombstones were reset, a public right-of-way was established around the Fensterer property (doubtless to Mr. Fensterer's vast relief), and the cemetery was enclosed by a wire mesh fence with a locked iron gate. On Patriots' Day, in a drenching downpour, a wreath was placed on Robert Townsend's grave, and an Army squad from Fort Totten fired the traditional military salute of eight rifles in three volleys. The sober young Quaker, who was never permitted to wear the uniform of his country, would have smiled a little sardonically at this final tribute.

✿✿✿
Acknowledgments and Bibliography

SOME years ago J. J. Schubert, theatrical producer and noted twister of words, rested a hand on my shoulder and told me solemnly: "My boy, the theater is not a labor of love, it is a labor of drudgery." Well, this book has been a labor of drudgery, but it is also a labor of love; and as I bring it to a close I should like to express my personal thanks to all those who helped me with my happy burden. For their generous advice and assistance in my research, I am immeasurably indebted to

The staff of Dartmouth College's excellent Baker Memorial Library, who not only allowed me to borrow several tons of books from their shelves, but cheerfully sent away for other books I requested.

The staff of Colonial Williamsburg, particularly William D. Geiger, director of craft shops, John J. Walklet, director of publications, Marietta Robbins, director of costumes, George Carroll, musick-master and specialist in Revolutionary War songs, and Gus Klapper, at the print shop, who showed me how to wreck a printing press.

The equally helpful staff of the New-York Historical Society, including Geraldine Beard, Wilmer Leech, and Shirley Beresford.

330 ACKNOWLEDGMENTS AND BIBLIOGRAPHY

The staffs of the manuscript division of the Library of Congress, who made the George Washington papers and other data available; the Houghton Library at Harvard University, who provided manuscripts from the Jared Sparks collection; and the Museum of the City of New York and the Metropolitan Museum of Art, who traced the changing fashions of the period and let me examine their collections of originals.

William C. Steere, director of the New York Botanical Gardens, and Miss Elizabeth C. Hall, research librarian, who supplied the names of shrubs and flowers found in New York in 1775.

The staff of the Fairfield, Connecticut, Historical Society, who furnished background material on Brewster's whaleboat raids.

Professor Richard B. Morris, former Chairman of the History Department at Columbia University and outstanding authority on the Revolutionary period, who contributed his invaluable help and suggestions.

Roland Baughman, Director of Special Collections at Columbia, who put the William J. Donovan collection at my disposal.

Dr. Catherine Snell Crary of Finch College, discoverer of Rivington's link with the secret service, who generously gave me access to her own research material.

John Bakeless, author of *Turncoats, Traitors and Heroes*, who also turned over his exhaustive reference files.

Amy O. Bassford, librarian of the Long Island Collection at East Hampton Free Library.

Arthur S. Maynard, assistant librarian of the New York Genealogical and Biographical Society.

Colonel Edward P. Hamilton of Fort Ticonderoga, recognized authority on early guns and weapons.

Mrs. Miner C. Hill of Oyster Bay, who provided information on the Townsend family history.

George A. Gibson of Oyster Bay, who devoted his personal time and energy to the search for the identity of 355.

Arthur M. Zich of Time, Inc., for his loyal help and advice on nautical problems.

The late Professor Albert Demaree of Dartmouth College, for his aid at the outset of my project.

Professor Herbert Faulkner West of Dartmouth College, who criticized this book as it progressed, and stubbornly kept me on the track.

Dorothy Olding of Harold Ober Associates, whose encouragement and enthusiasm saw me through some dark moments.

Norma Bouchard of Hanover, New Hampshire, who patiently typed and retyped this manuscript so many times that she knows it better than I do.

And, finally, my deepest gratitude to A. Richard Barber of the History Department at The Phillips Exeter Academy, who served faithfully as my research assistant. During the three years of preparation, he covered countless miles and spent endless hours organizing and gathering reference material, including a complete file of the Culper correspondence brought together from various sources for the first time. This book would not have been possible without him.

Certain published works have been of such particular value that I want to acknowledge my debt by giving them special mention here. *The Spirit of 'Seventy-Six*, edited by Henry Steele Commager and Richard B. Morris, is an indispensable anthology of Revolutionary War speeches and writings, which furnished me with many of the contemporary quotations used in this book.

Stoke's *Iconography of Manhattan Island*, the most exhaustive record of the period ever compiled, was a boundless source of factual information. Esther Singleton's *Social New York Under the Georges* contains minute details of New York life which made the whole era more real to me. Mather's *Refugees of 1776* afforded a wealth of otherwise unavailable material on Long Island and its residents at the time, and Lamb's *History of the City of New York* gave intimate details and anecdotes to color the story: the paint-and-fabric skin of the dinosaur. Baker's *Itinerary of George Washington* enabled me to follow the General's movements from day to day, and relish the illuminating comments he made in his diary. Dunshee's *As You Pass By* is a loving record of the early days, and his listing of the former names of streets and location of buildings helped me to trace the shape of yesterday. Abbott's scholarly *New York in the American Revolution* and Wertenbaker's readable *Father Knickerbocker Rebels* were both helpful guides. Dunlap's *History of the American Theater*, published in 1832, includes the author's own vivid recollections of New York, seen as a boy during the British occupation. Nor can I overlook Judge Thomas Jones's opinionated and vituperative *History of New York during the Revolutionary War*, which is so filled with sputtering rage and scathing sarcasm about his contemporaries that it is as alive today as when it was written in 1783. Two lengthy volumes failed to exhaust the Tory Judge's spleen at the "republicans, Presbyterians, and spawn of Yale," and his index bristles with further acid comments which the sight of the patriot names aroused anew. It is my favorite book of the Revolution.

For students of the period or amateur Revolutionary War buffs, who might wish to do additional research on the subject, my associate Richard Barber has appended the names of those books, pamphlets, and newspapers which aided us most in our effort to recreate the past. This does not pretend to be a complete bibliography of the Revolution, but is merely a suggested reading list for others interested in learning more about the city that was the center of American espionage for seven years.

MANUSCRIPTS

The Papers of General Sir Henry Clinton, The Clements Library, Ann Arbor, Michigan.

The Papers of Silas Deane, The New-York Historical Society.

The Papers of Major General Horatio Gates, The New-York Historical Society.

The Papers of Major General Nathanael Greene, The Clements Library, Ann Arbor, Michigan.

The Papers of Alexander Hamilton, Library of Congress.

The Papers of General William Heath, Library of Congress.

The Papers of Alexander McDougall, The New-York Historical Society.

Miscellaneous Townsend Family Manuscripts, The New-York Historical Society, and The Long Island Collection, East Hampton Public Library, East Hampton, Long Island.

The Papers of George Washington, Library of Congress.

GENERAL REFERENCE WORKS

BOOKS

ABBATT, William, *The Crisis of the Revolution; Being the Story of Arnold and André*. Issued under the auspices of the Empire State Society, Sons of the American Revolution, New York, 1899.

ABBOTT, Wilbur Cortez, *New York in the American Revolution*, New York, London, 1929.

ADAMS, James Truslow, *The Epic of America*, Boston, 1947.

ALDEN, John Richard, *General Charles Lee, Traitor or Patriot?* Baton Rouge, 1951.

———, *General Gage in America; Being Principally a History of His Role in the American Revolution*, Baton Rouge, 1948.

———, *The American Revolution, 1775–1783*, New York, 1954.

ANDRÉ, John, *Major André's Journal*, Tarrytown, New York, 1930.

André Court Minutes. *Minutes of a Court of Inquiry Upon the Case of Major John André*, J. Munsell, Albany, 1865.

ANDREWS, Charles M., *Colonial Folkways*, New Haven, 1919.

AUGUR, Helen, *The Secret War of Independence*, New York, 1955.

BAKELESS, John, *Turncoats, Traitors, and Heroes*, New York and Philadelphia, 1959.

BAKER, William Spohn, *Itinerary of General Washington from June 15, 1775, to December 23, 1783*, Philadelphia, 1892.

BARBER, A. Richard, "The Tallmadge-Culper Intelligence Ring: A Study of American Revolutionary Spies." Unpublished Master's essay, Columbia University, New York, 1963.

BARBER, John W., *Pictorial History of the State of New York*, H. & E. Phinney, Cooperstown, New York, 1846.

BARCK, Oscar Theodore, *New York During the War for Independence, With Special Reference to the Period of British Occupation*, New York, 1931.

BAYLES, William Harrison, *Old Taverns of New York*, Frank Allaben Genealogical Co., New York, c. 1915.

BEARD, Mary R. (ed.), *America Through Women's Eyes*, New York, 1933.

BENSON, Mary Sumner, *Women in Eighteenth-Century America*, New York, 1935.

BILLIAS, George Athan, *General John Glover*, New York, 1960.

BLIVEN, Bruce, Jr., *Battle for Manhattan*, New York, 1955.

BLUMENTHAL, Walter Hart, *Women Camp Followers of the American Revolution*, Philadelphia, 1952.

BOLTON, Charles K., *The Private Soldier Under Washington*, New York, 1902.

BRIDENBAUGH, Carl, *Cities in the Wilderness*, New York, 1938.

BRYAN, George S., *The Spy in America*, Philadelphia, 1943.

BURNABY, Andrew, *Travel Through the Middle Settlements in North America*, T. Payne, London, 1775.

CALVER, William Louis, and Reginald Pelham Bolton, *History Written with Pick and Shovel*, The New-York Historical Society, New York, 1950.

CAMPBELL, Maria, *The Revolutionary Services and Civil Life of General William Hull*, D. Appleton and Co., New York; G. S. Appleton, Philadelphia, 1848.

CAREY, A. Merwyn, *English, Irish and Scottish Firearms Makers*, New York, 1954.

COMMAGER, Henry Steele, and Richard B. Morris (eds.), *The Spirit of 'Seventy-Six*, New York, 1958, 2 vols.

CRUICKSHANK, Helen Gere (ed.), *John and William Bartram's America*, New York, 1957.

CUNNINGTON, C. Willett, Phillis Cunnington and Charles Beard, *A Dictionary of English Costume*, Adam & Charles Black, London, 1960.

CUNNINGTON, C. Willett and Phillis, *Handbook of English Costume in the Eighteenth Century*, Faber & Faber, London, 1958.

———, *The History of Underclothes*, Michael Joseph, London, 1951.

CUSTIS, George Washington Parke, *Recollections and Private Memoirs of Washington*, Derby and Jackson Company, New York, 1860.

DAVIDSON, Philip, *Propaganda and the American Revolution 1763–1783*, Chapel Hill, 1941.

DAVIS, Matthew Livingston, *Memoirs of Aaron Burr with Miscellaneous Selections from His Correspondence*, Harper & Brothers, New York, 1836–1837, 2 vols.

DAWSON, Henry Barton, *New York City During the American Revolution*, Privately printed for The [New York] Mercantile Library Association, New York City, 1861.

———, *Record of the Trial of Joshua Hett Smith, Esq., for alleged complicity in the treason of Benedict Arnold — 1780*, Broadstreet Press, Morrisavia, New York, 1866.

DILLIN, John G. W., *The Kentucky Rifle*, National Rifle Association of America, Washington, D.C., 1924.

DRING, Capt. Thomas, *Recollections of the Jersey Prison-Ship*, Greene, Albert G. (ed.), H. H. Brown, Providence, 1829.

DUNLAP, William, *A History of the American Theatre*, J. and J. Harper, New York, 1832.

DUNSHEE, Kenneth Holcomb, *As You Pass By*, New York, 1952.

EARLE, Alice Morse, *Costume of Colonial Times*, Charles Scribner's Sons, New York, 1894.

———, *Home Life in Colonial Days*, The Macmillan Company, New York, 1898.

———, *Two Centuries of Costume in America 1620–1820*, The Macmillan Company, New York, 1903, 2 vols.

EINSTEIN, L. D., *Divided Loyalties*, New York, 1933.

ELLET, Elizabeth Fries (Lummis), *The Women of the American Revolution*, C. Scribner, New York, 1856, 3 vols.

FITCH, Jabez, *Prison Ship Martyrs*, New York, 1892.

FITZPATRICK, John C., *Calendar of the Correspondence of George Washington — Commander in Chief of the Continental Army — With the Officers*, Government Printing Office, Washington, 1915, 4 vols.

———, *George Washington's Accounts of Expenses*, New York, 1917.

———, *The Diaries of George Washington 1748–1799*, Volume II 1771–1785, Boston and New York, 1925, 4 vols.

——— (ed.), *Writings of George Washington*, Government Printing Office, Washington, 1931–1939, 36 vols.

FLEXNER, James Thomas, *The Traitor and the Spy*, New York, 1953.

FLICK, Alexander Clarence, *Loyalism in New York During the American Revolution*, Columbia University Press, New York, 1901.

——— (ed.), *The American Revolution in New York*, Albany, 1926.

——— (ed.), *History of the State of New York in Ten Volumes*, Vols. 1 and 3, New York, 1933.

FORCE, Peter, *American Archives: Documentary History of the Origin and Progress of the North American Colonies*, Series 4 and Series 5, Published by Act of Congress, Washington, D. C., 1848–1853.

FREEMAN, Douglas Southall, *George Washington — A Biography*, Vols. 4 and 5, New York, 1951–1952.

FRIEDENWALD, Herbert, *A Calendar of Washington Manuscripts in the Library of Congress*, Government Printing Office, Washington, 1901.

GEGENHEIMER, Albert Frank, *William Smith 1727–1803*, Philadelphia, 1943.

GIPSON, Lawrence H., *The American Revolution as an aftermath of the great war for the Empire, 1754–1763*, Bethlehem, Pennsylvania, 1950.

———, *The Coming of the Revolution*, New York, 1954.

GOTTESMAN, Rita Susswein (ed.), *The Arts and Crafts in New York, 1726–1776*, The New-York Historical Society, New York, 1938.

——— (ed.), *The Arts and Crafts in New York, 1777–1779*, The New-York Historical Society, New York, 1954.

GRAYDON, Alexander, *Memoirs of His Own Time, with Reminiscences of the Men and Events of the Revolution* (ed. John Stockton Littell), Lindsay and Blakiston, Philadelphia, 1846.

GUITERMAN, Arthur, *Ballads of Old New York*, New York, 1920.

HALL, Charles Swain, *Benjamin Tallmadge, Revolutionary Soldier and American Businessman*, New York, 1943.

HARLOW, Alvin F., *Old Bowery Days*, New York and London, 1931.

HARRINGTON, Virginia D., *The New York Merchant on the Eve of the Revolution*, New York, 1935.

HAVEN, Charles T., *Shooting Muzzle Loading Handguns*, Guns Incorporated, Falmouth, Massachusetts, 1947.

HEADLEY, Joel Tyler, *Washington and His Generals*, Baker & Scribner, New York, 1849.

HERBERT, Henry William, *Frank Forester's Field Sports of the United States and British Provinces of North America*, Stringer and Townsend, New York, 1849.

HEWLETT, Leroy, "James Rivington, Loyalist Printer, Publisher & Book-seller of the American Revolution 1724–1802: A Biographical Biblio-graphical Study." Unpublished Doctoral dissertation, University of Michigan, Ann Arbor, Michigan, 1958.

HILDEBURN, Charles Swift Riche, *Sketches of Printers and Printing in Colonial New York*, Dodd, Mead, and Company (De Vinne Press), New York, 1895.

HILL, Frederick Trevor, *The Story of a Street*, New York, 1908.

HOFELAND, Otto, *Westchester County during the American Revolution 1775–1783*, Westchester County Historical Society Publications, Vol. III, White Plains, N.Y., 1926.

HOLLIDAY, Carl, *Women's Life in Colonial Days*, Boston, 1922.

HOWE, William, *General Sir William Howe's Orderly Book*, B. F. Stevens, London, 1890.

HUGHES, Rupert, *George Washington — the Savior of the States*, New York, 1930.

JANVIER, Thomas, *In Old New York*, Harper & Brothers, New York, 1894.

JOHNSON, H. P. (ed.), *The Correspondence and Public Papers of John Jay*, G. P. Putnam's Sons, New York, London, 1890–1893, 4 vols.

JOHNSTON, Henry Phelps, *Nathan Hale, 1776*, New Haven, 1914.

JONES, Thomas, *History of New York during the Revolutionary War*, Vols. I and II, The New-York Historical Society, New York, 1879.

KETCHUM, Richard M. (ed.), *The American Heritage Book of the Revolution*, New York, 1958.

KOLLER, Larry, *The Fireside Book of Guns*, New York, 1959.

LABAREE, Leonard Woods, *Conservatism in Early American History*, New York, 1948.

LATHROP, Cornelia Penfield, *Black Rock, Seaport of Old Fairfield, Conn., 1644–1870*, New Haven, 1930.

LEAKE, Isaac Q., *Memoir of the Life and Times of General John Lamb*, J. Munsell, Albany, 1850.

LEFFERTS, Charles M., *Uniforms of the American, British, French, and German Armies in the War of the American Revolution 1775–1783*, The New-York Historical Society, New York, 1926.

LEFFMAN, Henry, *Notes on the Secret Service*, Publication of the City History Society of Philadelphia, No. 7, Philadelphia, 1910.

LEWIS, Berkeley R., *Small Arms and Ammunition in the United States Service*, The Smithsonian Institution, Washington, D.C., 1956.

LODGE, H. C. (ed.), *The Works of Alexander Hamilton*, Houghton Mifflin and Company, Boston, New York, 1882, 12 vols.

LOSSING, Benson John, *The Pictorial Field Book of the Revolution; or, Illustrations, by Pen and Pencil, of the History, Biography, Scenery, Relics and Traditions of the War for Independence,* Harper & Brothers, New York, 1859–1860, 2 vols.

————, *The Two Spies,* New York, 1886.

LUNDIN, Charles Leonard, *Cockpit of the Revolution; The War for Independence in New Jersey,* Princeton University Press, Princeton; Oxford University Press, London, 1940.

McCLELLAN, Elizabeth, *History of American Costume 1607–1870,* New York, 1937.

McGEE, Dorothy Horton, *Sally Townsend — Patriot,* New York, 1952.

McMASTER, John Bach, *A History of the People of the United States,* Vol. I, D. Appleton & Company, New York, 1883.

MARTIN, Joseph P., *Private Yankee Doodle,* Boston, 1962.

MATHER, Frederic Gregory, *The Refugees of 1776 from Long Island to Connecticut,* J. B. Lyon Co., Albany, New York, 1913.

Memoirs of the Long Island Historical Society, Vol. II, *The Battle of Long Island,* Brooklyn, New York, 1869; Vol. III, *The Campaign of 1776,* Brooklyn, New York, 1878.

MILLER, John C., *Origins of the American Revolution,* Boston, 1943.

MOORE, Frank, *Songs and Ballads of the American Revolution,* D. Appleton & Company, New York, 1855.

NELSON, Henry Loomis, *Uniforms of the United States Army,* New York, London, 1959.

NEVINS, Allan, *American Social History,* New York, 1923.

NEW YORKER, A, *New York — Metropolitan City of America,* Carlton A. Phillips, New York, 1853.

New York State University Division of Archives and History, *The American Revolution in New York,* Albany, New York, 1926.

NYE, Russel B., *The Cultural Life of the New Nation, 1776–1830,* New York, 1960.

O'BRIEN, Michael J., *Confidential Correspondent of General Washington — Hercules Mulligan,* P. J. Kenedy, & Sons, New York, 1937.

————, *George Washington's Associations with the Irish . . . ,* P. J. Kenedy & Sons, New York, 1937.

OLDBOY, Felix, *A Tour Around New York by John F. Mines,* Harper & Brothers, New York, 1893.

ONDERDONK, Henry Jr., *Documents and Letters,* Vol. I, Leavitt, Trow and Co., Newport, Rhode Island, 1846; Vol. II, L. Vandiwater, Hempstead, Long Island, 1884.

OSBORN, Gardner, *The Streets of Old New York*, New York, 1939.

PENNYPACKER, Morton, *General Washington's Spies on Long Island and in New York*, Long Island Historical Society, Brooklyn, New York, 1939–1948, 2 vols.

——, *The Two Spies*, Boston and New York, 1930.

PENNYPACKER SCRAP BOOK, *Historical Notes Relating to Long Island*, Vol. I (Mrs. Pennypacker, Library at East Hampton, Long Island).

PETERSON, Harold L., *Arms and Armor in Colonial America 1526–1783*, Harrisburg, Pennsylvania, 1956.

POWNALL, Thomas, *A Topographical Description of the Dominions of the United States of America*, Pittsburgh, Pennsylvania, 1949.

PRESTON, John Hyde, *A Gentleman Rebel*, New York, 1930.

——, *A Short History of the American Revolution*, New York, 1933.

PRIME, Nathaniel S., *A History of Long Island*, Robert Carter, New York, 1845.

RICHMOND, Rev. J. F., *New York and Its Institutions 1609–1872*, E. B. Treat, New York, 1872.

ROBERTS, Kenneth and Anna M. (eds.), *Moreau de St. Mery's American Journey 1793–1798*, Garden City, New York, 1947.

ROSCH, John, *Historic White Plains*, White Plains Historical Society, White Plains, New York, 1939.

SABINE, William H. W. (ed.), *Historical Memoirs of William Smith*, Vol. I and Vol. II, New York, 1956–1958.

—— (ed.), *The New York Diary of Lieutenant Jabez Fitch of the 17th (Connecticut) Regiment from August 22, 1776, to December 15, 1777*, Colburn & Tegg, New York, 1954.

SARGENT, Winthrop, *The Life and Career of Major John André*, Ticknor and Fields, Boston, 1861.

SCHACHNER, Nathan, *Alexander Hamilton*, New York and London, 1946.

——, *Aaron Burr*, New York, 1937.

SCHARF, J. T., *History of Westchester County*, L. E. Preston & Co., Philadelphia, 1886, 2 vols.

SEYMOUR, G. D., *The Documentary Life of Nathan Hale*, New Haven, 1941.

SHELTON, W. H., *The Jumel Mansion*, New York, 1916.

SHERWIN, Oscar, *Benedict Arnold — Patriot and Traitor*, New York and London, 1931.

SHIELDS, Joseph W., *From Flintlock to M1*, New York, 1954.

SIMCOE, John Graves, *Simcoe's Military Journal*, Bartlett and Welford, New York, 1844.

SIMMS, Jepheta Root, *The Frontiersmen of New York*, G. Riggs, Albany, New York, 1882–1883, 2 vols.

SINGLETON, Esther, *Social New York Under the Georges, 1714–1776*, D. Appleton and Co., New York, 1902.

SMITH, Joshua Hett, *An Authentic Narrative of the Causes which led to the death of Major André, Adjutant-general of His Majesty's Forces in North America*, Matthews and Leigh, London, 1808.

SPARKS, Jared (ed.), *The Diplomatic Correspondence of the American Revolution*, Little, Brown and Company, Boston, 1853, 4 vols.

——— (ed.), *The Writings of Washington*, Russell, Odiorne & Metcalf and Hilliard, Gray and Co., Boston, 1834; also Harper & Brothers, New York, 1843, 12 vols.

STEVENS, B. F. (ed.), *Facsimiles of Manuscripts in European Archives Relating to America, 1773–1783*, London, 1889–1895, 24 portfolios.

STEVENS, John Austin, *The Evacuation of New York by the British, Monday, Nov. 26, 1783*, J. J. Little & Co., New York, 1885.

STOKES, Isaac Newton Phelps, *The Iconography of Manhattan Island 1498–1909*, Compiled from Original Sources and Illustrated by Photo Intaglio Reproductions of Important Maps, Plans, Views and Documents in Public and Private Collections, Vol. 4, R. H. Dodd, New York, 1915–1928, 6 vols.

SYRETT, Harold C. (ed.), *Alexander Hamilton Papers*, Vols. 1–3, New York, 1961–1963.

TALLMADGE, Benjamin, *Memoir of Colonel Benjamin Tallmadge, Continental Light Dragoons, 1776–1783*, Gilliss Press, New York, 1904.

THAYER, Theodore, *Nathanael Greene — Strategist of the American Revolution*, New York, 1960.

THOMPSON, B. F., *History of Long Island*, Port Washington, Long Island, 1962, 3 vols.

TILGHMAN, Oswald, *Memoir of Lieut. Col. Tench Tilghman, Secretary and Aide to Washington*, J. Munsell, Albany, New York, 1876.

TODD, Charles Burr, *The Story of the City of New York*, G. P. Putnam's Sons, New York, 1888.

TOWNSEND, Margaret, *Townsend-Townshend, 1066–1909*, Broadway Publishing Co., New York, 1909.

VAN DOREN, Carl, *Secret History of the American Revolution*, New York, 1941.

VAN TYNE, Claude Halstead, *The Loyalists in the American Revolution*, Peter Smith, Gloucester, Massachusetts, 1959; The Macmillan Company, New York, 1902.

WARWICK, Edward, and Henry C. Pitz, *Early American Costume*, New York, 1929.

WERTENBAKER, Thomas Jefferson, *Father Knickerbocker Rebels: New York City during the Revolution*, New York, 1948.

———, *The Golden Age of Colonial Culture*, Ithaca, New York, 1959.

WHITELY, Mrs. Emily (Stone), *Washington and His Aides-de-Camp*, New York, 1936.

WILLARD, Margaret W., *Letters on the American Revolution, 1774–1776*, New York, 1925.

WILSON, James Grant, *Memorial History of the City of New York and the Hudson River Valley*, Vol. II, New York History Company, New York, 1892.

WINSOR, Justin, *Narrative and Critical History of America*, Vol. VI, Houghton, Mifflin and Company, Boston and New York, 1888.

ARTICLES

BURNETT, Edmund C., "Ciphers of the Revolutionary Period," *American Historical Review*, Vol. XXII (Jan. 1917), 329–334.

CRARY, Catherine Snell, "The Tory and the Spy: The Double Life of James Rivington," *William and Mary Quarterly*, Vol. 16, No. 1 (Jan. 1959), 61–72.

JOHNSTON, Henry P., "The Secret Service of the Revolution," *Magazine of American History*, Vol. 8, Pt. 1 (1882), 95–105.

O'BRIEN, Michael J., "Hercules Mulligan, Confidential Agent of George Washington in New York During the Revolution," *Journal of the American Irish Historical Society*, Vol. XXVI (1927), 96–104.

PEARL, Nathalie, "Long Island's Secret Agents of General Washington during the Revolutionary War," *The Nassau County Historical Journal*, Vol. VIII, No. 1 (1945), 5–12.

UNDERHILL, Augustus P., "William Underhill, His Ancestors and His Descendants," *The New York Genealogical and Biographical Record*, LVIII (1927), 356.

VAIL, R. W. G., "A Revolutionary Spy Reports to his General," *The New-York Historical Society Quarterly*, Vol. XXXIII, No. 1 (Jan. 1949).

NEWSPAPERS

Rivington's *New York Loyal Gazette*, name changed in 1777 to *The Royal Gazette*.

(New York) *Royal American Gazette*.

New York Mercury.

Boston Gazette.
(Boston) *Evening Post.*
(Boston) *Continental Journal.*
(Philadelphia) *Pennsylvania Gazette.*
(Philadelphia) *Pennsylvania Journal.*
(Philadelphia) *Pennsylvania Ledger.*

Index

Index

Liberty Bell, 302
Liberty Boys, 5, 23, 34, 168
Liberty Elm, 51
Liberty Poles, 22, 24, 34
Lincoln, General Benjamin, 209, 279, 292, 316
Lispenard Meadows, 6
Litchfield, Conn., 66, 322
Livingston, Robert R., 14, 59, 221, 224
Livingston, William, 295
Livingston Sugar House, 157
Lloyd's Neck, 147
London (ship), 24
Long Clove Mountain, 235
Long Island, 5, 65, 87, 88, 94, 99, 100, 102–104, 106, 147–148, 179, 188, 197, 203, 226, 265, 278, 300, 309; battle of, 136, 159
Long Island Sound, 45, 102, 108, 120, 190–191, 202
Long Wharf (New Haven), 190
Loring, Elizabeth Lloyd (Mrs. Joshua), 85, 109, 138, 139
Loring, Major Joshua, 85, 138, 158
Louis XVI, King of France, 77
Lower Bowery Lane, 56
Lower Bay, 73
Lower Salem, 240
Loyalist Volunteer Corps, 205, 319
Lutheran Church, 134
Lyon, Rev. James, 69, 149, 326–327

Mabie's Tavern (Tappan, N.Y.), 249
Macaroni, defined, 17
Mackenzie, Captain Frederick, 129
Madison Avenue, 8, 9
Maiden Lane, 6
Mall, the, 13, 18, 133, 160
Malone, Mrs. Virginia Eckels, 322
Manhattan Island, 72, 99, 102, 103, 104, 106, 111, 124, 171; battle of, 4
Marbleheaders, the (regiment), 94–95, 96
Marcus, son of Cato, 41–42
Marion, Francis, 274–316
Marks, Nehemiah, 265, 266, 271
Martin, Daniel, 19
Martling's Tavern, 57
Massachusetts Assembly, 268

Mastic, L.I., 90, 258, 259
Matthews, David, 66, 302
McDougall, Colonel, 70
McGown's Pass, 8, 117, 309, 312
McLane, Major Allan, 286, 287, 323
Medford, Mass., 46
Meigs, Lieutenant Colonel Return Jonathan, 188
Merchants' Coffee House, 11, 20, 24, 26–27, 70, 168, 175
Merchant's Exchange, 12, 175
Mercury (Hugh Gaine's newspaper), 136, 166
Meschianza, 181, 200–201
Mifflin, Major General Thomas, 86, 91, 96–97, 166; brigade, 104, 112
Miller House, 142
Mills, James, 20
Miner's Tavern (New London, Conn.), 43–44
Minetta Street, 6
Misery Point, 227
Molyneux (boxer), 180
Monk (pseud. of Benedict Arnold), 182, 200
Monmouth, N.J., 159, 188
Montaigne, Widow de la, tavern, 22
Montgomery (ship), 122, 123
Montresor, Captain John, 31–40, 116, 139, 140, 324–325; quoted, 22
Montresor's Island, 8, 32, 53, 83, 102, 130
Moore, Mr. (pseud. of Benedict Arnold), 200
Moravian Church, 133
More, Hannah, quoted, 16
Morgan, Private Charles, 288
Morgan, General Daniel, 272, 316
Morris, Gouverneur, 14, 20
Morris, John, 19
Morris, Robert, 223
Morris, Roger, 166; mansion, 4, 112, 114, 118, 137
Morrisania, N.Y., 103
Morristown, N.J., 204, 210–211, 221, 269
Mortier, Abraham, 106
Mott Street, 5
Moultrie, Major General William, 316

DATE DUE	

GAYLORD   PRINTED IN U.S.A.

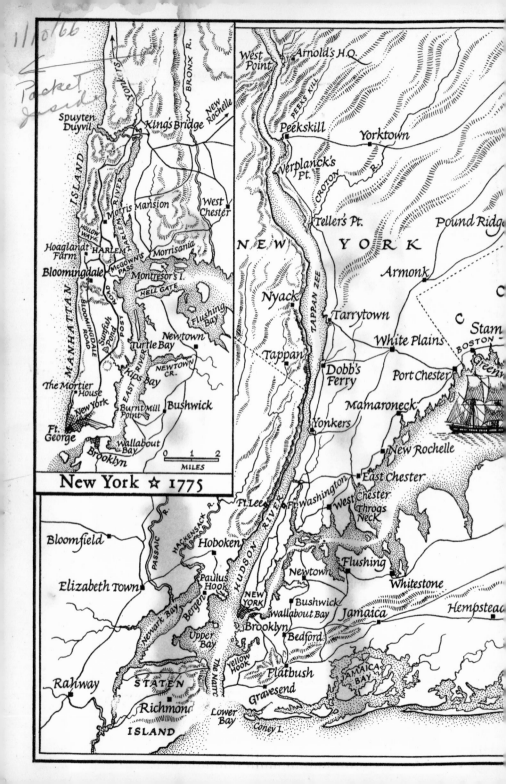

1/10/66

Pocket
inside

Inset map (upper left): New York ☆ 1775

Spuyten Duyvil

King's Bridge

YONKERS

BRONX R.

New Rochelle

West Point

Arnold's H.Q.

PEEKS KILL

Peekskill

Yorktown

Verplanck's Pt.

CROTON

Teller's Pt.

Pound Ridge

Morris Mansion

West Chester

NEW   YORK

Armonk

Hoaglandt Farm

HOLLOW WAY

HARLEM

HARLEM RIVER

Morrisania

McGOWN'S PASS

Nyack

TAPPAN ZEE

Tarrytown

White Plains

Stam

BOSTON

Green

Bloomingdale

Montresor's I.

HELL GATE

Tappan

Dobb's Ferry

Port Chester

MANHATTAN ISLAND

BLOOMINGDALE ROAD

POST ROAD

Sunfish Pond

Flushing Bay

Newtown

Turtle Bay

NEWTOWN CR.

Yonkers

Mamaroneck

New Rochelle

The Mortier House

New York

EAST RIVER

Kips Bay

Burnt Mill Point

Bushwick

East Chester

Ft. George

Wallabout Bay

Brooklyn

0   1   2
MILES

Ft. Lee

Ft. Washington

West Chester

Throgs Neck

Lower map

Bloomfield

PASSAIC R.

HACKENSACK R.

Hoboken

Hudson River

Flushing

Newtown

Whitestone

Elizabeth Town

Paulus Hook

Bergen

NEW YORK

Bushwick

Wallabout Bay

Jamaica

Hempstead

Newark Bay

Upper Bay

Brooklyn

Bedford

JAMAICA BAY

Rahway

STATEN

The Narrows

Yellow Hook

Flatbush

Richmond

Lower Bay

Gravesend

Coney I.

ISLAND